D0680713

"Tanenbaum's inquiry . . . blends well-documented research, interviews, and personal reflection in a lively, accessible style."

—*Library Journal*

"Tanenbaum relates her own experiences and interviews a variety of women and psychologists to explore the seemingly eternal adversarial relationships that exist among women despite many recent feminist gains." —*Booklist*

"Tanenbaum provides the latest in academic research. . . . An entertaining mix of examples from pop culture, newspaper and magazine articles, and original fieldwork. She makes the subject personal. . . . [*Catfight*'s] approach to the contradictions between feminist rhetoric and women's real experiences is sure to attract even more attention for this fast-rising social critic."

—*Publishers Weekly*

"Tanenbaum illustrates with empathy and humor the insidiousness of competition. . . . The book's blend of analysis and activism gives a smart, considered voice to a subject that still remains largely in the shadows, and encourages all of us to drag it into the light."

—*Bitch* magazine

"Tanenbaum's prose is provocative. . . . She succeeds beautifully at getting women to think about the role competition plays in their daily lives." —*San Francisco Bay Guardian*

"*Catfight* is an incisive exploration of a long-taboo subject—how and why women sabotage one another. Tanenbaum is a witty young woman, wise beyond her years. Her insights and lively stories explain the essence of women's resentment of other women; how to spot sabotage by the Other Woman; why rape victims are often disbelieved even by woman friends; and much more. Since competition is a learned behavior, not innate, Tanenbaum is able to guide us toward healthy competition. *Catfight* will prompt women to confront—and cure—their own feelings of competitiveness."

—GAIL SHEEHY

"Tanenbaum's first book, *Slut! Growing Up Female with a Bad Reputation,* was the precursor to all the books about indirect aggression among teenage girls. In *Catfight,* Tanenbaum is especially sensitive to adult female-female competition, cruelty, and cooperation among young, educated, professional women who are new mothers or who are thinking about how to balance careers and mothering. Tanenbaum herself balances biblical narrative, myth, social science research, literature, original interviews, and personal memoir in a graceful and feminist voice."

—PHYLLIS CHESLER, PH.D., author of
Woman's Inhumanity to Woman

© Cheung Ching-Ming

About the Author

LEORA TANENBAUM is the author of *Slut! Growing Up Female
with a Bad Reputation* and a rising young talent of journalism today. She has written for *Newsday*, *Seventeen*, *Ms.*, and
The Nation, among others, and appears regularly on a variety of national television programs. She lives in New York
City with her husband and two children.

CATFIGHT

CATFIGHT

Rivalries Among Women—from Diets to Dating, from the Boardroom to the Delivery Room

LEORA TANENBAUM

Perennial

An Imprint of HarperCollinsPublishers

The excerpt "A Woman of Valor," Proverbs 31:10–29, on page 255 is taken from the *Tanakh* © 1985 by the Jewish Publication Society. Used by permission.

Except for those who have given the author permission to use their names, the people quoted in this book have had their names changed. In a few instances, occupations and geographic locations have been changed to ensure anonymity. All ages and ethnicities remain unchanged.

A hardcover edition of this book was published in 2002 by Seven Stories Press. It is here reprinted by arrangement with Seven Stories Press.

HarperCollins books may be purchased for educational, business, or sales promotional use. For information please write: Special Markets Department, HarperCollins Publishers Inc., 10 East 53rd Street, New York, NY 10022.

First Perennial edition published 2003.

Designed by M. Astella Saw

Library of Congress Cataloging-in-Publication Data
Tanenbaum, Leora.
    Catfight : rivalries among women—from diets to dating, from the
    boardroom to the delivery room / Leora Tanenbaum.
    —1st Perennial ed.
        p. cm.
    Originally published: New York : Seven Stories Press, 2002.
    Includes bibliographical references and index.
    ISBN 0-06-052838-9
    1. Women—Psychology. 2. Women—Social   conditions.
    3. Competition (Psychology). I. Title.

HQ1206.T2143 2003
305.42—dc21

                                                   2003053591

03 04 05 06 07 ❖/RRD 10 9 8 7 6 5 4 3 2 1

In memory of
SASSI LONNER

CONTENTS

introduction 13

chapter one: THE ROOTS OF THE PROBLEM 37

Learning to Compete.....................................39

Women Divided by Class and Race 49

Women and Resentment.................................55

Women's "Essential" Nature 58

Indirect Aggression 61

Members Only...64

Healthy Competition 70

chapter two: BEAUTY 77

The Beauty Bind 82

Young, Thin, White... 88

...And Well Dressed 94

History of the American Beauty Ideal 98

Miss America 105

Feminism and Beauty 113

Cosmetic Surgery 116

Who's the Thinnest of Them All? 119

Eating Disorders 126

Dieting Mothers, Dieting Daughters...........................130

chapter three: DATING 135

The Other Woman in Literature 139

Dollars and Dependence 145

The New Singles Culture...151

The Other Woman Today 159

When the Other Woman Is Your Friend 165

Here Comes the Bride 169

chapter four: WORK 173

Sex Discrimination: Yes, It Still Exists 178

Job Insecurity..183

Tough as Nails 192

The Powerful Woman 196

The Female Advantage 204

Soft as Silk...209

Caution: Women at Work...218

chapter five: MOTHERHOOD 225

The Isolation of New Mothers 228

The Sacrificial Mother 236

The Biggest Antagonism 249

Working Mothers 255

Stay-at-Home Mothers 267

chapter six: WHEN WOMEN WORK TOGETHER 275

The Suffrage Movement 275

Women in Sports Today...283

The Most Feminine Athlete Wins 291

epilogue 303

notes 307

acknowledgments 325

index 327

CATFIGHT

INTRODUCTION

Competitiveness between women is a fact. It has a history and function in American society that does not benefit women. So why does it persist? And can we make it go away? Before tackling these questions we need to understand the role of competitiveness on a personal level.

I've long been fascinated by the issue of competitiveness between women because I've long been, well, competitive with other women. Growing up I wanted not only to get A's, but to get more A's than others. In junior high, when I developed an hourglass figure, I felt awkward about my burgeoning physique, but also good about getting more attention from the boys than the other girls did. In college I lived with a woman who possessed many traits I wanted in a friend—she was smart, witty, reflective, adventurous—but her beauty made her a magnet for men, plus she was talented as a journalist, a career I wished for myself. All of which led my envy to trump our friendship. My loss.

Another college friend now lives just blocks away from me, on Manhattan's West Side. We each have young children and we work in similar professions. Only her apartment is a *Friends*-worthy "classic six" with a terrace overlooking Central Park; her little girls rarely fuss or whine; and her career (travel writer) is glamorous and gives her the opportunity to take expenses-paid vacations around the world. And, oh yes, she is beautiful; wears gorgeous, perfectly fitting, up-to-the-minute clothes; has a good-looking, successful husband; and never has a chipped manicure. She seems so…perfect. I find it difficult to spend time with her.

When I was thirty, my husband and I decided to have a child, and I became pregnant. My status as Mother-To-Be was considered open for discussion by every woman I knew. Even strangers on supermarket checkout lines felt totally at ease asking me: would I have an epidural, would I breast-feed, would I continue to work? My answers—yes, I'm not sure, yes—elicited judgmental eyebrow raises, if not outright condemnations. Labor is *supposed* to feel like you're being ripped in two! Breast milk is best! Only a negligent mother would *think* of working before her child enters first grade, and even then a mother should only work part time! Feeling under attack, I began obsessing about the choices that other mothers made. To protect my fragile ego, I imagined that anyone who diverged from my path was a mindless baby machine without an ounce of ambition.

It was actually the most trivial part of my pregnancy that held particular fascination: the rate and size of my weight gain. I had gained too much too fast, I was told. Or, I hadn't gained enough— was I one of those crazy, misguided women who actually *diets* while pregnant, thereby harming the health of the fetus?! I couldn't win with anyone. When you're pregnant and wearing the same five outfits over and over, it would be nice for others to compliment you on your looks, even if they don't really mean it. Of course, lots of women (and men) did indeed tell me that I looked glowing and happy and wonderful. But just as often, I experienced exchanges like this one, with a colleague:

"You look so big; how far along are you?"

"Five and a half months," I mumbled.

"You're only *five and a half* months? Hmmm…You know, my daughter gained only nine pounds during her entire pregnancy."

I declined to mention that with three and a half months to go, I had already surpassed her daughter's total gain. Instead, I went immediately to the nearest women's room, which fortunately had a full-length mirror, stared at my out-of-control belly, and pondered my options if I outgrew my maternity clothes. Later, on the street, I saw another, larger pregnant woman. I reckoned the number of pounds *she* had gained, and felt better.

As you can see, I measure myself against other women. I constantly need to prove my worth, show everyone (especially myself) that I am capable, deserving, a woman who should be paid attention to. At some level, this is an expression of inadequacy. I worry I can never measure up. I am not smart, fashionable, thin, savvy, or maternal enough. The success of another woman translates into my failure. And my success translates into her failure—which makes my success all the more sweet. Although I am a feminist, committed to the idea that every woman should be given the opportunity to succeed in whatever endeavor she chooses, there is also a part of me that feels reassured if a woman on the same playing field stumbles. Such behavior is damaging. It never soothes my anxieties and always wields the potential to harm my relationships with others.

Why don't I feel competitive with men? I discount them as true rivals because, in most arenas, they either have more power than I (such as in their ability to earn more money or to rise in their professions) or they're not striving for the same things I am (such as being a good mother). I don't regard men as rivals because their successes in life have more to do with their privilege than with my failure.

For my own sanity, I needed to inspect the roots of my competitiveness. But I found that it was not my problem alone. Essayist Anne Taylor Fleming has perfectly expressed this problem faced by so many contemporary American women:

> Whenever I enter a room of people these days, I am conscious that it is the women, not the men, who give me the once-over, a quick, slightly veiled, not entirely ungenerous instant appraisal. I look back at these women across the room as if it were empty of men. Who are you, our eyes say to one another, what joys and sorrows have you known, what do you do, where do you work, where do you buy your clothes, but mostly, mostly, we ask one another, are you successful, do you have what you want, do you have what I want? There then ensues a kind of amiable grilling, a sizing up, a comparing of husbands, children, children's schools, numbers of miles run that day: the underlying question always: is she farther ahead than I? [1]

This book is an exploration of a phenomenon that affects nearly every American woman at every stage of life, beginning with the teenage years, when she feels competitive with other girls over fashion and the attention of boys, to midlife and older years, when she feels competitive with younger women rising in the workplace. It also influences the life of every woman who builds a family, especially if she tries to advance her career at the same time. In this book I focus on women in their twenties and thirties because they face this phenomenon most acutely. But American women of all ages will recognize the dilemmas of woman-against-woman competitiveness.

Envy and competitiveness are close cousins, but they are not the same thing. Both stem from societal inequality and an ensuing psychological sense of inadequacy. But envy—the feeling that I want what she has—leaves open the possibility of cooperation. I may covet what she has, but that doesn't make her a better person and it doesn't mean that we can't work together. I can usually rise above my envy because I recognize that cooperation has the potential of eliminating the inequalities that bred the envy in the first place. Competitiveness, however—the feeling that I want to surpass her—usually precludes cooperation. When women feel competitive, we want to feel superior and we want our rivals to be inferior. As a result, we do not believe we have anything to gain in cooperating because we want to perpetuate the inequality between us.

A person can feel envious but still be content. We live in a world filled with inequalities, and we all recognize that some people possess attributes or things that we would also like to possess, but do not. It is possible to long for these attributes or things yet remain fulfilled. Being envious isn't fun—it is, fundamentally, the recognition of the unfairness of inequality—but it isn't, in and of itself, destructive. (Besides, though I may envy what she has, I may possess something she lacks, so there is a sense of balance to our worlds.) Competitiveness is different. It is envy transformed into a destructive feeling of one-upmanship.

Sometimes, of course, competitiveness can be a positive thing—if it is out in the open rather than covert. A rival can spur a person to achieve heights she might not achieve on her own. When I swim laps at the Y, I always swim harder and faster when there is another, better swimmer in the lane with me. If a friend lands an assignment to write an article for a high-paying, prestigious magazine, I am encouraged to try to get such an assignment myself. My ambition is kindled by others who become, unintentionally, my rivals. Without realizing it, they show me what is possible and attainable.

This book focuses on the negative, destructive elements of competition because those are what must change. It is precisely the negative side to competition that is also undiscussed and unresolved. Much of the time, our competitiveness is tacit, underground. The covert desire to surpass another necessarily becomes bound up with resentment, bitterness, pettiness, and, in some cases, all-consuming obsession. One does not feel fulfilled with her lot. What she has is not enough. She needs more. She needs to be better than others.

What does she gain from being competitive? Initially, a woman feels a sense of purpose, even excitement. It feels good to have a goal. But when that goal is at the expense of another woman, fulfillment is usually short-lived. For as long as competitiveness continues, the insecurities that sparked it will continue to gnaw at her and destroy any sense of self-worth. She will also become divided from other women.

We feel competitive with one another because of our confused place in society. On the face of it, we are equal to men. Thanks to the tireless work of women's-movement activists in the late 1960s and 1970s, and to the continuing work of feminists today, we live lives far different from those of our mothers and grandmothers. We can have sex with far less anxiety about having an unwanted child, work in many of the same professions as men, and see ourselves represented in national sports leagues and rock bands, as well as among television news anchors. Many of us don't have to wear hose, heels, and girdles if we don't want to. We cannot legally be fired from jobs when we become pregnant or when we rebuff the sexual advances of a boss. We have attained high positions on the Supreme Court, in Congress, in presidential cabinets. Having been born in 1969, I can take all of these achievements for granted. Yet I also know that without these gains, my life would be intolerable.

And yet…at the same time that we are gaining liberties, we are also expected to conform, more or less, to a narrow role. According to the contemporary, middle-class American feminine script, we are supposed to attain the highest educational level possible, develop a meaningful career, get married, quit or slow down our career to have children, stay at home with them, return five or seven years later to work in a job that lets us get home in time to make dinner (and that therefore tends to go nowhere), and somehow always manage to look sexy. This script is conveyed in subtle and blatant ways. Our First Lady is proud that she lacks career ambition and is content to glide on her husband's coattails. The legal right (and, depending on where you live, the logistical ability) to terminate an unwanted or dangerous pregnancy, already precarious, is eroding at a steady clip. Mothers do not have earning parity with fathers, nor do they typically achieve the professional heights that fathers do. Most women continue to work in the so-called pink ghetto as secretaries, cashiers, maids, clerks, waitresses, hospital and nursing home aides, and elementary school and day-care teachers—jobs characterized by pitifully low wages and little, if any, prestige. The national media tell us that all child care provided by anyone other than the mother is deficient and that mothers should stay home with their young children. Mothers mistakenly believe they have to raise their children without assistance from anyone; to ask for help is evidence that one has failed as a mother. Keeping one's home reasonably clean and organized is no longer enough; authors like Cheryl Mendelson (*Home Comforts*) and icons like Martha Stewart instruct middle-class women on the joys of excessive domesticity. Women's fashions are at their clingiest, with low-rider, belly-button-baring outfits the norm, while men's fashions are at their baggiest. (Could it be, as many feminists have suggested, that women's fashions become more feminized the more power women accrue?)

Given the freedoms that women have attained over the last three decades, the traditional female role seems outdated. Many women, therefore, either defy it, ignore it, or just fall out of it. But its allure snares most of us eventually in some capacity. Besides, whether we end up following the American feminine script or thumbing our noses at it, it exacts a toll on our attitude toward other women: We become divided from one another and competitive with each other. This is because femininity and competition go hand in hand. By definition, the female role is something a woman "wins" at. Being feminine entails being attractive (more than other women); dating, living with, or marrying a "good catch" (who earns more money or is better-looking than other women's men); and having faultless children (who are smarter, cuter, more creative, and better behaved than her peers' children). If she works in a career surrounded by men, she has to do a better job than the other women so that she can be the perfect token female who is almost as good as the guys. When women's traditional role is exalted, a woman feels pressured to "win" at being the most feminine woman possible.

Yet when we think about competition, we hold a double standard. Men by their nature are supposedly ambitious and competitive; women by their nature are supposedly devoid of ambition and competitiveness. Women are caught in an impossible bind: We need to be competitive in order to be truly feminine, yet we can't be competitive because that would make us unwomanly. The only way out, as we will see, is for a woman to be competitive but to *pretend* that she is not. Covert competition, in my opinion, is unhealthy competition. This state of affairs explains why few women are willing to discuss their competitiveness. Even if we are self-aware enough to recognize our competitive feelings, we don't like to admit that we have them.

To understand and analyze their conditioning as women, members of Redstockings, an influential, early feminist activist group, developed the idea of consciousness-raising: In a group, women shared personal experiences. They discovered that others experienced the same hardships, and they analyzed the roots of their problems. "The personal"—problems that had seemed private and exclusive to oneself—were in fact "political"—linked to wider social forces. For instance, if a woman endured cruel comments from her husband—she was fat, needed to go on a diet, and was not sexually attractive to him—she internalized the belief that she was indeed ugly and unfeminine. But when she discovered that other women, who were far from unattractive, were experiencing the same abuse, she came to realize that restrictive beauty standards, combined with men's expectations—not her physical appearance—were the real problems. Women's eyes and minds were opened to the fact that their oppression was connected with their conditioning and that they were not alone. They found liberation through linking with other women, through their shared astonishment at how they were being manipulated to comply with what society wished them to do or be.

We could still benefit from consciousness-raising. We rarely, if ever, acknowledge how competitive we still are. Ashamed of our behavior, we refuse to discuss it openly, or we place blame on another woman—"*She's* competitive with *me*" or "Sure I'm competitive, but only with *myself*." But today, consciousness-raising has devolved into recovery-movement-style sharing. The energy created by the awareness that "the personal is political" has been replaced by an emphasis on personal challenges for improvement; the political element has largely disappeared. (At my local Barnes & Noble bookstore, ten bookcases are devoted to "Self-Improvement." Four are filled with books on "Women's Studies.") Yet an emphasis on self-improvement—rather than group improvement—serves to keep women isolated from one another. It makes everyone's problem appear individual, not collective or societal. This isolation compounds our inclination to compare ourselves with others and find ourselves lacking.

Today, pockets of feminist activism exist, but it is generally rare to find collaboration among women trying to advance the interests of women as a class of people. Notable exceptions include young "third wave" feminist activists, who continue the momentous battles for abortion rights and protection from sexual violence but who are only beginning to collide with the challenge of having children and working and therefore generally (and understandably) have not focused on bread-and-butter issues like subsidized child care. There are also religious women who are making amazing strides in chipping away at sexism in religious life but who limit their struggle for women's rights to their narrow milieu. More typical is the collaboration of mothers who join forces not to press for women's rights but to assert their moral authority as mothers on an unrelated social issue such as gun control. The mothers who participated in the Million Mom March on Washington in 2000, for instance, only reinforced our country's perception of women's traditional role as the moral guardians of our youth.

Does the idea of universal sisterhood have validity? On one hand, all women share a fundamental commonality and understanding of one another because we all experience (or have the potential to experience) menstruation, birthing, nursing, and the cultural expectations of being a woman. But when taken to an extreme, this thinking loses focus: Does a poor black married woman in Somalia share any common ground with a white lesbian Internet editor in San Francisco? Still, there is some basis of commonality among women. All women, after all, experience sexism. We are all defined by our reproductive capacity because so many cultures equate having a uterus with being a mother. Even if we do not give birth or become adoptive mothers, we are expected to "mother" others through nurturing or enabling behavior (taking care of an elderly parent, preparing meals for our families). We are all subjected to the sexual double standard: Any one of us could be called to task for our sexuality. And without effective, safe, cheap, easy, and widely available contraception, our reproductive biology impedes our physical safety and social mobility, whether we are heterosexual or lesbian.

Yet, as we will see, women—even those of similar backgrounds—do not automatically understand each other and empathize with one another simply by virtue of experiencing these hardships. If there is any doubt, psychologist Phyllis Chesler lays it to rest in her comprehensive book, *Woman's Inhumanity to Woman*. Chesler exhaustively chronicles the hostility that women around the globe are capable of—from shunning and maliciously gossiping to being complicit in acts of rape or murder.[2] By and large, "woman" is not a class of people with the same values, ideals, and assumptions. However, I believe that there is enough shared ground to allow us to join forces and minimize the antagonisms.

The truth is, women remain divided. On some level, we are trained—by mothers, fathers, friends, religions, the media—to value male opinion and attention, even at the expense of sisterhood. As feminist theorist bell hooks has observed, "We are taught that women are 'natural' enemies, that solidarity will never exist between us because we cannot, should not, and do not bond with one another."[3] Sadly, many females—even "you go, girl" types who otherwise are the first to show support for feminist causes—can be very quick to malign other girls and women. Our secret hope is to raise our own value. But in the face of competition with other women, do any of us feel better about ourselves? Of course not. We are left feeling envious, resentful, and inadequate. And yet, it doesn't take long before we're competing again. In a sense, we cooperate in our own subordination.

Whose interests are served by our relentless compulsion to belittle other women? By and large, a small number of privileged, individual women benefit from this state of affairs. They reap the rewards of "winning" at femininity. They remain at the top of the feminine social pecking order. Still, even the stature of these fortunate few is quite limited when compared with the stature of the group that truly benefits from our situation—men in power. Because of competition among women, men in power, usually white, get to safeguard their high-echelon jobs in business, medicine, law, government, and the military. Unless they are single fathers, they get to have children without doing half the scut work. They can afford to be choosy about whom they marry, if they marry at all. They get to ogle women in revealing outfits on the street and in their offices without having to expose a proportionate amount of their own physiques. They get to earn more money. They can divorce knowing that, most of the time, their standard of living won't drop dramatically. They can keep their jobs after having a baby without worrying that they are negligent parents. The elevation of the traditional female role, and the ensuing division of women from one another, serves a society run primarily by men. While women are shopping for a new outfit, on the Stairmaster, or dragging their three-year-old from music class to art class, men in power are making decisions that ensure their place at the top of the social order.

There is no reason to put down every facet of traditional femininity. I enjoy wearing makeup, high heels, low-cut camisoles.

There's nothing I find more relaxing than getting a manicure. I love taking care of my young sons; indeed, I often find it impossible to concentrate on my work knowing that they are in the next room, their delicious, plump legs just begging to be squeezed. But I enjoy these things precisely because I have chosen them. If they were mandatory, I would feel oppressed. And, in fact, I do feel oppressed that I earn so much less money than my husband, even though I work equally hard. I do feel oppressed that my character alone is judged on the basis of the achievements of our sons. I do feel oppressed that if, God forbid, I were to become widowed or divorced, I would be in really big financial trouble. I do feel oppressed that when we attend a formal event, my husband gets to wear the same suit he always wears, while I have to coordinate a not-worn-too-many-times dress with shoes, hose, jewelry, and handbag. I do feel oppressed that, even though I'm married, I still feel the need to be at least a little flirtatious and even a bit deferential with men—otherwise I am considered too serious, too uptight, or a bitch. I do feel oppressed that I have to go to the gym three times a week to stay in shape, lest I be condemned as a woman who has "let herself go."

Women are not inherently more competitive than men. Rather, our restrictive gender roles, combined with our relatively new liberties, create a confusing environment that sets us up as adversaries—and we have to compete with each other if we're ever going to succeed according to the rules of the mixed-up game we are living. And when we do compete, we tend to be more underhanded and personal in our attacks than men are. "There is data suggesting that males are much more direct expressors," says Solomon Cytrynbaum, Ph.D., a psychiatry and behavioral sciences professor at Northwestern University who has studied the relationship between gender and authority in groups for more than twenty-five years. "They compete more directly; they go head to head. If they undercut someone, they tend to do it more directly. Women are much more behind the scenes, much more subtle. If you ask women in the workplace about issues that trouble them, this is among the most frequent concerns they report."

In part women are more "behind the scenes" because we have few, if any, legitimate arenas in which we *can* openly compete—forcing our ambitions for power, money, and control underground. As writer Elizabeth Wurtzel puts it, "Women, you see, like any other group obstructed from paths to power, tend to get their action on the sly."[4] Men, on the other hand, have many opportunities to compete and excel. A male friend hits the nail on the head when he jokes, "I watch *Jerry Springer* for the catfights. If I want to see men fight, I'll watch the news."

Being competitive, catty, and cunning are part of the stereotype of femininity. At the same time, however, women are said to cooperate in gentle sisterhood and to shun any ambition that might pit one against another. These stereotypes contradict each other, providing girls and women with clashing messages. But it's the former stereotype—the ruthlessly competitive woman—that has captured more attention throughout the centuries. That women are competitive is considered a given—so much so that Nancy Reagan felt entitled to claim, when she was accused of engaging in the unethical practice of taking twenty-thousand-dollar couture gowns from designers while First Lady, that "some women aren't all that crazy about a woman who wears a size 4, and seems to have no trouble staying slim."[5]

The stereotype of the competitive woman has a long history. In the Bible, we read of Sarah banishing Hagar from her home to languish in the desert, Leah disguising her identity to marry Jacob in place of her sister Rachel, Peninah taunting Hannah (her husband's other wife) about her infertility, and two prostitutes fighting over an infant before King Solomon.[6] The Trojan War, legend has it, was caused by female competitiveness. Aphrodite desperately wanted to outshine her rivals in beauty, and lured Paris (who had the power to declare her "the fairest") to Helen of Troy. Paris stole Helen away from her Spartan husband, and the ensuing war lasted ten years.

Twentieth-century cinema served up, again and again, representations of women who are ruthless and cunning in every aspect of their lives. Classics like *The Women* (1939) and *All About Eve* (1950) portrayed cartoonlike predatory females circling each other. *Rich and Famous* (1981) and the French film *Mina Tannenbaum* (1993) thoughtfully and seriously explored the complexities of women's friendships and the undercurrent of competitiveness and envy flowing through them. *Working Girl* (1988) gave us the portrayal of a secretary who struggles for her big break on Wall Street at the expense of her (conniving) female boss. *The Hand That Rocks the Cradle* (1992) showed us that a woman who dares to leave her child with a nanny deserves what she gets: a psychotic and jealous female caregiver. *The First Wives Club* (1996) and *Stepmom* (1998) exposed antagonisms between first and second wives.

The noun *catfight*, used in a mocking, derogatory way to describe a vicious clash between women, dates back to 1919 but only became popular in the 1970s. Cultural historian Susan Douglas describes how the national news media, in an effort to downplay the women's liberation movement, portrayed it not as a dignified struggle for women's rights but as a silly squabble between homely hippies and happy housewives.[7] But the noun *cat*, according to the Oxford English Dictionary, has been used as a term of contempt for a spiteful or backbiting woman as far back as the early 1600s, while the adjective *catty* to describe a woman who denigrates another woman in a malicious way dates back to 1886. In the United States, *cat* was also used as a term of vulgarity to refer to a vulva or vagina; it was sometimes a synonym for a sexually promiscuous woman or prostitute. Beginning in the early 1900s, the term *cat-fit* was used to describe a fit of anger or hysteria that was expected from a child or woman.

Today, pop culture teems with references to backbiting "other women." In one week alone in May 2001, I watched an episode of *The Sopranos* in which Tony Soprano cheats on his wife with an "other woman," and went to the movies to see *Bridget Jones's Diary*, in which Bridget discovers that the man she pines for is sleeping with another woman. I also sat through the off-Broadway production of *Cinderella*, in which stepsisters fight over whose foot fits in the glass slipper, and listened to the Ani DiFranco song "32 Flavors," which includes the lyrics "everyone harbors a secret hatred/for the prettiest girl in the room."

Advertising agencies, magazines, and television screenwriters continue to exploit the stereotype to the fullest. An ad for Aquafina bottled water shows two women in a boutique viciously grabbing for the same pair of shoes. (That's right, it's an ad for *water*.) The spring 1999 Louis Vuitton ad campaign showcased young models, fierce determination in their eyes and posture, fighting each other over the designer handbags. *New York* magazine recently ran a profile of a beautiful socialite scorned by other women in her social milieu because she is a Latina from Queens, as opposed to a white, uppercrust Wasp, while the cover of *W* magazine's June 2002 issue trumpeted, "Meow! Fashion's Best Catfights."

Meanwhile, the characters on *Sex and the City* blithely refer to young, beautiful women as "bitches"; Carrie buys five-hundred-dollar Manolo Blahnik mules and a Bergdorf's dress costing her a month's rent in order to outdress the organizer of an arts luncheon, who happens to be the wife of her ex-boyfriend. *Ally McBeal* was similarly rife with women's jealousies; Ally was for a number of seasons in love with a married ex-boyfriend who was a colleague at her Boston law firm (and whose wife was another colleague). In one episode, Ally and the wife, Georgia, who had finally attempted to become friends, took a kickboxing class together and almost killed each other after a friendly sparring session escalated, their unresolved aggression pouring out. But Ally's competitiveness with Georgia was surpassed by her competitiveness with just about every other woman with whom she crossed paths. Typical episode: Ally tells everyone that the opposing counsel on a case, a beautiful woman, is a "bitch"; after the commercial break, said bitchiness is confirmed when the lawyer says to Ally, her saccharine-sweet smile belying her hostility: "Ally, forgive me for saying this. But don't you think it's a little inappropriate to wear such a short skirt in a courtroom?"

When media critic and University of Buffalo professor Elaine Rapping showed a segment of *Ally McBeal* to her "Gender and Media" class, her male students were shocked by the negative stereotypes. They couldn't believe that the women on the show were so competitive and catty. To Rapping's dismay, the female students, even smart and outspoken ones, insisted that "that's how women really are" and "that's what you have to do to be successful."[8]

Rapping was appalled that to these young, impressionable women, *Ally McBeal* is a reflection of reality. And I, too, am deeply unsettled by their uncritical endorsement of backstabbing behavior. It seems to me that the stereotype of the competitive female gains cultural force as women accrue societal power, because the more power we have, the more threatening we become. But if a highly educated lawyer such as the Ally McBeal character is portrayed as competitive and deeply neurotic, she obviously can't be all that competent. On the other hand, I don't believe that the stereotype is sheer misogynistic fantasy, something wholly dreamed up by Hollywood and Madison Avenue. The competitive women of media land are caricatures rather than concoctions. While the machinations of Ally McBeal and company are obviously exaggerated—and, very troublingly, influence how men and women come to regard real-life women—are they entirely different from the competitive maneuvers of many ordinary women?

I say no. Tempting though it may be to dismiss the stereotype as part of a sexist plot or backlash, it doesn't do anyone, least of all women, any good to do so. Rather, we must confront the stereotype. We must be honest about the fact that, to some extent, American women *are* guilty of occasional acts of covert competition. Of course, we tend to be more subtle than the cinema's Eve Harringtons or television's Ally McBeals—we are more likely to make a cutting comment here, a sizzling scowl there. But let's face it: Feeling insecure, many of us really do resort to backstabbing and other manipulative behaviors as a pitiful way to make ourselves feel, however fleetingly, more powerful. And, with the media-generated, highly exaggerated images of competitive women everywhere around us, it can become difficult for women to maintain a sense of which behaviors are appropriate in daily life.

Today, American women have more power than in the past. Shouldn't we be grateful? Aren't we lucky in comparison to past generations of women? Yes and yes—but the fact is that we still do not have enough power. No matter how high a woman may rise, there is almost always a man above her who makes the final, bottom-line decisions. Condoleezza Rice may have risen to National Security Advisor, but it's men such as Secretary of State Colin Powell and Defense Secretary Donald Rumsfeld who step in to make the *real* decisions about the war. No wonder women's insecurity today is so complex and volatile. It is fraught with contradictions.

Most women enjoy intimate, emotionally satisfying relationships with female friends, colleagues, mothers, and sisters—relationships they couldn't possibly experience with men. But most women also feel beleaguered by adversarial, competitive relationships with female friends, colleagues, mothers, and sisters—relationships they also couldn't possibly experience with men. American women of different ethnicities, economic backgrounds, and sexual orientations have stories of becoming a target of envy after losing a lot of weight; experiencing peer pressure from other mothers to be a stay-at-home mom instead of a return-to-paying-job mom (or vice versa); and encountering the resentment of female mentors who tried to quash their success at work. Many women of color can talk for hours about tensions between dark-skinned and light-skinned women, and about competing with white women in the workplace. Many single women can spell out in excruciating detail the delicate negotiations necessary when dating a friend's ex. Many new mothers spend more time at baby play-groups defending their decision to bottle-feed (or breast-feed, depending on the peer group) than they do humming "The Wheels on the Bus" to their little miracles.

When I began work on this book, a trusted male colleague suggested I focus in depth on one competitive arena—the workplace, say, or motherhood—and drop the others. To me, the idea was unthinkable. When a woman feels competitive with another woman, she generally does not isolate one area for evaluation. She does not judge another woman only on the basis of her physique or her title at the office. Rather, she compares herself to the other woman as a complete package. Women are pushing themselves to excel in every arena at the same time. "A decade ago, the feminist ideal was to have a great career and a family," says Susan Bordo, author of several books on body image. "Now the ideal is to have a great career and dress like a sex kitten, too."[9]

Thirty years ago, in the inaugural issue of *Ms.* magazine, Letty Cottin Pogrebin wrote a landmark essay in which she assailed the patriarchal system that positions women as competitors. When a woman's identity is "deprived of nourishment," she wrote, "it fights; and the most convenient target is another victim." The rules, she explained, are straightforward. First, "if you feel depressed, don't examine your discontent—find a woman who's worse off than you are." Second, "if you doubt your attractiveness, don't question the standards of beauty—outdo and outdress every woman in sight."

Next, if you're worried that you're not "feminine" enough, don't question feminine norms; instead, "point a finger at some tough cookie and call yourself a powder puff by comparison." And finally, "if you believe that you're intellectually lacking, don't embark on the Harvard Classics—ridicule other women for sublimating their frustrations in affairs of the mind."

The rules are as relevant today as they were three decades ago during the bloom of the women's liberation movement. We've achieved so much in these three decades: the right to an abortion, gender parity in law and medical school enrollments, the popularity of black women's literature, the passage of Title IX. Yet too many of us are still mired in the age-old game of one-upmanship.

In her final paragraph, Pogrebin advised, "It might be useful to figure out precisely when I got hooked on competing with women. But, frankly, I can't spend any more time speculating about it. I, like you, have more important things to do."[10] I respectfully disagree. I believe that we *must* spend time speculating about competitiveness between women. It is important and necessary to explore the roots of this competition, which at best makes one woman covet another woman's designer handbag and at worst thwarts her in the development of her career and her ability to raise children with sanity. Women can't afford to remain divided from each other.

"The power we get from this competition between women is really petty power," sighs Jill Nelson, *USA Today* columnist and author of *Straight, No Chaser: How I Became a Grown-Up Black Woman* and *Volunteer Slavery: My Authentic Negro Experience*. "It's easier to get caught up in the struggle for petty power than in real power. We have to challenge ourselves about that. Why does it make me feel better because I sliced up some woman when she walked into the room? We need to affirm each other. Instead of looking for what we can criticize about a woman, let's look for something we can celebrate."[11]

We must not be consoled with the bread crumbs of petty power. If we want the next three decades to be as productive as the last three, we must begin celebrating each other and, in doing so, take the reigns of real, raw, raging power.

CHAPTER ONE
THE ROOTS OF THE PROBLEM

The more complicated a woman's life becomes, the more likely she is to take stock of her life and compare it with that of other women. And women's lives are complicated indeed. Women born and raised in the wake of modern feminism live in a contradictory cultural climate. We have been taught clashing messages about what it means to be a woman. We are caught in a threshold between two paradigms, the old and the new.

☞ Regarding beauty, we have learned from our parents, magazines, advertising, and other women: It's important to be thin and pretty and wear the latest fashions and always be well groomed. We have also learned (often from the very same sources): Such concerns are frivolous. Inner beauty, not superficial appearance, is what counts.

☞ When it comes to romance, we've been told: We need to find a good man and get married. We've also been told: We don't need a man to be complete as a person—and with women's rise in the workplace, we don't need his money, either.

☞ In the workplace: We need to compete like a man to get ahead. And yet: It's important for women to share, to be cooperative, and to be nice—otherwise we are seen as castrating bitches.

☞ What about our source of identity? Becoming a full-time wife and mother is a woman's finest achievement, we have been taught.

But at the same time we know: A woman needs a career to pay the bills and to feel fulfilled, regardless of marital and parental status.

With all these mixed messages, women are caught in perpetual vertigo. We face internal battles about the "right" way to live our lives. No matter which path we choose, we are going against something deeply ingrained in us, against a path that many other women we know are following, against a path our mothers may have followed, even against a path we may have followed ourselves in the past. As a result, we feel defensive. To defend ourselves, we go to great lengths to justify our decisions, to validate ourselves, to prove to ourselves and to others that our chosen path is the right one. Along the way, any ambivalence we might have about our life course hardens into certainty that our path is the only correct and appropriate one.

Of course, no one can live her life by checking off a series of boxes. Many women today strive to achieve a balance between the old rules and the new—by wearing lipstick and mascara but unapologetically eating lasagna and ice cream; by getting married but striving for an egalitarian partnership; by mentoring other women but strategically moving up the corporate ladder; by raising children but continuing to put in full-time hours at the office. If juggling all this sounds easy, you probably think that Linda Tripp tattled on Monica Lewinsky to protect her young friend from an unhealthy relationship. Living as a woman today is difficult, fraught with pressures, with many of us desperate for a sense of control and direction. An easy way to delude ourselves into thinking we've achieved mastery over our lives is to compete with other women. By competing, we place ourselves and others into neat little categories—"I'm a doting stay-at-home mom; *she's* a workaholic who neglects her kids" or "I work out four times a week; *she's* let herself get out of shape"—that serve to organize our lives and deliver them from chaos to complacency.

Women also, perversely, compete over who is worst off. We listen to a friend complain about her evil boss, her boyfriend's "commitment problem," and her fat thighs—and then we checkmate her by telling her that we've got all the same problems ourselves, *plus* our mother has broken her hip and our credit cards are maxed out, so of course our situation is truly worse and we deserve more sympathy. Many of us can't help but strive for the Biggest Martyr award. If we can't get the recognition we crave for our achievements, at the very least let us get some recognition for our burdens and sorrows.

Competition, of whatever form, is caused by feelings of inadequacy. When a person feels threatened, her instinct is often to go on the defensive. But the cause is more than psychological. A sense of inadequacy is fostered by a very real societal situation: women's restrictive roles.

LEARNING TO COMPETE

Are competitive power struggles inevitable? We live, after all, in a world of finite resources and limited conceptions of status and beauty—don't these circumstances necessitate competition to weed out the losers and reward the victors, to determine how desirable resources will be distributed? A number of different thinkers have grappled with these questions and have come to different conclusions.

First and foremost, writer and former educator Alfie Kohn declares a loud and emphatic no: We don't need competition. In his brilliant critique of competition, *No Contest: The Case Against Competition*, Kohn skillfully and exhaustively debunks the widely held myth that competition is part of human nature. Competition—or, as Kohn terms it, "mutually exclusive goal attainment" (the concept that my success equals your failure)—is not necessary for evolution. Herbert Spencer's soundbite on Darwin's theory of evolution, "survival of the fittest," conjures up images of the kind of violent struggles between animal species portrayed on public television. But in fact, survival generally requires that individuals work together, not against each other.

Competition is learned behavior. No one is born with an ingrained motivation to compete with others, says Kohn. Drawing on his background in education, he poignantly cites example after example of schoolchildren encouraged by their teachers to compete over who has more gold stars, whose drawings made it to the bulletin board, who got higher grades. Yet when children learn to study and play cooperatively, they learn better—and they prefer the cooperative arrangement. Success through competition is not necessary for one's psychological health. A woman does not have to compare herself to another in order to gain a personal sense of competence. As Kohn says,

> All of us enjoy the sense of accomplishment that comes from being particularly good at something. Sometimes it is convenient to assess that performance by comparing it to those of other people. But the individual who feels good about herself and is simply interested in doing well does not go out of her way to outperform others. She does not seek out relative judgments. She is content with a sense of personal satisfaction, sometimes buttressed, depending on the activity, by a consideration of absolute standards.... The desire to be better than others feels quite different from this desire to do well. There is something

inherently compensatory about it. One wants to outdo in order to make up for an impression, often dimly sensed, of personal inadequacy.... If competition has a voice, it is the defiant whine of the child: "Anything you can do, I can do better."[1]

The healthier one is, psychologically speaking, the less she feels the need to compete. The more she needs to compete, the more worthless she feels.

But what about productivity and the achievement of excellence? Don't we need to compete in order to do our best? Again, Kohn cites study after study showing that we do not perform better when we are trying to beat others as opposed to working with them or alone. It turns out that cooperation promotes higher achievement than competition. "Competition need never enter the picture in order for skills to be mastered and displayed, goals set and met," he concludes. [2]

Kohn's debunkings are eye-opening. But let's face it: No matter how much some of us might happen to despise competition, our culture celebrates it everywhere, from the schoolyard to the sports field to the partnership track at work. The CBS *Survivor* shows, which have pitted people against one another in challenging environments, have been a mega-success, proving that competition equals high ratings. Whether they enthusiastically embrace competition or resign themselves to it, both women and men live in a system that rewards those who rise to the top, and therefore both women and men compete in various ways.

Women sports enthusiasts, in contrast to Kohn, generally agree that competition is a fact of life and that instead of decrying it, we should focus our energy on learning to compete healthfully. Since the passage of Title IX in 1972, which prohibits sex discrimination in educational institutions, including school-sponsored athletic activities, more and more girls are growing up engaging in sports with as much intensity as boys have for decades. To women sports enthusiasts, this is a welcome phenomenon that will only help new generations of women, who learn that life, like sports, is a game with rules. To win, you have to cooperate with your team—and there is always a victor and a loser.

Mariah Burton Nelson, a former pro athlete and feminist author who has explored the advantages of competition for women, defines competition as "seeking excellence together." She writes in her book *Embracing Victory*:

> Boys learn to compete through sports. Now girls too are learning through sports what it takes to succeed: practice, teamwork, consistency, flexibility, stamina, and hard work. We're learning how it feels to be victorious, to be the best, to be subordinate to no one. We're noticing that winning is fun but that losing is no disgrace. We're developing respect, even gratitude for our rivals. We're learning that the harder we push our teammates, the stronger the team becomes.[3]

I agree with Nelson that sports can teach positive lessons about healthy ways of competing. But sports can also teach negative lessons about the importance of winning as often as possible, being ruthless, and the need to maintain a certain weight and physique. Still, women's sports enthusiasts are advancing women's status by publicly snubbing and disproving the stereotype that females are weaker than males.

Historically, most feminists have tended to side with Kohn and have argued that competition is usually a destructive force. In her

1915 utopian novel *Herland*, Charlotte Perkins Gilman imagined a country containing three million girls and women—and no boys or men. Three men on a scientific expedition enter the civilization and are astounded to discover that it is highly advanced, with beautiful architecture and landscaping. "Everything was beauty, order, perfect cleanness, and the pleasantest sense of home over it all." There was no crime, poverty, or inequality. There was also no competition. Instead, there was an "extremely high sense of solidarity" and a "limitless feeling of sisterhood."[4] Through her vision of the perfect civilization, Gilman expressed her belief that societal evils such as crime or competition are caused by men and that if women ruled the world, it would consist of one great sisterhood.

Activists in the early days of the women's liberation movement felt the same way. They consciously tried to avoid the hierarchical leadership model that was then prevalent in the male-dominated New Left. Feminism, as they saw it, would be a nonhierarchical movement of equals without any leaders. Naturally, this naïve and optimistic vision was impossible to put into practice. How do you hold a meeting or come to any consensus without a leader? Who gets to be a spokesperson when *Time* magazine comes calling? Feminists who spoke to the media and became anointed leaders were criticized by fellow activists for betraying the cause. In her memoir, *In Our Time*, activist and author Susan Brownmiller recalls numerous vicious attacks:

> Getting your name in the paper was "personal publicity" that made you a "star," guilty of the sin of personal ambition. Verbal fluency and confidence were defined as the "advantages of class privilege." Writing for a mainstream publication, even putting

your full name on your work in a countercultural paper, was castigated as "ripping off the movement's ideas."[5]

When Brownmiller told the women in her weekly feminist group
that her groundbreaking book, a history and analysis of rape, *Against
Our Will*, was almost complete, one woman exploded: "Do you have
to put your name on this book? Rape doesn't belong to you, it
belongs to the movement. You should take a stand and be the first
feminist author to do away with personal ego." Brownmiller never
returned to the group.[6]

Clearly, if women ruled the world, there would still be competition. Humorous and satiric it may be, but Gilman's utopia also
comes across as inauthentic and dishonest. The women of *Herland*,
after all, do have a hierarchy with leaders, and motherhood itself is
a status symbol, since not every woman is allowed to reproduce. It
strains credulity to think that such a society would not be beset by
competition, no matter how immaculate its landscaped lawns.
Women will always have differences in income, education, ability to
conceive, physical attractiveness, and health. We must do our best
to minimize those inequalities that are fluid (such as education), and
to accept those inequalities that are fixed (such as fertility). Along
the way, we must do our best to compete in a healthy way. Gilman
was naïve to imagine a culture without any competition whatsoever,
but surely we can strive for one that places a premium on cooperation
along with honest, above-board competition.

The psychoanalytic explanation of female competitiveness provides an alternative perspective. According to psychoanalysis, we
learn to mistrust other women through our relationship with our

mothers. To Freud, this behavior isn't so much learned as it is ordained. Girls are fated to experience conflict with their mother, Freud believed, because of the way they experience the Oedipus complex. When young girls realize they lack a penis, they "hold their mother responsible" and "do not forgive her for their being thus put at a disadvantage." Girls "feel seriously wronged" and develop an "envy for the penis" because they recognize that boys have "far superior equipment."[7] Blaming their mother for being "castrated," they now turn away from their "powerful" attachment with their mother and form a new and strong attachment with their father. "The turning away from the mother is accompanied by hostility; the attachment to the mother ends in hate," wrote Freud.[8]

Female psychoanalysts such as Helen Deutsch and Nancy Chodorow persuasively reworked Freud's idea of penis envy to make it plausible. To them, girls envy not an actual penis but what a penis represents: power, status, and a sense of self-worth. Noting that a middle-class daughter in twentieth-century Western culture most likely has been raised by her mother, not her father, Chodorow argues that the daughter has identified with a parent who lacks real power in the larger society, regardless of the amount of power the mother may have seemed to have within the household. The daughter has rejected identifying with a "devalued, passive mother," but in so doing she also has rejected and devalued herself. (Chodorow emphasizes, however, that the girl has retained a strong connection to her mother and it is through her mother that she has gained a sense of what it means to be female, as well as an ethic of connectedness to others.) Mother-daughter conflict, then, is not inevitable. It is rooted in a family structure in which the mother is the primary parent and the father is the primary breadwinner. Change gender stereotypes and parenting arrangements—by getting men very involved in child care and letting girls grow up seeing a mother who, in addition to being a skillful parent, also has "a valued role and recognized spheres of legitimate control"[9]—and circumstances can be altered. Today, women do have quite a bit of power in the larger world (though still not as much as men). As a result, today's young daughters do not grow up devaluing themselves, as per Chodorow's theory. Instead, they grow up brimming with self-confidence—which often deflates when they realize women are not allowed to be as strong as they had supposed.

Psychologist Phyllis Chesler similarly implicates the mother-daughter relationship. To Chesler, all women's relationships with other women are, to some extent, reflective of the mother-daughter bond. "Most women unconsciously expect other women to mother them and feel betrayed when a woman fails to meet their ideal standards," she writes in *Woman's Inhumanity to Woman*. "Most women are no more realistic about women than men are. To a woman other women are (supposed to be) Good Fairy Godmothers, and if they are not they may swiftly become their dreaded Evil Stepmothers."[10]

From Kohn to Nelson, and Gilman to Chodorow and Chesler, many pieces of the puzzle of woman-against-woman competitiveness have been explored. To my mind, however, it is crucial not to overlook the power of gender roles and the effect these roles have on our psyches. No matter how a girl is raised, as she grows up, she finds that the power of gender stereotypes is enormous and incredibly difficult to escape. No matter how egalitarian-minded a woman is, chances are that she still behaves, at least in some aspects, according to the old stereotype of femininity, which dictates that she separate from her mother and define herself in relation to men and to what men want. Thus, we grow up longing for male approval because men are the ones with the power. Many women compete over things they think men value, such as looking sexy. On the other hand, according to the stereotype of masculinity, a man can be self-assured whether or not women value him, so he doesn't need to compete over things he thinks women value, such as remembering an anniversary.

Society still conditions girls and women to believe they are inferior to boys and men—in terms of emotional stability, physical strength, psychological fitness, sexual behavior, mathematical ability. The implications of this message are enormous and far-reaching. The most dangerous outcome of this is self-hatred: girls and women disparage themselves and disassociate from other females. Self-hatred is common among subordinated groups of people. When power is withheld, those with power are resented. Yet their values and norms are internalized. Frantz Fanon, the influential West Indian philosopher, psychiatrist, and revolutionary who analyzed the condition of being black in a white world, wrote in 1952,

> In [children's] magazines the Wolf, the Devil, the Evil Spirit, the Bad Man, the Savage are always symbolized by Negroes or Indians; since there is always identification with the victor, the little Negro, quite as easily as the little white boy, becomes an explorer, an adventurer, a missionary "who faces the danger of being eaten by wicked Negroes."…There is identification—that

is, the young Negro subjectively adopts a white man's attitude.... As a schoolboy, I had many occasions to spend whole
hours talking about the supposed customs of the savage
Senegalese.[11]

Being black while living in a culture with negative stereotypes of
blacks leads to an alienation from and rejection of other blacks.
According to Fanon, it leads also to shame, self-contempt, even
nausea. "If the signals I get from the dominant culture are that I am
a person deserving of disdain," asks writer Jill Nelson, "is it any
wonder I begin to hate myself?"[12]

Being a woman of any color in a sexist culture leads to similar responses. The archetypical woman is self-sacrificing, nonin-
tellectual, soft and pretty, and derives utter contentment from
taking care of others. I don't identify with these traits, and yet I
am not a man. How do I reconcile this paradox? By viewing
myself as different from (read: better than) other women who do
appear to live the stereotype. A male friend who enjoys wry
humor always seems pleasantly surprised when I come up with a
well-timed deadpan. "You're the only funny woman I know," he
says. It's a compliment to me but an insult to women. Despite
myself, I eat it up every time.

When I was growing up, I thought it was cool not to like the
other girls but to hang out with the boys: The girls were, well, *girlish* and sort of prissy, while the boys beckoned with their mischief.
Many of my girlfriends remember feeling the same way. As
women, we come to believe that male approval is more significant
than female approval, and that a relationship with a man confers
more status than a relationship with a woman. Thus, many women

believe that supporting other women is suicidal if they want to achieve success in a male-dominated milieu. It's one small step away to thinking that they should cut down other women who might stand in their way.

WOMEN DIVIDED BY CLASS AND RACE

Economic and ethnic differences, in particular, breed mutual suspicions. The late 1990s' boom on Wall Street widened the income gap between the richest and poorest families, according to a 2000 report by two Washington think tanks, leading the earnings for the poorest fifth of American families to rise less than 1 percent between 1988 and 1998, while the earnings of the richest fifth jumped 15 percent.[13] The richest 2.7 million Americans, the top 1 percent, have as many after-tax dollars to spend as the bottom 100 million.[14] It goes without saying that the majority of the richest Americans are white, while the majority of the poorest are people of color.

Class differences affect the way women live more dramatically than the way men live. A poor man and an upper-middle-class man are both apt to work long hours most of the time, though the poor man probably works more than one job and might not even get to take weekends off, while the upper-middle-class man can take one, maybe more, luxury vacations each year. But contrast their lives with that of a poor woman and an upper-middle-class woman; for the sake of argument, make them both mothers of young children. The poor woman works at a dead-end job, possibly workfare-mandated, and races home to spend whatever shred of time she can with her children. After the kids are all asleep, she stays up late to do the household chores. The woman who is well-off through inheritance or because her husband earns a tremendous salary, on the other hand, doesn't need to work in a paying job if she chooses not to. She can hire a full-time, live-in nanny (possibly even one nanny per child) and a maid, which frees her up to do fulfilling volunteer work, shop, and play with her children when the time is convenient for her. For a woman, money makes a huge impact on her lifestyle.

Cultural critic Barbara Ehrenreich laments how class polarization affects relationships among women. In 1972, she writes, a college "junior faculty member's living room looked much like that of a departmental secretary," and both the faculty member and the secretary easily mingled, discussing "everything from the administration's sexist policies to our personal struggles with husbands and lovers." But today, "the secretary is likely to accessorize her home at Kmart, the professor at Pottery Barn."[15] Thirty years ago, the majority of American women stayed home to raise their kids; today, more than 70 percent of women are in the work force.

Of course, this represents tremendous progress, since a financially independent woman doesn't have to rely on an abusive or uncaring husband. At the same time, though, it creates a deep divide among women who used to share the status of "housewife" and who performed "similar daily tasks—housecleaning, child care, shopping, cooking. Today, in contrast, the majority of women fan out every morning to face vastly different work experiences, from manual labor to positions of power. Like men, women are now spread throughout the occupational hierarchy (though usually not at the very top), where they encounter each other daily as unequals."[16] A female attorney and the administrative assistant who answers her phone and types her correspondence very often are of different ethnicities, live in different neighborhoods, have different types of health insurance plans, buy clothes and shoes at different stores, eat different types of food, have different forms of child care, and may even enjoy different forms of entertainment. As a result, they may not recognize any common ground between them.

No matter how much money you have, it's hard not to envy those around you with more money, whether you're a man or a woman. This is particularly true in a city like New York, where I live: The affluent, the poor, and the huge muddle in the middle all share sidewalk space, so it's painfully easy to compare yourself to your Gucci-clad fellow pedestrians. In the mid-1990s and up through September 11, 2001, more and more Americans openly desired luxury goods, status symbols, and expensive designer clothing with identifiable logos—and more and more well-to-do people were all too happy to display them. (In the wake of recession and war, however, consumer overindulgence has been losing its appeal.) *Money* magazine trumpeted on its cover, "Everyone's Getting Rich!,"[17] suggesting that if you weren't getting rich yourself, you were either stupid or a loser or both. Movies routinely depict ordinary, middle-class people who just happen to live in multimillion-dollar homes, wear designer clothes, drive tony cars, and send their children to the best private colleges. It's difficult to leave the theater without feeling inadequate. Affluent men and women alike can be guilty of conspicuous consumption, but affluent women in particular often fall prey to competitive consumption. Isn't showing off your purchases, after all, part of what it means to be an American? Susan Faludi blames the whose-outfit-is-more-exclusive ethos on our culture of "commercialized feminism," in which women's independence "is the freedom to buy." The ever-growing rise of consumer culture has infiltrated the ideals of the feminist movement, leading to the belief that "feminine happiness equals other women's envy of your purchased glamour. Or, in modern terms, who has the better Chanel bag."[18]

Today there are about eight million people in the country worth $1 million or more.[19] Some multimillionnairesses seem to exist in their own universe with their own reality. The owner of a Beverly Hills salon told *The New York Times* that she has become accustomed to emergency calls from clients, just off the Concorde, who *must* have their eyebrows waxed immediately. One client called her at midnight and "was desperate" for an immediate appointment. The charge: $400 for a five-minute session. Other women fly their linens to Paris to be dry-cleaned; in some homes the tab runs to $6,000 a month.[20]

But apparently these luxuries are not enough; even the super-wealthy are apt to feel that their net worth is lacking, at least as compared with that of the extra-super-wealthy. Being rich does not make one happier than being merely middle-class, since added wealth brings with it a concern about keeping up the appearance of being wealthy, particularly in relation to one's neighbors. In a *New York* magazine article that has been nearly memorized and oft-cited to hoots of laughter by many of my New York City–based peers, several multimillionaires complain that they don't have enough money to live comfortably. Justine, the wife of an investment banker who earns one million dollars annually on Wall Street, and who had earned half a million herself before she quit when she had a baby, told the magazine, "Even if my husband is making over one million dollars, that's not much, you know, compared to a lot of our friends. Especially when you realize that he gets more than a third of his compensation in stock and we can't flip it for five years." Two-thirds of a million dollars not enough? Here is how she explains her plight: "We have a nice apartment on the Upper East Side—we paid over $2 million, for eight rooms—but it is not a mansion at all," she says. "You would be shocked. It is not at all palatial. We have a house in the Hamptons, a very basic thing, again, nothing palatial, not on the water. We pay $40,000 or $50,000 for the summer, for three months."

Justine can afford to spend $20,000 a year on clothes, $23,000 a year on a full-time housekeeper, and $40,000 a year on a full-time nanny. So what does she lack that her friends don't? A car and driver. "A driver is a big help if you have kids. It is just sick and wrong to have babies on the subway, so I take taxis."[21]

Regardless of her economic circumstances, a white woman in this society always has advantages that a woman of color does not possess. Yet white women often feel threatened by women of color, particularly in school or at the office, where they may go head-to-head for a limited number of scholarships or promotions. It goes without saying that white women have the upper hand, since whites are the majority and in power. Affirmative action is not put into practice as often as whites think. But just as there are many, many occasions when a lesser-qualified white woman is offered the job over a woman of color, there are also instances in which a lesser-qualified woman of color is awarded the scholarship. The result is suspicion that racial privilege, rather than fairness, is dictating these decisions.

In my senior year of college, I applied for a fellowship and internship position at a major publishing company, to begin after graduation. Only one person from my college would be offered the position, although five of us—all women—applied. I was certain that I was a shoo-in, as I had extensive experience: I had served as editor-in-chief of two separate campus publications and was a regular contributing writer to several others. I had also worked as an editor for the publishing arm of a nonprofit organization during my summer vacations. What more could they want from a twenty-one-year-old? When I didn't get the fellowship, I was more surprised than disappointed. I was told the name of the classmate who did receive the offer, and I looked her up in the "face book," the student directory containing photographs of each undergraduate. She was black.

Had she not been black, I remember thinking, I would have been the victor. Immediately I felt guilty and ashamed: I had no proof that she was any less qualified. I didn't know the woman or anything about her. I had made a racist assumption that this woman was less deserving than I. Part of me recognized that it would be nice and friendly to look her up and congratulate her; since we both sought professional futures in the world of words, we might have had a lot in common. But I never did. The situation made me too uncomfortable. I felt uneasy about my assumption that she possessed an unfair advantage over me and chastened by my inability to crack the number-one spot. In short, I felt unworthy.

WOMEN AND RESENTMENT

It's easy to feel resentful toward someone who appears to have an unfair advantage. It can be difficult to be happy for another woman when she succeeds, because the question nags us: What's stopping me from achieving the same thing? It's not a big leap from resentment to believing she doesn't deserve this success, that she deserves to fail. Nietzsche's notion of resentment is useful in understanding this thought process. Admittedly, it may seem perverse to refer to a philosopher who romanticized competition and survivalism. Nevertheless, his concept of resentment strikes me as helpful in making sense of how one individual can turn on another. According to Nietzsche, resentment occurs when one lacks some value, yearns to be the person who possesses it, and then seeks to undermine that person. It is part of a "slave morality" of the weak, who don't like themselves and attempt to bring down the strong. In *The Genealogy of Morals*, Nietzsche asked,

> Is there anyone who has not encountered the veiled, shuttered gaze of the born misfit, that introverted gaze which saddens us and makes us imagine how such a man must speak to himself? "If only I could be someone else," the look seems to sigh, "but there's no hope of that. I am what I am; how could I get rid of myself? Nevertheless, I'm fed up." In the marshy soil of such self-contempt every poisonous plant will grow, yet all of it so paltry, so stealthy, so dishonest, so sickly-sweet![22]

The essence of resentment is a real or imagined powerlessness, which can lead to the denigration of everything you are not. If you are weak and financially struggling, you malign the strong and the prosperous as evil and immoral. After all, you can't *both* be good and moral—and it's not fair if your nemesis is blessed with both a fat bank account and moral virtue. You must be the saint, which explains why the interest due on your credit card exceeds the cost of your purchases.

There is a sense of satisfaction when someone you resent is put in her place. That's how Carolyn Kates's two best friends appear to have regarded their friend. Their example is extreme, yet at the same time completely ordinary. Carolyn likes to wear short skirts, which show off her long legs, with clunky black boots. That's her style, she will defiantly tell you: She likes to look feminine, but with an edge. Several years ago, in her sophomore year of college, Carolyn was raped. And from the way her friends reacted, it was almost as if they were glad that someone had finally taught her a lesson for looking so damn good.

Carolyn woke up in her friend's bed with a strange man on top of her, having sexual intercourse with her. Hours before, she had gone to visit her friend, drank too much, and fallen asleep. Now, at six A.M., Carolyn was in pain and asked the man to stop. He didn't. She was paralyzed with fear and couldn't scream or move. After two more hours, he jumped up, pulled up his pants, and left. Carolyn gathered her clothes and walked home.

When Carolyn mustered the courage to tell her two best friends what had happened, they were far from supportive. The first asked, "What do you expect, getting drunk in those little skirts?" The other queried, "Carolyn, are you sure you're not making this up because you feel bad about a one-night stand?" As Carolyn puts it, "They acted like I did not say the word 'rape' and they would not use that word when mentioning the incident. I felt like I was in the twilight zone." Indeed, it is alarmingly common for rape victims to be disbelieved, even by friends and family.[23] Carolyn didn't want to press charges—part of her believed her friends that she deserved it—but she did spread the word about the rapist; she wanted to warn other women about him. The only person who was supportive was a gay male friend.

A week later, Carolyn saw the rapist at a club. He was dancing with two women, a smirk on his face, when he spotted Carolyn. He pointed in her direction. The women he was with laughed and called over to her, "Lying bitch." Carolyn was telling me this story over the phone. Her voice lowered to a whisper so that her room-mate wouldn't be able to hear; I had to press my ear to the phone. "I overheard one of them say, 'Look at what she's wearing. She was asking for it.' I was horrified because these women were competing with me over a rapist! After that, I became very depressed through-out college and isolated myself for months. I feel very vulnerable about my relationships with other females. I feel that my friends in college betrayed me because they never confronted the rapist."

To Carolyn's friends, and to the rapist's friends, it was easier to believe the man who claimed he was innocent than to believe the woman who said she was the victim of a crime. Even though they could just as easily have been raped themselves, they could not imagine themselves in Carolyn's place. Carolyn, after all, has the audacity to want to look attractive—a quality that, no doubt in the backs of their minds, they wished they could pull off. And so they distanced themselves from her—*She's not one of us.* "Slave ethics," wrote Nietzsche, "begins by saying no to an 'outside,' an 'other,' a non-self, and that no is its creative act. This reversal of direction of the evaluating look, this invariable looking outward instead of inward, is a fundamental feature of resentment."[24] The weak cause the strong to desire weakness, to turn against themselves. And that is precisely what Carolyn's friends did to her: They caused her to doubt herself, to agree that she deserved to be raped.

WOMEN'S "ESSENTIAL" NATURE

But wait a minute—how can women be so callous? Aren't women supposed to be sensitive and gentle, empathetic and interconnected with people? At least, that's what a large group of feminist scholars says: that there is something special about women's nature, that they are more sharing and caring than men. Women are commonly believed to operate on a higher moral plane and to be more attuned to others' feelings. After all, only women can be mothers—and mothers, as everyone knows, are more nurturing than fathers. Indeed, in her influential feminist treatise, *Maternal Thinking*, author Sara Ruddick went so far as to maintain that mothers are necessarily pacifist because "maternal attentive love, restrained and clear-eyed, is ill adapted to intrusive, let alone murderous, judgments of others' lives." She contrasts motherhood with the male-controlled military. "Mothers protect children who are at risk; the military risks the children mothers protect."[25]

Psychoanalyst Nancy Chodorow has argued that since mothers are generally the primary parents, their daughters have a role model with whom they can easily identify (albeit a role model who is "devalued" and "passive"), while their sons do not. As a result, this theory goes, girls emerge from childhood with a strong sense of connectedness to others, while boys see themselves as separate from others. Psychologist Carol Gilligan, building on Chodorow's theory, has advanced the idea that females' relational character makes them feel a stronger sense of justice and responsibility to the world than men do. To Chodorow and Gilligan, women's relational character propels them to be, among other considerate things, caring citizens who are active in community affairs and who better circumstances for others. These ideas have been so popularized (and watered down) that they seem to be invoked in nearly every lecture, course, and even conversation on the subject of women's and men's supposed essential differences.

Yet it is a well-known fact that women can be appallingly aggressive and violent, toward women and children as well as toward men. In the United States, men are overwhelmingly responsible for violent crime: they commit 90 percent of the murders, 80 percent of the muggings, and nearly all the rapes. But women do their share too: They commit the majority of child homicides, a greater share of physical child abuse, an equal rate of sibling violence and assaults on the elderly, about a quarter of child sexual abuse, an overwhelming number of the killings of newborns, and a fair amount of spousal assaults.[26]

Of course if women alone possess caring characteristics, then men needn't bake the holiday cakes or wake up for the three A.M. baby feedings. Carol Tavris, social psychologist and author of *The Mismeasure of Woman*, is concerned about this "growing tendency to turn the tables from us-them thinking (with women as the problem) to them-us thinking (with men as the problem)." She argues that it is "a misguided belief that there is something special and different about women's nature, an attitude that historically has served to keep women in their place. It continues to use the male norm, although this time to define what is supposedly right with women instead of what is wrong with them."[27]

Tavris points out that many people *think* that women are kinder and gentler, so that when they rate themselves on empathy, women score higher than men. While it's true that women, on average, are better able to intuitively interpret male behavior than men are female behavior, "this is not a female skill," writes Tavris. "It is a *self-protective* skill, and the sex gap fades when the men and women in question are equal in power." Psychologist Sara Snodgrass conducted an experiment that proved this to be the case. She paired men and women in work teams, sometimes assigning the man to be the leader, and sometimes the woman. The person in the subordinate position was more sensitive to the leader's nonverbal cues than the leader was to the subordinate's cues—regardless of whether a man or a woman was the leader or follower.[28] Habitually jumping up to serve your husband coffee while he lounges on the sofa is the result of a power imbalance and social conditioning, not hormones. Empathy, in other words, is about power, not gender.

"Much of the stereotype of women's innate advantage in empathy derives from the different jobs that women and men do and their different average levels of power. Women are more likely than men to be the caretakers and monitors of relationships," continues Tavris. "Although there is no question that mothers spend far more time, on the average, than fathers in terms of the daily care of their children…it does not follow that mothers are necessarily more empathic about understanding their children's feelings or actions."[29]

Feminist commentator and *Nation* columnist Katha Pollitt adds that it's no accident that women may be more "relational" and men more "autonomous": These characteristics are borne from inequitable work arrangements. Most women need to rely on a wage earner so that they can survive, leading them to be more deferential and therefore empathetic, while most men need someone to care for their children and manage their emotional life so that they can do the work, leading them to be more independent and therefore less attached to others.[30]

As a result of the "kinder, gentler" myth, many men come to believe that they don't have to be sensitive and caring to be considered good and decent people. Women, meanwhile, have been encouraged to develop themselves in relation to others, making their rivalries intensely personal.

INDIRECT AGGRESSION

There is another pernicious consequence to the "kinder, gentler" myth: the double standard in competition. Girls and women internalize the idea that being aggressive is acceptable only for men, so we direct our aggression underground. Rather than confront the people whom we feel have wronged or unfairly bettered us, we express our aggression indirectly, through social sabotage, gossip, or vague double entendres. Indirect aggression is aggression that appears unintentional, such as when a supervisor pats you on the back and says, "Your report is excellent; I'm so glad you were able to understand the assignment"; a friend exclaims, "Oh, you've lost twenty pounds? How wonderful! Are you going to lose the rest?"; a colleague accidentally-on-purpose misplaces something that you're responsible for, like an important file or phone number. These actions could be interpreted as hostile, but they also could be construed as just clueless—the result of someone who perhaps has good intentions but just doesn't know the proper way to convey them, or of someone who is simply disorganized. Women are masters of this sort of competitiveness.

Indirect aggression is slippery, impossible to nail down; it is disguised beneath a veneer of politeness or gentleness. If confronted, the aggressor has an accessible backdoor: "I didn't mean it the way it sounded" or "Of course I'm not angry with you" or "You're too sensitive" or even "You're paranoid." The recipient is left paralyzed. She has no proof, just her suspicions. If she confronts the aggressor with her doubts, she may very well be blamed for causing conflict herself.

Meg, a manager at an insurance company, relates that Jackie, a woman she supervises, is supposed to show her materials before they are mailed to clients. Jackie often doesn't show Meg the materials beforehand. Meg interprets this as a way for Jackie to undermine her authority. When Meg confronts her, Jackie's reaction is always, "I'm sorry, I forgot to show it to you, but I can't believe you think that I would ever intentionally go behind your back." Meg complains that Jackie never deals with the substance of the accusation. "I end up agreeing with her because it's easier. I end up saying something like, 'I never thought you were against me; I'm just telling you that if you do have a problem, you should come to me to discuss it.'" Jackie puts Meg on the defensive so that she doesn't have to account for her actions. It gives her the upper hand because now she is in a position where she can turn the accusation around and suggest that her supervisor is the one with the problem: She is delusional.

Dana Crowley Jack, author of *Behind the Mask: Destruction and Creativity in Women's Aggression*, observes that

> Many women feel they cannot overtly express their feelings, oppose others, or exercise their wills. Instead, much like the brightly painted Russian dolls that nest one inside another, they hide their intent inside a different form, and another, and another, placing feelings within charming exteriors that hold surprising contents. The recipient ends up with a doll that appears to be one form, most often that of good femininity, but that contains a complexity of hidden intentions. [31]

Jack identifies the factors that lead women to mask their aggression. First, there is women's unequal amount of power. Many of the women Jack interviewed expressed fear of physical, economic, or emotional retaliation if they openly expressed overt opposition to someone more physically or socially powerful, or they feared negative professional consequences. Second, there is women's socialization. While boys are given permission to punch and kick to express negative feelings, girls are taught to avoid direct conflict. The third cause is cultural expectations. Women told Jack that they masked their aggression in order to give the appearance of being nonaggressive, so that they can conform to the myth of the kinder, gentler female and not come across as bitchy.

Many girls master the hidden machinations of indirect aggression: They know, even at a young age, that they are supposed to appear good and demure and deferential, not overtly aggressive. But of course, says science writer Natalie Angier with exasperation, girls have aggressive impulses that need to be uncorked from time to time. "They're alive, aren't they?" she writes. "They're primates. They're social animals. So yes, girls may like to play with Barbie, but make the wrong move, sister, and ooh, ah, here's your own Dentist Barbie in the trash can, stripped, shorn, and with toothmarks on her boobs."[32] As adults, women are supposed to be sisterly, to "relate" to one another. Feeling angry or hostile toward another can be scary for anyone, but especially for a woman: Since the female role is to prize and nurture relationships, she doesn't want to be regarded as hampering those relationships. She does not feel entitled to express her anger. So what does she do with it? She either suppresses it or she reroutes it.

MEMBERS ONLY

As children of both sexes grow up and form friendships with others, they learn the golden rules of conformity: To be included, you must accentuate similarities and wipe away differences. You have to be accommodating, willing to please. And you can't always express what you really think. The desire to be liked, then, leads to self-effacement. Adult women continue to follow these rules, with men as well as with women. How many times have I said "I totally agree" even when I couldn't have disagreed more? Occasionally I do it to gracefully end a painful conversation, but most often I do it to be accepted. My gut impulse, always, is to be conciliatory. When I'm a guest on a radio program, discussing an issue from a feminist point of view, and a caller baits me with an opposing perspective, I grasp for some shared shred of opinion so that I can tell him, "You have a point." It's a protective gesture: By pointing out that the caller and I share some common ground, I can diffuse the tension. Only after

I've established that I'm on his side do I proceed to defend my perspective. Perhaps this is strategic debating. But it is also a ploy to ensure that I am liked, even by someone who thinks I represent the destruction of civilization.

You'd think that the desire to be liked would make girls and women bloom beneath the rays of another woman's admiration. Yet the opposite is often true: We worry that admiration could lead to envy and resentment. When a female friend or colleague tells us how much she respects our work, we're inclined to say, "Oh, it's not as important as what *you* do." If she admires our outfit, many of us habitually respond, "*This?* Uch, it's just something I got on sale five years ago" or "Really? *You do?*" The words "thank you" don't occur to us. God forbid we come across as complacent or proud.

In her novel *Eating the Cheshire Cat*, Helen Ellis describes Nicole, a Southern teenage girl besotted with Sarina, a popular and beautiful classmate who is destined for great things, such as sorority queenship. Nicole desperately and pathologically wants Sarina's approval.

> When Nicole showed up at the Summers' house before their dates, Sarina would gasp, "Oh my God, Nic, you're so much prettier than me. I hate you," she'd laugh. "I really, really hate you."
>
> This sort of reaction made Nicole have to pee. She'd go to the bathroom, then wash off her mother's paint-by-numbers. Sarina never said a word, but when the dates arrived and both complimented her, she gave her approval by saying, "Nicole looks nice too."
>
> With Sarina, Nicole made an effort to play down her beauty. She didn't powder her nose. A zit was like a door prize that

she'd never try to hide. Who cared what her date thought? Not Nicole—one single bit. Her unfinished face put Sarina at ease. When Sarina was at ease, she was more attentive to Nicole. She accompanied her to the restroom, to get popcorn, refill their drinks. Anytime Nicole could steal Sarina from her date.[33]

The ironic thing about being included is that it necessarily entails exclusion. What's so great about being accepted if everyone is? A gatekeeper is necessary to ensure the sanctity of the friendship or group. "A girl who is able to exclude another," write Terri Apter and Ruthellen Josselson, authors of *Best Friends: The Pleasures and Perils of Girls' and Women's Friendships*, "holds the key to who is included, and can set the rules. This provides the authority to teach other girls how to dress, how to speak, whom to approach, and whom to avoid. A girl may come to believe that only if she can follow these rules, she, too, can become the ideal girl, the girl whom everyone likes and always wants to be with—the girl who is always safe in friendship."[34] When girls recognize the power of exclusion, they begin to experiment with it and see how far they can go within the limits of acceptable female preadolescent behavior: hence the exchange of nasty notes, the bribing of someone to "be my best friend" at the expense of another, the routine excommunications of whoever doesn't fit the flavor of the month or week.

Exclusion is one of the most sinister forms of aggression and one of the most popular among young girls. Boys roughhouse with each other to vent their aggression. Girls, who aren't supposed to get into rough-and-tumble fights, instead form hate clubs, shunning some poor girl for being different or weird. Many of us experienced this painful period firsthand; it is also well represented in contemporary fiction. Margaret Atwood masterfully recreated the drama of girls' exclusive clubs and sadistic ostracism in her novel *Cat's Eye*. The protagonist, Elaine Risley, grows up in an eccentric family: Her father is an entomologist and the family moved from motel to tent to cottage during her first eight years, never rooted to one place. When they move to a new, middle-class suburb of Toronto in the postwar years, Elaine is not prepared. Her new friend, Cordelia, lives in a two-story house and has a cleaning woman, a powder room, napkin rings, and egg cups.

Cordelia and two other girls terrorize Elaine. They bury her alive in Cordelia's backyard. They hold meetings about her to discuss her failings, the way she eats and walks and laughs. They throw her hat down an icy ravine; when Elaine descends into the freezing water to fetch it, she becomes immobilized and nearly freezes to death. And what does Elaine do? She submits. Cordelia, after all, is her friend. She must mean well. And Elaine, who has never had girlfriends before, who wants to learn about the accoutrements of middle-class life, desperately wants to please Cordelia. "Hatred would have been easier," she muses years later as an adult. "With hatred, I would have known what to do. Hatred is clear, metallic, one-handed, unwavering; unlike love."[35]

As a teenager, Elaine switches places with Cordelia: She becomes mean and domineering as Cordelia turns meek and submissive. The more abrasive Elaine becomes, the more other girls want to be her friend; her obnoxious behavior is an attraction. Elaine's parents, seeing that their daughter is miserable, offer to take her out of public school to attend an all-girls' private school.

Elaine is aghast: "The idea fills me with claustrophobic panic: a school with nothing in it but girls would be like a trap."[36]

Unlike Elaine, many young women yearn to be accepted by exclusive, female-only cliques, such as college sororities. Students who want to be accepted into a sorority endure a process of evaluation by the sorority's members. Judy Hecker, a curator at a prestigious art museum in New York, recounts her experience at Wellesley, an all-women's college. In her sophomore year she tried to gain entrance into the "society" (Wellesley's version of a sorority) that most closely matched her interests, the Arts and Music Society. Judy was an art history major and wrote for the arts page of the college paper, so she figured she would be asked to join.

"My roommate was a member, and she came and told me that I didn't get in," remembers Judy. "At first I didn't believe her. I guess I didn't fit whatever criteria they were using. I don't know if I didn't have the right hairstyle, the right clothes, the right friends, the right attitude, or what. All my friends were in it, yet this group of women judged me and decided they didn't want me. The decision was clearly based on things other than my commitment to art and music and what I could bring to their programming. Because I could have brought a lot. And phooey on them," she says with amusement. "Now I'm a curator at the Museum of Modern Art."

Lisa Steinberg, thirty-one, was a member of an exclusive sorority when she attended Syracuse University. "If I could do it again, I would never be part of a sorority. In fact, I rarely even admit to being in a sorority," she says. "I didn't feel any sense of sisterhood. People weren't necessarily nice to you just because you were 'sisters.'"

The rush process, she recalls, "was horrible. It was very mean.

In my particular sorority, they were looking for attractive, cool, popular girls." Potential pledges had to attend mixers at the sorority house and mingle with the "sisters." If a particular woman was well liked, she would be introduced to everyone else. Otherwise, she was ignored. "At the end of the night, after they closed the doors, there was a big meeting where the 'sisters' said, 'Did you see her outfit?' or 'Did you see that girl's hairstyle?' or 'She fooled around with my boyfriend in summer camp, so we can't have her in the house.'" When you have the ability to exclude, you hold enormous power, and that means that, like it or not, you have a responsibility to make those excluded maintain a sense of dignity. (But that's not that much fun, now, is it?)

The agony of not fitting in stabs at us throughout our lives. Ruthellen Josselson recounts an incident when a friend, Janice, told her she was invited to present a paper at a conference in Paris. Janice had been invited by a shared friend, Lydia. Immediately Josselson was swept back to the anguish of the shifting alliances of adolescence. She worried that she wouldn't also be invited, that Janice was pleased to be singled out, that Lydia and Janice would become closer, and that she, Josselson, would become the odd woman out.[37]

Indeed, panicked flashbacks of being left out by other girls at the school playground are so strong that they have inspired a popular adult Internet-based game, Sissy Fight. The rules posted on www.sissyfight.com explain, "Three to six girls can play in a game. Everyone starts with 10 Self-Esteem points. When other girls humiliate and abuse you, you get really embarrassed and lose your self-esteem. If your Self-Esteem goes down to zero, you become, like, totally mortified and a loser and have to sit out for the rest of the game." Players log on from all over the world to recreate the act of ganging up on other girls and wresting the seesaw. To win, you must strategically become friends with the most popular girls and join forces with them to crush the "worthless dweebs" who are your enemies. Clearly, we never fully recover from the exclusivity games of our teenage and young-adulthood years.

HEALTHY COMPETITION

I believe that competition can work for us rather than against us. The mistake is to think that it serves no positive purpose, that its flow should be stanched. Some educators, in response to the work of Alfie Kohn, attempt to eliminate all forms of competition from their class-rooms—an endeavor that does not necessarily prepare students for the real world or give them the tools they need to channel the com-petitive impulse into healthful activities. In gym class at the Sunrise Drive Elementary School in Sayville, New York, for example, students are not allowed to pick their own teams for ballgames lest anyone picked last feel bruised. "No one ever gets their feelings hurt in my class," says Joanne Hamilton, the gym teacher. Hamilton prohibits all games involving elimination of players. In baseball, the teams do not switch roles after three outs; instead, each team gets ten minutes at bat, then ten minutes in the field. Players are allowed to choose between having the ball pitched to them or hitting it off a tee.[38] I enthusiastically support Hamilton's decision to ban the long-painful practice of allowing student captains to choose their teams (years of being picked last or nearly last took their toll on my own self-esteem), but I also think she goes too far. Baseball and other widely played games have rules that, like it or not, involve competition. Children who are never exposed to these rules will likely face ridicule once they graduate from the safe haven of Sunrise Drive Elementary School and encounter real-world sports. Besides, sometimes we all need an outlet in which we are allowed to compete. Sports, if not taken too seriously, can provide the perfect vehicle for channeling aggression in an aboveboard way. It would be preferable to introduce cooperative games and rules without eliminating competitive ones entirely.

Rather than deny or hide our psychological response to an unequal world, we must allow it to spur us to do our best work; to be devoted friends, partners, and parents; and to look as attractive as we can and desire—without obsessing. If we are in touch with and unashamed of our motivations, if we admit that we are, after all, only human, then we don't have to resort to manipulative games and cutting remarks.

One woman, Maria, offers the story of her friendship with a soul mate named Carmen as a cautionary tale. When Maria was introduced to Carmen four years ago, they immediately hit it off. Maria thought Carmen was an "amazing" woman: clever, hard-working, beautiful. "She's a banker, but she's fun," laughs Maria, a thirty-two-year-old freelance journalist living in New York City. "I thought she was too good to be true." The two women come from strikingly similar backgrounds. They are both Latinas raised by strict, traditional parents who expected their daughters to get married and have children. They are both well educated and have lived abroad and traveled widely. Acquaintances and colleagues assume that the women, who have fair complexions, are white, which annoys both. As a result, they have shared a special bond.

How did such close friends become estranged? "We started competing over our relationships, how we look, and our jobs. We both envy each other. She's jealous because I have a great relationship with my boyfriend and he asked me to marry him. Carmen lives with her boyfriend, but it's not a good relationship. He cheats on her. I think she knows but just doesn't want to deal with it. She wants to marry him anyway."

Maria and Carmen used to always flatter each other with comments like, "You look beautiful, girlfriend!" But now "We look at each other like, 'Does she look prettier than I do?'" notices Maria. "And I feel insecure because she's got a steady job and she and her boyfriend make ridiculous amounts of money, while I can't even afford health insurance. But she's jealous of me because I work for myself. I'm not making any money but I'm doing what I love, while she hates her job and is stuck there twelve to fourteen hours a day. We're like on different tracks. It's like, 'My lifestyle is better.' 'No, *my* lifestyle is better.'" When Maria and Carmen felt that they were on the same team, they supported each other and created a powerful connection unlike any other. But once they felt threatened and vulnerable, they began to reevaluate each other, even turn on each other.

I asked Maria if she thought there was a chance she could salvage this friendship. "Yes, definitely," she told me. "I'm totally committed to it. I think we need to sit down and talk. It was nice the way it was before, when we created a safe haven from everything else. We were fighting for the same things. Now our lives are different. I think we're still fighting for the same things, but in different ways."

Unresolved competition, not competition per se, is what destroys relationships between women. We can't afford to deny our emotions. If a woman tells her friend that she resents her because the friend has a great job and a wonderful family and a beautiful home, the friend should thank her. She has handed the friend the opportunity to explore the different ways that each has achieved success, and the different paths that are available to, and restricted from, women today. But she has handed the friend more than the chance to explore the psychological ramifications of envy and competitiveness; she has also opened the door to think about the societal consequences of inequality. And now that the two women are having a conversation about inequality, they can choose to take actions in response. They can refuse to play along with the rules that foster competitiveness in the first place—by sitting out of the competition with other women over a man or demanding that women's magazines run photos of women who aren't stick-thin.

If left unresolved, competition can destroy us. Sylvia Plath, who committed suicide in 1963 at the age of thirty-one, was a famously ambitious and competitive poet. Throughout her college and post-college years in the 1950s, she regularly sent out batches of poems to *The New Yorker*, *Mademoiselle*, and *The Atlantic*. More often than not, her poems were rejected—spurring her to devote more effort to her craft but also to compare, compare, compare her work with that of anyone who did get published. She wrote in her journal, "I am jealous of those who think more deeply, who write better, who draw better, who ski better, who look better, who live better, who love better than I."[39] Self-aware she certainly was, but Plath's competitiveness reached a dangerously obsessive level. Pages and pages of her journals are filled with comparisons with others—with women. Plath recognized that as a young woman in the 1950s, her life choices were limited: She would be considered, and would consider herself, incomplete without a man and children. But how was she to become a great poet while tending children? She very much identified herself as a woman with a woman's lot. Plath would achieve enormous success only posthumously, with *The Bell Jar* (published one month before her death) and with the publication of such works as "Lady Lazarus" and "Daddy." While she was still struggling for recognition, she looked to other women, especially other women poets, to ascertain how they managed it all.

Plath was a manic-depressive in an age before effective treatment for this disease, and therefore suffered from dramatic highs and lows that most of us, thank goodness, never have to experience. Nevertheless, her competitive response to her second-class status as a "woman" poet is instructive. Plath was enormously self-critical. She was also incredibly mean. In one journal entry, Plath compares her own writing to Linda, "the sort of girl you don't remember when you meet her for the second time. She is rather homely, and nondescript as an art gum eraser." Plath feels "sick" and astonished that Linda could write so much better than she.[40] When she felt superior but unrecognized, Plath unleashed a torrent of venom. Reading the six women poets in a volume of *New Poets of England and America*, she wrote in her journal that their work is "dull, turgid" and that "Except for May Swenson & Adrienne Rich, not one better or more-published than me. I have the quiet righteous malice of one with better poems than other women's reputations have been made by."[41] Of course Plath wasn't even allowed to compete with men, and we don't know how she would have felt toward other women if she had been allowed into the larger arena with men.

I can't help but wonder what might have been. If Plath had been able to channel her competitiveness in a different direction, she might have recognized that she could learn from other female poets and might have seen them as worthy people with real talents of their own. What if she had made the attempt to connect with other women? What if she had been able to express her anxiety about never being good enough to another woman and not merely in a notebook? Could her tenuous ego have been nourished, and might she still be alive today?

CHAPTER TWO
BEAUTY

Across the street from my old apartment on Manhattan's Upper West Side is a trendy women's clothing boutique. The windows display mannequins wearing curvy-cut outfits in beguiling bright colors. It is exactly the kind of store I never used to shop in: I had made a habit of wearing grungy, loose sweaters and skirts in colors like gray, beige, and black. But, well, one day a few years ago I decided that I needed something new, and I lived right across the street, so there I was in this achingly hip shop. I scanned the racks and plucked a few pairs of pants and some sweaters in my usual two-sizes-too-large and brought them into the dressing room. There was no mirror: I was forced to open the folding doors and scrutinize my image in the public mirror hanging in the middle of the shop, price tags dangling awkwardly from my elbow and waistband.

The saleswoman observed me. She was pretty and stylish and not intimidating. "May I make a suggestion?" she gently asked. She rummaged in the racks, found the same outfit in a smaller size, and handed it to me. No way, I told her: It would be too tight. She gave me a look. I can't remember exactly what she said, so I'll paraphrase; her actual words were far more diplomatic. "You're not fooling anyone by wearing clothes that are too large. People can still figure out that you've got a big bust and big hips. Besides, you don't look very good." I knew that she had a point. But I felt comfortable in oversized clothes. I was reluctant to wear clothes that announced, "Hello everyone, I've got a voluptuous body, come and take a look for yourself." I left the store without buying anything.

At home, I threw my clothes from the closet onto the bed and tried them on in front of my bedroom mirror. That saleswoman knew what she was talking about. I was making myself appear twenty pounds heavier than I really was. Yes, this sounds like some silly, girly-girl *Marie Claire* magazine story, but here's the true tale of what happened: I returned to the store and asked the saleswoman to help me put together several outfits in sizes that fit. I bought them. For the first time, I realized I could look good in clothes that followed the lines of my body rather than hid them. It didn't take long before I became interested in clothes and made a habit of flipping through the pages of *Vogue*, *Marie Claire*, and *Harper's Bazaar*, looking longingly at the fashion spreads and ads. I started peering into the windows of all the women's shops dotting upper Broadway (and since Manhattan is practically one gigantic shopping mall, there sure are a lot of them). More and more often, I made my way inside and bought various items.

Having flattering clothes has been transformative for me—for better and for worse. I have become comfortable with and confident about my body. It is the same body as before—with the same ten pounds I'd love to lose as long as I don't have to work too hard losing them—yet now I feel a certain measure of control. If I'm having a romantic dinner with my husband, I wear something with a low V-neck; if I'm going to synagogue, I wear a tailored suit; if I'm spending the day typing in front of my computer, I wear jeans, a T-shirt, and a cardigan. In each instance, I take on a different persona: I am a sexy goddess, a demure and pious Jewess, a journalist hot on the trail of an exposé. There is liberation in malleability.

But of course, a sense of self goes well beyond one's costume. Clothes do not make the woman; rather, the woman fills the costume. Still, as much as I try to fight it, I do buy into the consumer mythology of the power of clothes.

Now when I evaluate my appearance, I think about how I must appear to others—which spurs me to buy more clothes. This takes its toll. There are the obvious problems with money and time, always in short supply. More significantly, keeping up with fashion means participating in a tacit and ongoing, often quite ruthless, competition with other women. I never used to care what other women wore, since I didn't care much about what I wore. Now I check out what they're wearing and make assessments accordingly: "Oooh, that's so nice; I wish I could afford that/pull that off/look that good" or "Uch, that totally doesn't work; does she have any idea how ridiculous she looks?" Of course, women are checking me out too—and I don't want anyone thinking I look ridiculous.

These competitive feelings compel me to compare not only my shoes but also my thighs, nails, breasts, and eyeglasses with those of the women I encounter in offices, restaurants, sidewalks. I'm happy with my appearance on its own merits; when I look in the mirror, I like what I see. But when everyone else is in Pilates-fit shape, my rounded belly suddenly seems mountainous. I wish I could just focus on how I feel about my looks, but I always end up scrutinizing myself in relation to other women. As a result, there are many days, I confess, when my vanity gets the best of me—when I insist on putting on lip gloss and mascara before making an emergency run to the corner drugstore to buy diapers, or I refuse to wear a hat in frigid weather because I don't want flattened hat-hair when I have to take it off indoors.

Does my husband notice my pedicures? You've got to be kidding. But women do. We walk around in a tacit beauty contest with other women. Writer Pam Houston relates,

> I am walking down the street in Manhattan, Fifth Avenue in the lower sixties, women with shopping bags on all sides. I realize with some horror that for the last fifteen blocks I have been counting how many women have better and how many women have worse figures than I do. Did I say fifteen blocks? I meant fifteen years.[1]

I never dwell on what men think of my appearance. Since I'm married, I'm not out to hook men's sexual attention (although, of course, it's always a nice bonus to receive it anyway). In any event, even if I were single, heterosexual men don't generally notice the details of women's appearance. Sure, they know if a woman looks sexy or dowdy, but how many straight men do you know who can recognize if your suede boots have chunky or kitten heels, or if your bag is Coach or Kate Spade?

My urge to compare and contrast my looks springs from our culture's narrow conception of beauty. Of course, the definition of beauty is inherently subjective. We all have our own ideas about what constitutes beauty, and many people habitually see beauty where others see plainness or even homeliness. Regardless, beauty tends to be regarded as a universal, changeless thing—as obvious to the eye as the setting of the sun. For women, it is equated with certain privileged characteristics: being young, white, blond, fashionable, thin—as well as intangibles such as being virginal, innocent, and nurturing. In our hierarchical, competitive culture, only a small minority of women are deemed beautiful. Only a few are privileged to possess the seemingly magical ingredients of beauty, as it is narrowly defined. If everyone were considered beautiful, beauty would lose its power to control. By definition, then, beauty is regarded as if it were a scarce commodity. As Naomi Wolf explained in *The Beauty Myth*, beauty is treated as if it "objectively and universally exists. Women must want to embody it and men want to possess women who embody it."[2]

I've often joked that I waste a lot of brain activity on the trivial issues of appearance, and it turns out, in fact, that I really have. A fascinating and unusual study shows that how a woman feels about her body can affect her cognitive abilities. University of Michigan psychologist Barbara Fredrickson had male and female college students wear bathing suits as they took a math test. The women scored lower than men also in swimwear, and they also scored significantly lower than other women who took the test wearing street clothes. Meanwhile, the men in bathing suits performed just as well as the men in normal attire. Women's self-image was damaged during the test, which consumed their mental resources and disrupted their cognitive performance.[3]

The point of the study, Fredrickson explains, was to induce a state of self-objectification—when a person evaluates her body from a third-person perspective (How do I look?), as opposed to a first-person perspective (How do I feel?). To Freud, a woman's attention to her appearance is evidence of narcissism;[4] to

Fredrickson, it is an "adaptive strategy," though not necessarily consciously chosen. "Rather," she writes, "repeated exposure to the array of external pressures to enhance physical beauty could effectively socialize girls and women to experience their attentiveness to appearance as self-chosen or even natural."[5] Self-objectification "coaxes girls and women to adopt a peculiar view of self.... [T]he cultural milieu of objectification functions to socialize girls and women to, at some level, treat themselves as objects to be looked at and evaluated."[6] Since a woman's perspective of her physical self is that of an observer, she vigilantly monitors her physical appearance.

Thus, I feel pressured to evaluate myself by the way I imagine my body appears to others. As a result, I feel validated when I receive flattery for my appearance, which makes me care even more about looking good to others. My appearance has become a central part of my identity. This feels totally normal: Is this not what it means to be a woman?

But I not only treat myself as an object to be evaluated; I also treat other women in the same light. So if my mental resources are interrupted by worrying about my own appearance, to what extent are they diminished by judging other women at the same time?

THE BEAUTY BIND

Men today are becoming accustomed to being judged on the basis of their appearance. They have long turned to bodybuilding to bulk up, but recently they have also increasingly embraced hair transplants, teeth whiteners, even penile implants. Still, a woman is categorized by her looks in a way that a man is not. A man is evaluated mainly by his achievements in the workplace, while a woman is judged primarily by her success in maintaining an ornamental appearance. Unlike a man, she is caught in a double bind—a beauty bind: Whether she is considered ugly or beautiful, her looks can be used to justify withholding the recognition she deserves. In either instance, she is reduced to a stereotype.

If a woman is unattractive, she can be dismissed as unfeminine and undesirable. Even if she demonstrates without a shadow of a doubt that she is a capable person, a good mother, and a tough cookie, she still lacks a fundamental essence of womanhood. If she is unattractive and disliked, then she deserves to be mistreated. Take Linda Tripp: The media considered it acceptable to ceaselessly humiliate her because of her looks. Had she been good-looking, or a man, people would have grumbled for a few days, a week at most, about her reprehensible taping of Monica Lewinsky's conversations. "I, too, wish she could have had a character transplant," wrote Gloria Steinem in a *New York Times* op-ed. "But being born less than conventionally attractive is hardly a bigger crime than taping the confidences of a friend (plus entertaining your bridge group with them)." Steinem reported that Tripp blamed herself for her media skewering—"I was responsible for the portrayal in the media by the way I looked," she reportedly said—and therefore underwent plastic surgery.[7]

Likewise, Florida's conservative Republican secretary of state, Katherine Harris, was vilified for her obvious partisan favoring of George W. Bush in the hotly contested 2000 presidential elections. But it was her thick makeup that really drove people crazy. A fashion reporter for *The Washington Post* wrote: "Her lips were overdrawn with berry-red lipstick—the creamy sort that smears all over a coffee cup and leaves smudges on shirt collars. Her skin had been plastered and powdered to the texture of pre-war walls in need of a skim coat."[8] Can you imagine the press snickering so at an unpopular male politician because of his obvious and unsuccessful combover? Even the most liberal news reporters, who before the terrorist attack on the World Trade Center considered New York City mayor Rudy Giuliani a tyrant, never stooped to that level.

In fairy tales, an ugly woman is an evil witch and a beautiful woman is a kind fairy. In real life, an ugly woman is an evil bitch and a beautiful woman is kind of scary. Yes, a beautiful woman is also a victim of stereotypes. This is the other side to the beauty bind. If she is successful, she is sleeping her way to the top. ("If this were possible," notes Steinem dryly, "there would be many more women at the top."[9]) Or, she got a lucky break because of her looks, so her achievements don't really count that much. Plus, she has a difficult time being taken seriously as an authority figure.

When George W. Bush chose the attractive Condoleezza Rice as National Security Advisor, *The New York Times* ran a profile that belittled "her girlish laugh and gushes of Southern charm." The article continued, "She either eats a bagel or cereal every day for breakfast. She is always impeccably dressed, usually in a classic suit with a modest hemline, comfortable pumps, and conservative jewelry. She keeps two mirrors on her desk…apparently to check the back as well as the front of her hair." Colin Powell is quoted as saying that "Condi was raised first and foremost to be a lady." And, in case you were wondering, her dress size vacillates between a 6 and an 8, because of "muscle mass."[10] By contrast, an article that ran the preceding day in the *Times* on Colin Powell did not divulge how the Secretary of State maintains the back of his hair.

To whom can an attractive woman turn for comfort? Not other women. When I spoke with beautiful women—women whose faces and bodies most of us would characterize as unusually attractive—I heard story after story of envy and bitterness. Joy, a Manhattan legal secretary, has big dark eyes, long dark thick hair, and a sexy, voluptuous body. "The way I look causes tension with everything, everything, everything. I have problems with my male friends' girlfriends and wives. My best friend, Louise, always had this competitive thing with me. She's always had to outdo me in dressing. She says things like, 'Oh, you're putting on weight.' She is very insecure with herself and I guess to make herself feel secure she makes me feel insecure."

It can be difficult for an attractive woman to befriend women: She is seen more as a threat than a comrade. I still shudder with shame, remembering how I coldly treated a stunning woman in one of my college seminars. She made numerous attempts to reach out to me, but her beauty intimidated and threatened me. If I'd walked around campus with her, who would have ever given a second glance to me? Jessica Williams, a twenty-six-year-old administrative assistant in San Francisco, was thin with long blond hair during her college years. "I frequently felt stabbing looks from women because I represented a threat," she recalls. "In mixed social situations where there were both men and women, I frequently ended up hanging out with the men because they were the only ones who would engage in conversation with me. I started having dreams with a Samson and Delilah theme, where my hair held my power and other women wanted to strip it from me."

Jennifer Baumgardner is definitely someone you would look at twice: She is tall, blond, slender, and blessed with both prominent cheekbones and an uncanny fashion sense. She also happens to be razor-sharp smart. She worked her way up at *Ms.* magazine from unpaid intern to editor (later co-authoring *Manifesta*, a call to arms for young feminists), and was one of the only employees who dressed up and wore makeup (many of her colleagues wore jeans every day). "Usually I was complimented on how I looked, but there were a couple of people who I felt were sexually competitive with me and would say things like, 'God, you always have to wear a see-through shirt.'" When Jennifer's sister, similarly tall, blond, and beautiful, came to New York and Jennifer was showing her around the office, one of the colleagues said, "Oh my God, it's the attack of the killer Barbies." "She said it in front of everyone," recalls Jennifer. "It really rankled me. She made it clear that she was trying to diminish me because I liked to dress up, which only made me want to dress up and compete with her [over clothes] even more."

It's hard enough when a colleague puts you down because of your looks; when your own sisters and mother do it, the pain can be enormous—and there is no escaping it. Miriam, a labor organizer in Manhattan, wears absolutely no makeup—nothing—and she certainly doesn't need it. She has flawless skin, black hair, bright blue eyes, and naturally red lips. She is a middle sister, with one ten years older and another four years younger. "I have always felt tremendous resentment from my older sister," sighs Miriam. "The resentment has a lot to do with appearance. I think she really felt that I had been dealt a better hand. When I was a teenager, she would criticize me for being vain because I wore makeup. Last year we had this big birthday party for our grandmother. My grandmother introduced me to someone and she said, 'This is the pretty one I was telling you about.' And my sister was standing right there. I almost died. I was like: Oh no! I'm going to have to pay for this for another five years!"

Miriam's looks have also played a role in her relationship with her younger sister. When they were both young, people would tell them that they looked alike. But as they grew up, the younger sister became very heavy. When she was in college, she went to a photography studio, had her hair and makeup done professionally, and had some glamorous shots taken. She showed the pictures to Miriam, who, unthinkingly, said, "Is that *you?*" With a pained look, Miriam explains to me, "I know it was a terrible thing to say, but I mean, it really didn't look like her! And then she said, 'Yes. I think these pictures make me look like you.'" And then there is Miriam's mother. Miriam's parents separated when she was twelve and were later divorced. When Miriam was a teenager, her mother's male friends would often comment on Miriam's attractiveness. But instead of taking pride in her attractive daughter, Miriam's mother felt upstaged.

Now age thirty-two, Miriam very consciously eschews makeup; she also pays zero attention to fashion trends, preferring to wear years-old oversized clothes. "I rarely go shopping. I buy a sweater once in a while if I'm walking by and I see it in the window. I do care about my appearance, but there is always that underlying feeling that it doesn't really matter, so I'm not going to spend much time and effort on it." Miriam has decided to completely distance herself from the competitive arena of beauty and fashion. It's not worth it to her to risk alienating her family. And to tell you the truth, she seems very much at peace with her decision.

Some women are honest about their own resentment of others' beauty. One thirty-one-year-old woman admitted to me that when she and her roommate were put in a triple room during their soph-omore year at Harvard, and first met the woman who would join them, they couldn't stand her. "She was very attractive and very fashion-conscious. She was a runner and was very aware of her body. So my friend and I agreed: If we didn't like her, we were just going to be so mean to make her move out. We would make her life miserable." Luckily, the three women ended up getting along very well and are still close, twelve years later.

YOUNG, THIN, WHITE...

If a woman is young, thin, white, with Western facial features, she has the chance to pass muster as attractive in this country. Of course, millions of women—the majority of women—do not fit these criteria. Yet, we ludicrously internalize this narrow ideal and believe that if we work hard enough, we can look this way.

Because we live in a celebrity culture, many of us judge our looks in relation to the models and actresses we see in magazines, on TV, and in the movies: people who are larger than life with pro-fessions that require them to be beautiful. And yet, we are encour-aged to believe that we, too, can look like them because we are women. When the star of the TV show *Felicity*, Keri Russell, had her long, thick hair cut very short for the show's second season, the rat-ings plummeted. J. J. Abrams, co-creator of the show, declared with grave seriousness, "We take full responsibility for the idea of cutting her hair." And why did ratings fall like a loose hair extension? A spokesman for the WB network explained, "Women kind of identified with [Russell's character]. When she cut her hair, they basically said, 'I don't want to be that person; it ruins the illusion for me.' We heard that over and over again."[11]

The celebrity machine wants ordinary people to believe that the glamour can rub off on us. Thus, untold numbers of women mistakenly think that they can achieve the same look as celebrities (who have their own exercise trainers, makeup artists, hairdressers, facialists, yoga instructors, manicurists, and fashion stylists). Millions of women waste precious resources, including self-worth, following the diet and beauty tips of the stars. But it's not the ideal of beauty per se that is so damaging. It is the narrow conception of beauty that causes women to chase down an impossible and expensive dream.

I find celebrity culture particularly unbearable when it ups the ante on how pregnant women should look. Magazines like *People* and *In Style* showcase photos of stars like Iman, Madonna, Josie Bissett, and Reese Witherspoon looking perfectly chic right until they check into the delivery room. They have established an ideal that has trickled down to ordinary women. Tent dresses and functional flat shoes, which had been perfectly acceptable maternity wear in the past, are now considered déclassé. *In Style* features four-page spreads of maternity clothes favored by the celebrity set from designers Nicole Miller, Liz Lange, Lilly Pulitzer, and the store A Pea in the Pod. Prices start at two hundred dollars for clothes that, keep in mind, a woman wears only for a few months. A thirty-one-year-old writer sighs in *New York* magazine, "It's no longer cool to be pregnant with black stretch leggings and your husband's shirt. You have to do better than that." Adds a twenty-four-year-old who works in advertising, "Being pregnant is not an excuse to go around looking like a slob."[12]

Moreover, after a woman gives birth, she is expected to bounce right back into shape as if her body were made of rubber. Melissa Rivers, fashion commentator on the E! channel, complained that she still felt fat less than four months after having her first child. "Before my pregnancy, I was a size 0 or 2," she said. "Now I'm a size 4 or 6 and feel that I still have ten pounds to lose."[13] No wonder that Julia Roberts, when asked why she hasn't had children yet, replied, "I like my flat little belly."[14] Unlike Catherine Zeta-Jones, who lost her pregnancy pounds in three months (just in time for her wedding to Michael Douglas), and Marlee Matlin, who lost sixty-two post-baby pounds in five months, it took me six months to lose most of the weight from my first pregnancy. The rate of my weight loss was fairly typical, but given the media images around me, how could I have felt anything other than a failure?

The mass media are not omnipotent and women are not cultural dupes. On an intellectual level, we know that the models who clothe their lollipop-thin bodies in glamorous, expensive outfits represent a fantasy life. But at the same time, we internalize their standard of beauty because, unlike men who get to see a variety of male images in the news and other media, we don't have a broad range of feminine images available to us. Women over the age of fifty are exposed to a particularly narrow slice of feminine imagery. Hollywood tells us that women in midlife are not beautiful and therefore do not deserve mass attention. Over-fifty male stars are routinely paired romantically with actresses young enough to be their daughters. (Some of the more ridiculous couplings in recent years were Harrison Ford with Anne Heche in *Six Days, Seven Nights*, Michael Douglas with Gwyneth Paltrow in *A*

Perfect Murder, Richard Gere with Winona Ryder in *Autumn in New York*, Sean Connery with Catherine Zeta-Jones in *Entrapment*, and Warren Beatty with Halle Berry in *Bulworth*.) The fashion industry dictates that it's fashionable to wear tight, low-slung, hip-hugging pants, impossible for most older women to fit into even if they wanted to. Complains seventy-three-year-old novelist Judith Krantz, a woman who certainly has the means to buy as much clothing as she desires, "Older customers are heartlessly treated as if they have no right to new clothes for the many special occasions in their life. Do designers imagine that most women have the body of Jennifer Lopez?... Oh, don't get me started!"[15]

But being young doesn't necessarily get you any closer to the beauty ideal, either. You have to be slender, too. We all know that many American women engage in futile attempts to achieve a stick silhouette. They believe that thin equals feminine, that thin equals success, that thin equals power and control. Americans (men as well as women) spend roughly $40 billion a year on diet aids, from artificial sweeteners to liposuction. (Marilyn Wann, author of the delightfully fat-friendly 'zine and book *Fat!So?*, points out that with $40 billion each year, we could pay off the federal deficit twice, donate four times more money to charities than the combined charitable donations from all U.S. corporations, fund the National Endowment for the Arts for 250 years, and provide six times more federally funded day care to help working parents.[16])

The average American woman weighs 140 pounds and wears a size 14, though most clothing designers don't recognize her. They rarely manufacture sizes above 14, effectively telling large women that their bodies are not normal and that they are unworthy of fine clothes. If you absolutely can't be slender, the beauty ideal dictates that at the very least, your body should be toned. Even the size 16 models in *Mode*—a wonderful, body-affirming magazine that, until its recent demise, was revolutionary in showcasing images of "large" women of all colors—were curvy in only the "right" places. There was no stomach flab in those pages.

American women of color with "black" features often have been dismissed by the narrow American beauty industry. In the modeling business, things have improved somewhat over the past decade. "When I first started out, in the early nineties, it was harder to shoot a black model for a beauty story," a white beauty editor reveals to me. "The editors would say, 'Well, how many people can relate to her?' Sometimes if you had a black model on a shoot, the photographer would say, 'Oh, it's going to be hard to light that girl.'" If black *models* can't fit the beauty ideal, what does that say about the chances of ordinary black women?

As a white woman, I am obviously an outsider to the concerns of black women. But over and over again, black women report to me that a color caste system remains strong among American women of color, and that this system can have damaging consequences. In Nella Larsen's 1929 novel, *Passing*, a light-skinned woman of color is accepted into white society because she can "pass" as white, but her deception leads her world to unravel. Even today, I am told, light-skinned black women tend to be awarded privileges denied their dark-skinned sisters because they more closely conform to the narrow American beauty ideal, which continues to treasure whiteness. The conviction that life is easier when you resemble the white standard of beauty is perhaps most famously confronted in Toni Morrison's classic novel, *The Bluest Eye*. Pecola Breedlove, a lonely, neglected girl living in squalor in 1939, prays for blue eyes like Shirley Temple's. All the blacks around her revere white features and consider blackness ugly. When Pecola is raped by her father and becomes pregnant with his baby, she is beaten by her mother; her sanity deteroriates and she becomes even more obsessed with having blue eyes. By the novel's end, Pecola is abandoned, alone, and bereft of any shred of sanity. The townspeople still consider her ugly. Pecola believes she has blue eyes and creates an imaginary friend who confirms their existence.

Observes Ella Jamison, a researcher on Wall Street, "When you have the lightest skin and the best hair, you are desirable. It doesn't matter if you're a bitch." Desirable to men, that is. To other women, you are competition. It's another case of the beauty double bind: Being light-skinned awards you cultural advantages (people think you're prettier, smarter, better because you appear "white"), but it also makes others resent you and presume that you haven't had to work your way up.

Georgina Jones, a fair-skinned African American in Atlanta, tells me that an African-American colleague always makes cutting comments about her complexion. Recently the two women were talking about some racial incident in Boston that was making the news. The friend said, "Well, Georgina, you could go to Boston and you wouldn't have that problem. People would wonder if you're really black." With indignation, Georgina said to me, "I thought that that was absolutely ridiculous. This is a woman whose intelligence I respect. I think she is resentful of what I represent, that somehow I have it easier and better because I am fairer-complected."

Writer Jill Nelson observes that comparisons over who is darker and who is lighter are highly subjective anyway. She herself is light-skinned, but she's gotten all types of comments. "Someone once told me, 'You know, you're really dark, like me' and I didn't consider her really dark. So I realized that it's all totally crazy." It's just like when girls and women say to each other "I'm so fat" when they so obviously aren't fat at all. But at least saying "I'm so fat" unites girls and women (admittedly in a sick way). The color caste system is "the house nigger versus field nigger mindset," charges Nelson. "But if you're a nigger, you're a nigger. House or field, it doesn't really help you. I mean, slavery is slavery."

...AND WELL DRESSED

Let's say you truly are one of the blessed few deemed "beautiful." You can't just rest on your laurels. Women want evidence that beautiful women put some sweat and tears into looking great. Erin Shield, a Manhattan attorney, is working late one evening at her Battery Park office. I meet her at seven P.M., and our talk is her break from the work she will continue after I leave. Erin has a thoughtful face: She exudes trustworthiness. Erin grew up in southern California, where everyone seemed to look like Pamela Anderson. "And I am not blond, I do not have blue eyes, I do not have big boobs, and I did not have a lot of money," Shield says, "so I never felt like I fit in. Being female in southern California is hard. Everybody is beautiful and everybody is constantly eyeing you—you walk down the street and people scan you from head to toe. Remember that scene from *Pretty Woman* where Julia Roberts walks into that store on Rodeo Drive in her hooker clothes and the saleswomen are really mean to her? Well, salespeople were like that all the time! That was not an exaggerated scene. If you walked into a store dressed badly, they would look down on you." Shield's classmates were even more judgmental. So, to protect herself from their jibes, she kept a calendar of what she wore so that she didn't inadvertently wear the same thing too often. On each day she would note her outfit; for instance, Tuesday—white T-shirt, pink pedal pushers, white Keds.

Oh, the pressure of keeping up with fashion. Even if a woman does look like blond, buxom Pamela Anderson, she still has her work cut out for her: Every day, she must put together an outfit (top, bottom, shoes, handbag, accessories, jacket or coat) that (a) demonstrates to the world that she's up on the latest trends and has the money to buy them; (b) expresses her personal flair to show that she's not merely a fashion slave and knows the difference between tasteful and tacky; (c) shows off her body to its best effect; and (d) hasn't been repeated recently. My friends, this is hard work. Very hard work.

The anxiety of always looking put-together made my pregnancies a relief. I could retreat from the competition: I wasn't expected to keep up with the fashions as my belly swelled. I didn't want to spend a lot of money on clothes with a short lifespan, so for each pregnancy I amassed five outfits—a typical number for a pregnant woman. Plus, my swollen feet could slide into only one pair of shoes. I was thrilled with my easy clothing choices. Every morning I'd open my closet and pull out whichever outfit I'd worn least recently. I'd choose a scarf or necklace, and off I went.

Clothing styles change with breakneck speed. Ever since Christian Dior designed his 1947 "New Look" with its voluptuous silhouette, designers have created clothes with obsolescence in mind. Hemlines would be decreed short one season, long the next. Yet in the late twentieth century, fashion followed a cycle one could reasonably keep up with: New styles would be shown on the runways, then they would be described in fashion magazines and the style sections of newspapers, then they would appear in stores, then women would wear them, then women would tire of them. If you went shopping two or three times a year, you knew you could stay on top of the trends. But now, every month there are new styles clogging the stores. One retailer, Zara, can design a new, low-cost collection within four to five weeks and manufacture it in another week, allowing it to spot and react to trends immediately. The chief executive of Zara's parent company explains that "Fashion expires, much the same way yogurt does."[17] Moreover, clothes today are very revealing of women's bodies, adding to the cutthroat pressure to stay in shape. And because of improved manufacturing, all the stores, at every price level, sell essentially the same styles—making the task of individualizing your look quite difficult.

Assuming you can afford to keep up, assuming you want to keep up, who has the time? "Initially, I liked the fact that everything was different each season," says a fashion editor. "Then I got tired of having to know what the next new thing is. It's exhausting." It's so exhausting, in fact, that a women's magazine has popped up to help women with the arduous task of shopping. Unlike other women's magazines, *Lucky* has forgone the stock copy of its sister publications: There are no articles about exotic locales, the evils of anorexia, or the plight of women in abusive relationships. There are no book or movie reviews. Every single article is about shopping:

what to buy and where to find it. In a way, *Lucky* is delightfully refreshing: It is the only women's magazine truly honest about its agenda. "Now there's a magazine that helps you shop more success-fully, more creatively, and better than ever!" trumpets its advertising campaign. Shopping is hereby declared an activity that you can strive to be more successful, creative, and better at.

Shopping is now even evidence of "girl power," the new feminist lite credo. "Unlike our feminist foremothers, who claimed that makeup was the opiate of the misses, we're positively pro-choice when it comes to matters of feminine display," writes Debbie Stoller, co-editor of *Bust* magazine, in *The* Bust *Guide to the New Girl Order*, a compendium of articles that originally appeared in the magazine. "We're well aware, thank you very much, of the beauty myth that's working to keep women obscene and not heard, but we just don't think that transvestites should have all the fun."[18] Somewhere down the line, though, the choice for a young urban woman to decorate herself for fun has become practically mandatory. The consumerist message to buy, buy, buy has now become tinged with the feminist goal of liberation: Buying cool things makes you a liberated woman. Conversely, in order to be a liberated woman you must buy cool things. Materialism has become an end in itself.

If you choose to participate in the world of fashion, as Stoller says, the goal is to have fun with it. Deciding what to wear each morning could be like creating an art project, layering materials and colors to form a cohesive image. And very often, it is fun. But the expectations that it carries can also make it a burden. Just as our colleagues judge us on the reports we turn in or the number of widgets we make, other women size us up based on the cut of our jacket and the heel of our boot. Sarah, an advertising account executive, works among a bevy of young women who always seem to wear the latest fashions. "Whatever is on the cover of the magazines, they all have it," she says sourly. "I wonder: They must go shopping every Saturday, all day. They must spend all their money on shopping. I would never spend hundreds of dollars on a shirt; I'd rather have the money in the bank. But when I'm in a meeting with them, I doubt myself. I think, 'My God, what am I wearing? My pants are pilly and my clothes should be left in the back of my closet.' I get kind of down on myself."

How we feel about our clothes reveals much about how we feel about ourselves in general. A saleswoman at a fashionable New York City boutique told me she likes to think of herself as a "retail therapist" because she spends so many hours in the dressing room with customers. "I have a regular client who comes in for jeans. She's always buying jeans. It always turns into a therapy session. She tells me all about her marriage. She doesn't need the jeans; usually I discourage her from buying them." If you feel like everything in your life is going wrong, at least you can exert some control by buying a new item of clothing.

HISTORY OF THE AMERICAN BEAUTY IDEAL

When marriage is the primary form of mobility, women often use how they look to compete for husbands. In our country's earliest years, white women felt competitive over who was "more beautiful" because they needed a well-heeled husband for their own economic survival. However, these same women were also urged to stifle signs of beauty or fashion because a "proper" woman was not supposed to pursue beauty and fashion in the first place. The Puritans who settled the Massachusetts Bay Colony in the 1630s believed that vanity was corrupt and prevented salvation.[19] The men and women who battled England's supremacy in the American Revolution likewise rejected the rouge, white powder, and other beauty preparations used by the male and female aristocracy (as well as elite colonists). To these new citizens interested in pursuing a democratic future, the vain rituals of self-presentation were a reminder of their class-based, hierarchical past.

In the 1800s, men who used makeup were scorned as lacking in authority and trustworthiness, since their genuine appearance was masked by artifice. Meanwhile, women were also advised to present a natural and unadorned appearance.[20] The ideal American woman in the 1830s and 1840s was a dedicated homemaker who rejected the extravagances of fashion and face painting. Even feminists who sought to expand women's role beyond the domestic sphere shunned makeup as artificial and insincere. In her 1845 feminist manifesto, *Woman in the Nineteenth Century*, which urged that all barriers to women's equality be removed, Margaret Fuller called on women to develop their minds instead of their appearances and to clear their souls "from the taint of vanity."[21]

Yet even without the assistance of makeup, the white nineteenth-century woman was still expected to be beautiful. She had to allow her inner beauty to radiate outward, explains Kathy Peiss, historian of beauty culture, in her book *Hope in a Jar*. Using cosmetics indicated that one was a "painted woman," a prostitute. Meanwhile, physiognomy, the quack scientific belief that one's physical appearance corresponds with her character, was popular, says Peiss, "reducing moral attributes to physical ones. Hair, skin, and eye color frequently stood as signs of women's inner virtue. The facial ideal was fair and white skin, blushing cheeks, ruby lips, expressive eyes." Black women, who never had any hope of achieving the prevailing, narrow beauty ideal, also avoided cosmetics, though they received no social rewards for their self-control. According to the ideal of the time, they could never be considered beautiful.[22]

Peiss argues that the mid-nineteenth-century distrust of women's cosmetics correlated with women's burgeoning rights. More and more women were working for wages and demanding equality with men, putting their role as family anchor in jeopardy. How could one distinguish between a good woman who knew that her place was at home and an immoral one who sought personal freedom? Through her appearance. A woman's looks told the world whether or not she was virtuous. Therefore, cosmetics were a deceptive tool that hid a woman's true nature. "Cautionary tales circulated about prostitutes disguised as shoppers, saleswomen posing as ladies, and light-skinned 'octaroons' passing into white society," writes Peiss. "Advice books gave bachelors hints on how to tell the authentic beauty from the fake."[23]

Cosmetics, together with beauty competition, became acceptable, however, with the rise of the Industrial Revolution and the emergence of an urban American bourgeoisie. Upwardly mobile women, seeking to announce their new status, increasingly turned to beauty aids—and overtly competed with other women in the beauty arena. Late-nineteenth-century middle-class women enjoyed strolling, shopping, and eating in public, requiring them to pay attention to how they appeared to others: They were now on display in public in a way they had never been before. Cosmetics, along with fashionable clothes, became much more accepted and enabled middle-class women to manufacture an image for themselves and take control of how they were seen. Physical beauty became a higher priority than spiritual beauty, and a new cosmetics industry grew to "help" women with their image. Notes Peiss, "What changed in the late nineteenth century was the attitude toward competitiveness. It became more accepted as a dynamic that women would likely engage in. That is, competitiveness became part of the cultural definition of femininity for the white middle class."[24]

The last *fin de siècle*'s emphasis on self-presentation resonates with our own turn of the century's voyeuristic concern with looks and style. A decade ago, Starbucks designed coffee bars with seats facing the window, allowing customers to gaze not on a companion sharing afternoon coffee but on strangers walking along the sidewalk. *Glamour* magazine snaps photos of unsuspecting women and deems their outfits "do's" or "don'ts." Joan Rivers mercilessly dissects the gowns worn at the Academy Awards, and pity the poor actress whose ensemble is ridiculed as déclassé. In the new millennium, men and women both are hyperaware of how others appear and how others perceive their own appearance. At the same time, there is a backlash of sorts (along with a sense of huge relief for many of us) with the Internet, where anyone can remain anonymous and a person is judged by her typos or grating usage of all-caps rather than by her outdated Banana Republic skirt.

Just as it does today, being on display in the early twentieth cen-tury bred insecurities. Cosmetics ads asked, "Do you wonder, when you meet a casual friend, whether your nose is shiny? Do you anx-iously consult store windows and vanity cases at every opportunity?" A 1922 soap advertisement that appeared in *Ladies' Home Journal* depicted a woman walking through an outdoor plaza where others are seated, eating and drinking. All eyes are upon her. "Strangers' eyes, keen and critical—can you meet them proudly—confidently—without fear?" Ads for Armand, a cosmetics company, stated omi-nously, "The great moments of your life are 'close-ups.'" [25]

Makeup was now considered an aid in personal transformation, accessible to everyone. "Beauty may have been considered the birthright of only wealthy or fortunate women in the nineteenth century," observes Peiss, but in the twentieth century "cosmetics advertising sold the idea that an attractive appearance was an accomplishment all could easily achieve. Mail-order and tabloid-style ads promised cheap, instant beauty to working women unable to afford the time and money leisured women spent on beauty cul-ture." [26] The new beauty culture fit in perfectly with the American ideals of democracy and personal fulfillment (even though the old one supposedly fit in just as well). It created an even playing field while allowing women to express their individuality.

There was one problem: More and more, women were not free to choose whether or not to use cosmetics, whether or not to play with their image. They were pressured to "put on a face" every day, whether they were at home or out at work. Beauty aids became compulsory and had an aura of medical authority. Advertisements implied that women were naturally unattractive and needed cosmetics to make them pretty. True femininity meant being attractive, and beauty indicated true femininity.

Thus, guidance counselors at Smith College noted in their records the "attractiveness" of graduating seniors. Telephone operators, whose appearance was irrelevant since the public never saw them, were forced to adhere to numerous grooming requirements. The H. J. Heinz Company instituted weekly manicures for its pickle packers and even instructed them on how to wear cosmetics properly. Beauty education spread through high schools and colleges, where students were instructed on the use of cosmetics, facial care, and cleanliness.[27] Black women had it the worst, since they were pressured to conform to the white ideal by bleaching their skin and straightening their hair. Beauty entrepreneurs such as Madam C. J. Walker and Annie Turnbo Malone, however, refused to adhere to the constricting ideal and promoted the attractiveness of African-American hair and skin.

Maintaining a slim physique also became compulsory. At the turn of the twentieth century, many middle-class white girls and women in Europe and the U.S. restricted their food intake in an effort to appear as thin as possible—and therefore to associate themselves with an upwardly mobile class identity. (The image of the dowdy Victorian matron was thought to symbolize a life of old-fashioned self-sacrifice rather than fast-paced modernity.)[28] The pressure to diet intensified in the 1920s when the hourglass silhouette for women's dresses was replaced with the popular "flapper" look, a chemise with a dropped waistline that looked best on thin, flat-chested, small-hipped women. The "flapper" look signaled a rise in women's rights: American women had fought for and won the right to vote in 1920, and more women than ever before were working outside their homes. Ironically, notes cultural historian Joan Jacobs Brumberg, "the new slim body, with its small breasts and narrow hips, symbolized increased rather than diminished sexuality.... [A] slender body and the willingness to wear more revealing clothes were taken as signs of increased sexual confidence, freedom, and enjoyment. A svelte female figure became, for the first time, the ultimate sign and symbol of heterosexual interest and success."[29]

In her history of girls' bodies and their relationships with them, *The Body Project*, Brumberg traces how teenage girls began to focus on losing weight as the answer to all of their problems. She quotes from the diary of Yvonne Blue, the daughter of an ophthalmologist and homemaker living in Chicago. Born in 1911, Yvonne began worrying about her weight in the summer of 1926, when she was fifteen. One of her best friends, Mattie, joined Yvonne in dieting. Mattie wrote to her during her summer vacation: "I had a dream with you in it. You wore a lumberjack blouse and a checked skirt and you were so thin I nearly died of envy. I am terribly fat."[30]

Before World War I, women who could afford new clothes visited a dressmaker, who fit each dress to the customer's body. In the 1920s, the clothing industry offered standard, ready-to-wear sizes, which women had to try on and accept or reject. Brumberg notes in her history of anorexia nervosa, *Fasting Girls*, that girls and women found clothes-shopping a frustrating experience, because they were now made aware of their "figure flaws." Those who didn't fit into stylish clothes felt embarrassed about their bodies. Being slim was part of the recipe for attractiveness, and its importance grew throughout the century.[31]

MISS AMERICA

As women became more self-conscious about their appearance, along came an institution guaranteed to feed their anxieties: the beauty contest. The most well-known and "respectable" beauty contest, Miss America, put not only the concept of "beauty" under a spotlight but "femininity" as well. Just as "beauty" had been defined in very narrow terms, now so too was "femininity," which increasingly came to mean a woman who was respectable, sexually pure, poised, active in charitable good deeds—as well as a looker in a swimsuit with gorgeous gams.

The Miss America pageant began as a "bathing beauty" contest in 1921 in Atlantic City (one year after women won the right to vote), designed to lure tourists to remain at the resort past Labor Day. Contestants were required to adhere to numerous restrictions so that they could be touted as high-class, modest, and honorable women who represented America, despite the fact that the contest had them parade half-naked wearing high heels, and that those who flocked to the pageant sought a cheap sexual thrill. Right from the beginning, beauty was entwined with nonaesthetic characteristics such as "innocence" and virginity.

To participate, a woman had to be single. Alcohol was prohibited, and each contestant was banned from bars and taverns. She also adhered to a nightly curfew, was constantly chaperoned, and was disqualified if seen alone talking to any man, including her own father, during pageant week. In 1938, the talent competition (always involving something performative such as singing, dancing, or playing a musical instrument) was inaugurated, and that year each contestant was also required to represent a geographic region.

By 1940, she was vying for scholarship money, another sign that this pageant was about more than just surface beauty. Each contestant was later required to have a "platform" that raises awareness about a social cause to which she could devote volunteer work.[32] (Charitable work, especially in the service of social issues such as breast cancer awareness or the prevention of teenage pregnancy, is considered respectable because it deals with private concerns and not with public ambition.) And she had to sign a statement vouching that she had never been married or pregnant.

The never-been-pregnant rule applies even today. In 1999, Miss America organizers realized that New Jersey law prohibits discrimination on the basis of marital status and pregnancy, so they lifted the old restrictions. The policy change would have required contestants to say only that they were not married nor the natural or adoptive parent of a child, opening the pageant to women with divorce and abortion in their past. The chief executive officer of the Miss America Organization who proposed the new rules was summarily fired, New Jersey laws be damned. The new CEO, an Atlantic City casino chief, declared that "Miss America is an icon owned by the American people, and anachronistic and puritanical as it is, a lot of people want her to be virginal and pure as the driven snow."[33] The only changes today that reflect our evolving times are the name change from "swimsuit competition" to "physical fitness competition" (which only puts more pressure on contestants than ever before: now they have to be toned and firm as well as shapely) and the lifting of the requirement to wear high heels with one's swimsuit.

Miss America's relentless equation of beauty with respectable femininity stands in contrast with the Miss USA, Miss Teen USA, and Miss Universe contests, co-owned by Donald Trump. The winners of these pageants are awarded money, a car, and a fur coat—but no scholarship (though obviously one can use her monetary award for tuition). The organizers of Miss America–related pageants are horrified by the suggestion that they have anything at all in common with Miss USA and its ilk. They are *scholarship* pageants, they emphasize, thank you very much. Indeed, when I telephoned the president of the Miss Connecticut Scholarship pageant (a feeder pageant into Miss America) to inquire how I could attend an upcoming pageant, I was not at that time well-versed in these distinctions, and I made the mistake of referring to it as a "beauty pageant." The president, whose voice identified her as older, was horrified. "Oh, my dear," she gasped into the phone, "we are *not* the Miss USA pageant! If I may be so bold, and I don't want to put anyone down, but they are a *beauty* pageant." To me the difference between a scholarship and a beauty pageant is negligible, since in either case you have to be beautiful and poised to have any chance of winning, platform issue or no platform issue, and the award is money, no matter how you look at it. But those associated with Miss America take these distinctions very seriously. Their reputation is on the line.

The Miss America pageant is not just about beautiful women belting out Broadway musical lyrics and gliding down a catwalk in beaded evening gowns, with poufy hair and plastered-on smiles. It is symbolic of what American girls and women are supposed to aspire to. The American beauty ideal is an impossible dream for most of us, but Miss America raises the stakes even higher by making beauty a stand-in for so much more. Miss America teaches girls and women that to be truly beautiful, they must also be respectable, poised, blessed with sopranic vocal chords, nurturing (through a concern with social issues), and virginal. Once again we see how elusive (and ridiculous) the American beauty ideal is.

Yet the Miss America organization wants us to believe that any woman can win. The crown, notes beauty pageant historian Sarah Banet-Weiser, is "held up to be supremely attainable; this crown, like commercial success, like the American dream, is there for those who try."[34] Since physical attractiveness is only one of the categories in which a contestant is formally judged—with 15 percent of the total score allotted to the swimsuit competition and another 15 percent allotted to evening wear—the consensus among those involved is that the winner is chosen not because she's beautiful but because she is an exemplary woman (who happens to be beautiful).

Recently I attended one of the small pageants that feed into the Miss America pageant, held in New York City. (The winner of this pageant would go on to compete in the Miss New York competition, and Miss New York would vie for the Miss America crown on national television.) There were twelve contestants of different ethnicities and body types. Indeed, only half had model-type physiques; the rest had fairly average-looking bodies, cellulite and all. All twelve women were physically attractive, some more so than others. In the middle of the pageant, I went backstage to the dressing room. Some contestants were visibly nervous, others were smiling wanly. To my surprise, I didn't detect any overt competition among the "girls," as they're called (although they are women between the ages of eighteen and twenty-four). In fact, they went out of their way to show support for one another by hugging and holding each other's hands.

Since this wasn't supposed to be a beauty pageant, I asked, what did they think about the fact that part of what they were judged on was their appearance? "I don't think there's much emphasis on appearance," said one young woman, tall, slender, black—and she really seemed to mean it. She also happened to be a sociology and history major at Yale University. "I was at the pageant last week in Queens and the women looked quite different. They were short and heavyset. It's not about blond hair, blue eyes, small waist, size 2 anymore. Swimwear and evening wear are 30 percent of the total, yes. But I think it's more about confidence and how you carry yourself than how you look."

Another contestant, a Latina pursuing political science and theater degrees from Fordham University, agreed. "I've seen many girls who are extremely competent but perhaps don't have the best figures," she said, "and they hold themselves with grace and with confidence. So what if they're not the most fit, if they are confident. And that's what it's really about. The pageant is really about health and physical fitness, and about grace and composure under pressure."

I would have dismissed these women's optimism as brainwashed pageant-speak, but then the winner, Tracy Nightingale, was announced.[35] A freshman at New York University, she was white with wavy dark hair. Most people would probably have described her as attractive, not breathtaking. She was not as slender as the others. She had sung a musical number from *The Phantom of the Opera*, and to my ears her voice was no better or worse than that of the other budding singers. Her chiffon gown had seemed flattering. (I had no idea how her interview had gone, since for this pageant, interviews were conducted privately backstage.) In short, I think that most people would have agreed that Tracy was cute with a good voice and a good eye for gowns but not the most conventionally "beautiful" of the bunch, according to the standards of the narrow American beauty ideal. She made winning a beauty pageant seem truly attainable.

The question, of course, is whether or not winning a beauty pageant is a desirable goal in the first place. Even if the standards of the contest have changed, participants are still paraded like dogs and then rated as objects. High ratings make them valuable objects, low marks render them valueless. As long as such contests continue, woman as object will continue.

When I spoke with her a month after the pageant, Tracy told me that the volunteers who had organized her pageant were pressuring her to lose ten to fifteen pounds.

> Everyone who has seen me has told me that if I want to win, I should lose [the weight]. When I go home [for the summer after the semester is over], basically that's what I will be doing. That's the one area that they think is my weakest. It's kind of hard to take. It's not a bad thing. It's looked upon as a good thing because it forces people that do need to do things like this to take control of something they can control, like losing weight and getting in shape. It's not like someone is yelling at me and saying, "If you don't do this, you won't win" or that they're being mean to me or anything like that. I've been treated wonderfully by the people who are in charge. It's just for, like, the purposes of being on stage—things look so much different on stage and on TV than they do [in real life]. You have to be smaller than normal.

"Do *you* think you need to lose weight?" I asked. "Actually, honestly, I would like to a little bit," answered Tracy, "but no, oh gosh, no, please don't think that I'm not comfortable with myself. I have high self-esteem, actually, and feel pretty good about my body and people's responses [to it]." She also revealed how all the "girls," herself included, made their bodies behave while onstage. Before they put on their bathing suits, they sprayed Firmgrip, used by tennis players to make the racket stick to their hand, on their behind so that the bathing suit wouldn't ride up. "It hurts when you rip it off," she offered before I had the chance to ask. "The next thing you do is for your chest. To make cleavage, you take medical tape and you put it across your chest to push yourself up and make a crease. And then you usually put padding around the sides to enhance your bust."

At the end of the summer, Tracy competed in the Miss New York pageant, where she made it to the top ten finalists, but didn't win the crown. When I spoke with her this time, she sounded shell-shocked from the experience. Yes, she had lost ten pounds, and that had given her a boost of confidence. But while at the pageant in Manhattan there had not been a sense of competitiveness, here the "girls" had gone "all-out." Many of them had spent tens of thousands of dollars on gowns, outfits, and professional photographs—belying the scholarship money as the reason contestants compete. Some of them appeared to Tracy as quite ruthless. One had even used "water boobs," as Tracy put it, in her bathing suit to enhance her cleavage. (This is apparently not against the rules.) The woman who won Miss New York State, Tracy observed, had poured a significant amount of money into the pageant. She was beautiful in a polished way, but her talent, playing piano, was far from superior. Still, said

Tracy, she was very confident onstage and seemed comfortable with herself, though some of her answers during the interview came across as "being memorized or a little fake."

Did the judges place more emphasis on the winner's looks than they should have? I asked Tracy.

> I think it's human nature that you cannot help but score higher for someone you find attractive. That's just normal; that's just human nature. The nice thing is that almost all the girls there were pretty attractive, but I think it's an unconscious thing that the one who looks a little more put-together is going to stand out to you.

I pointed out that that's why they spend thousands of dollars on their outfits.

> Yes. They're aware that if you're going to play this game, you're going to play it. And I guess that's what I learned from being there. That if I were ever to do this again, now I know: This is a game, and you've got to learn to play it if you're going to win.

Of course, the game of beauty—with the "winner" being judged most beautiful—extends to everyday life. You don't have to go to Atlantic City to be a contestant.

By the national level, any trace of attainable beauty had vanished like lipstick at the end of a long day. When I watched the Miss America pageant on TV that fall, I noticed that every contestant had flawless skin and blindingly white teeth. None looked like an "average" woman. There was no cellulite in sight, and all were quite thin but at least somewhat busty. Indeed, Miss America has become skinnier over the decades, and many winners have been undernourished, according to nutrition experts at the Johns Hopkins School of Public Health. In the 1920s, contestants had Body Mass Indexes [the BMI is a measure of weight relative to height] in the range now considered normal, which is 20 to 25. But increasingly since then the winners have had BMIs under 18.5, which is the World Health Organization's standard for undernutrition.[36]

FEMINISM AND BEAUTY

When the women's liberation movement erupted in the late 1960s, its first order of business was to attack the beauty industry. Feminists claimed that beauty ideals enslaved women by pressuring them to compete with other women for the attention of men, and thus formed the bedrock of modern women's oppression. The Miss America pageant was the perfect vehicle for a protest. New York Radical Women, one of the small but vital cells that made up the movement, mobilized one hundred activists to go to Atlantic City and to fill a giant trash can with eyelash curlers, garter belts, curling irons, cans of hairspray, and other beauty aids. On national television, they also crowned a live sheep America's beauty queen. The point of the demonstration was that all women are hurt by beauty competitions—including the women competing for the Miss America crown. But that message got lost, lamented Carol Hanisch, one of the organizers: "Posters which read 'Up Against the Wall, Miss America,' 'Miss America Sells It,' and 'Miss America Is a Big Falsie' hardly raised any woman's consciousness and really harmed the cause of sisterhood. Miss America and all beautiful women came off as our enemy instead of as our sisters who suffer with us."[37]

Bitch, a feminist magazine that is a refreshingly biting forum about how women are represented in popular culture, is always on my must-read list. But one recent article soured me. The author, Andrea Oxidant, discusses working as a skin care consultant at Sephora, the giant cosmetics store chain, and sneers that "About 80 percent of our clients are lemmings running in for the new flavor of the month." She also declares, "I truly believe that the average human IQ drops about twenty points upon entering a mall."[38] In a similar article in *Elle*, therapist and novelist Amy Bloom writes about her experience working behind a makeup counter. She categorizes the customers as Sample Ladies, who are "congenitally cheap" and press incessantly for free samples; Leisure Ladies, who "drop off their kids in the morning and hang around until early afternoon, spritzing a little of this, trying a fingerful of that" and who bring with them "the air of anomie and desperation"; and the Everything Ladies, who buy beauty products "the way bulimics eat, and even when the layers of goop will keep their faces not fresh but disturbingly damp, like rotisserie chicken, they want it all, and all at once."[39]

Oxidant and Bloom want us all to know that *they* buy and wear makeup in moderation because their self-esteem remains intact, that the beauty industry has not worn *them* down, and that it's perfectly acceptable to be contemptuous of other women who, perhaps lacking restraint and self-worth, yearn to achieve the American beauty ideal. What does their scorn say about me? Many a time I've bought eyeliners, eyebrow shapers, and blushes from Bobbi Brown sales reps after they've told me I should. Does that make me an idiot who enjoys throwing away money, or that like most women, I'm willing to spend some cash if it helps me achieve a few more degrees of confidence when I walk out my apartment door in the morning? And don't even those who overuse makeup deserve our understanding, not our scorn? They have come to believe that without beauty aids, they are powerless or worthless. Or maybe they just find makeup a lot of fun, and for them, spending money on lipliners and night creams that sit unopened in their medicine chests is an avocation, no more harmful than searching for and buying vintage books that are treasured yet go unread.

Some feminists have analyzed women's relationship with the beauty ideal without setting up "feminism" and "beauty" as contending forces. Debbie Stoller of *Bust* wholeheartedly embraces the two. "We love our lipstick," she writes of feminism's Third Wave, the generation of women under thirty-five, "have a passion for polish, and basically, adore this armor that we call 'fashion.' To us, it's fun, it's feminine, and, in the particular way we flaunt it, it's definitely feminist."[40] Ellen Zetzel Lambert offers a nuanced analysis in her book, *The Face of Love*. Lambert agrees that feminists shouldn't feel guilty for caring about appearance. But at the same time, she also wants feminists to recognize the inherent subjectivity of beauty. Feeling loved, and loving another, makes a woman feel beautiful; the recipe for beauty can never be found in women's magazines. The only way we can change our appearance is to change the way we feel about ourselves.[41] I admire Lambert for trying to forge a feminist path that acknowledges the importance of beauty without pitting women against one another. Of course, she is absolutely right that how we feel about ourselves is what really counts. Unfortunately, we live in a culture in which we are constantly judged on how we appear.

Yes, the beauty standards of our time are oppressive; yes, they take their toll on the self-esteem of countless women. But at the same time, beauty rituals can bring us together to supportively appraise one another as we experiment with colors and styles. I, too, enjoy applying blush to cheekbone and lipstick to mouth. But the problem has never been rouge or lipstick per se. The problem is that society makes women believe that without these aids they are not beautiful and therefore not important. In fact, without the aids, women are taught they are invisible.

COSMETIC SURGERY

Makeup is seductive because of its transformative possibilities. There's a reason that talk shows never tire of featuring women who get makeovers and who are applauded for their new looks (and, by implication, new identities). The idea that an individual has the power to remake himself or herself is part of our culture's Enlightenment philosophy: Everyone is entitled to pursue his or her own happiness, and self-transformation is regarded as an effective way of achieving it. The power of self-transformation can obviously be liberating, but it can also unleash competitiveness. If one woman can make herself beautiful, regardless of her natural attributes, then there really is no excuse for other women to remain plain Janes. They had better transform themselves, too; otherwise, they will get left behind.

Cosmetic surgery, in which an individual literally carves his or her body or face to conform to an ideal, is physical transformation *par excellence*. Historian Sander Gilman traces the roots of cosmetic surgery (he calls it "aesthetic surgery") in his book *Making the Body Beautiful*. He writes that aesthetic surgery was developed at the end of the sixteenth century to hide the stigmatizing disfigurement of syphilitics (whose nose cartilage and bone had been eaten away). By the late nineteenth century, cosmetic surgery was used to eliminate racialized characteristics, such as the hooked noses of Jews; most patients were men. Jews who could "pass" as Gentile, particularly in Europe, had the opportunity for great professional success. Since they looked like everyone else, their Jewishness was invisible. Writes Gilman, "'Passing' is a means of trying to gain control. It is the means of restoring not 'happiness' but a sense of order in the world. We 'pass' in order to regain control of ourselves and to efface that which is seen (we believe) as different, which marks us as visible in the world."[42]

Today, by far the majority of cosmetic surgery patients are women. They, too, want to "pass": They want to look attractive. Beauty is not generally the goal of cosmetic surgery: looking ordinary, the way a woman is "supposed" to look, is. Patients believe that their flaws—too-small breasts, large thighs, love handles, jowls—make them too visibly different from their idealized norm. Erasing these so-called flaws will give them an entrée into "normal" femininity. But, as Gilman points out, cosmetic surgeries are primarily attempts to disassociate with a particular racial or ethnic group (even though this is rarely the stated intent). The goal of most cosmetic surgeries continues to be the elimination of features associated with being Jewish, Asian, or African American. The goal, in other words, is to conform to the narrow American white ideal.

Until recently, most Americans disapproved of cosmetic surgery, but today the stigma is disappearing. Average Americans are lining up for procedures—two-thirds of patients report family incomes of less than $50,000 a year—and many of them return for more.[43] Younger women undergo "maintenance" surgeries in a futile attempt to halt time. The latest fad is Botox, a purified and diluted form of botulinum toxin that is injected between the eyebrows to eliminate frown lines. Although the procedure costs between $300 and $1,000 and must be repeated every few months, roughly 850,000 patients have had it performed on them. That number will undoubtedly shoot up now that the FDA has approved Botox for cosmetic use.[44] Even teenagers are making appointments with plastic surgeons: More than 14,000 adolescents had plastic surgery in 1996, and many of them are choosing controversial procedures such as breast implants, liposuction, and tummy tucks, rather than the rhinoplasties of previous generations.[45]

Many women would pay any price for the perfect body—but what about their lives? The safety of some procedures is questionable. Liposuction, the most popular cosmetic surgery, in which body fat is suctioned out through a tube, carries a fatality rate of one in 5,000—an incidence of death that is two to three times higher than that of dying from a normal pregnancy. More than 230,000 liposuction procedures were performed in 1999; 200,000 of the patients were women. Most fatalities are caused by blood clotting, complications from anesthesia, or errors by practitioners who may not have enough experience.[46] In 1997, the California Medical Board's plastic/cosmetic surgery committee traced most of the liposuction deaths in that state to the fact that doctors were going overboard, removing up to forty-seven pounds of fat and fluid from some patients.[47]

The second-most popular cosmetic procedure, breast augmentation, also poses health dangers. In 1999, more than 167,000 American women spent an average of $3,000 each to have saline sacs implanted in their chests. Implant manufacturers and the doctors who insert them generate roughly $800 million a year. Most implantees are satisfied with the surgery. However, nearly 50,000 women and doctors have reported problems, including 118 deaths, since 1985. Sixteen percent of patients suffered moderate to severe breast pain, and 9 percent developed painful hardening of tissue around the implants. Eight percent had improperly positioned implants, and 17 percent had either intense nipple sensation or numbness. These statistics come from a study conducted by one of the major American breast implant manufacturers, McGhan Medical[48] (so who knows what an unbiased study would turn up). To put things in perspective, saline implants are supposed to be an improvement over silicone-gel implants, now off the market except for medical reasons (such as reconstruction after mastectomy).

Cosmetic surgery gives a person a sense of control over her appearance in a world in which others judge her worthiness within ten seconds of meeting her. That even cancer survivors are willing to risk their lives to "pass" as attractive suggests how truly warped the beauty ideal is. Is it not obvious that it's better to have one breast, or two small ones, or a big nose, or chunky thighs—and remain in good health?

WHO'S THE THINNEST OF THEM ALL?

Let's be honest. When most women measure their looks against that of other women, they are really focused on one thing: who's thinner. How come *she* doesn't have cellulite? Does she ever eat anything besides salad? What does she weigh?

Many women perpetually fight their metabolisms in a usually futile quest for a body devoid of signs of femaleness—hips, thighs, rounded belly, any fatty tissue at all. Even if they do lose weight, chances are that they remain unsatisfied, since the "perfect" female body, according to the narrow American beauty ideal, is by definition out of reach.

It's easy to forget that many women around the world equate "thin" with "ugly." In some parts of Africa, for instance, fat is the beauty ideal for women. In Nigeria, brides are sent to "fattening rooms" or "fattening farms" before their wedding to gain weight. Some Nigerian women even go so far as to eat feed for animals in order to gain weight.[49] But here in the United States, most women are better able to relate to Helen Gurley Brown, the doyenne of women's magazine editors, who has famously said that "Skinny is sacred to me." Here's how sacred skinny is:

☞ A twenty-two-year-old recent college graduate moans to me about the plight of her friend who is going to the Caribbean for spring break with some girlfriends. "Last night I was talking to her, and she said, 'Uch, I had a whole slice of pizza tonight, and I'm so upset because I'm going away with a bunch of skinnies, and I don't know what I'm going to do. I'm going to have to starve myself before I go.' They're all her friends and they will all have a great time with her no matter what, but it's going to be tough. They're size 2s and 4s and she's probably a size 10. When they're on the beach and wearing their bathing suits, she's going to be very self-conscious. She told me that she might not take off her shorts and will probably go into the water in her shorts. I know that a lot of girls do that around guys, because they feel weird about exposing so much, but this is going to be all girls."

☞ A lesbian writer recalls her first relationship with a woman at the age of twenty. "For me, she was perfect, the ideal woman. She was five-seven, C-cup breasts, and in my mind she had this perfect body. And I felt ashamed of my body and I worried that if we ever slept together she would find my body unattractive because she would compare my body to her own body."

☞ An editor at a fashion magazine relates that in her business, run of course by women interested in beauty and fashion, "the big competition is over who's skinnier. I remember one girl saying that her boss hated her. I asked why. And she said, 'Because I'm skinny and pretty.' And you know what? I think it was true. Her boss really did hate her because she was skinny and pretty."

If she is skinny and pretty, an adolescent or preadolescent girl is rewarded with popularity. Other girls look up to her and want to be associated with her. It's amazing how often this narrative is repeated when girls and women talk about their junior high and high school dieting experiences. Lori Gottlieb, a former Hollywood executive who grew up in Beverly Hills, stopped eating in junior high. At lunch everyone noticed that she was losing weight and buzzed around her, wanting to know her secrets. "What do you eat for breakfast?" one girl asked. "Exactly nineteen flakes of Product 19 cereal, with two ounces of nonfat milk," Gottlieb answered, pretending that it tasted good even though she actually thought it tasted "pretty gross." "Then everyone started crowding around me and asking questions all at once, like I was a movie star or something,"

Gottlieb wrote in her diary, which she published as the book *Stick Figure: A Diary of My Former Self*. "They wanted me to look in their lunch bags and tell them how to stay thin or get thinner, like I was doing. I know this sounds conceited to say, but by the end of the lunch period, I was almost as popular as I used to be back in first grade when I still had blondish hair."[50]

Kate Dillon, now a plus-size model, remembers that in junior high everyone made fun of her for being overweight, even though she was just a little bit chubby. So Dillon began starving herself: Some days she would eat nothing but a piece of fruit, on others she would have some salad and frozen yogurt. There were days when she would eat nothing at all. After three and a half months she lost thirty pounds and gained popularity. Kids in school wrote in her seventh grade yearbook, "Sorry about all that weirdness before, but I'm really glad I know you now." For several years Dillon continued to eat next to nothing, consuming no more than 700 calories a day—and again she was rewarded, this time with a modeling contract and an internationally successful modeling career.[51]

It's really no surprise that so many girls starve themselves into the popular clique. Being overweight, especially in junior high and high school, generally makes you a target of ostracism and cruel jokes, unless you're lucky enough to remain completely unnoticed. The single largest group of high school students considering or attempting suicide are girls who think they are overweight.[52]

On the other hand, being thin also makes other females wary of you, particularly when you've grown to adulthood and they have outgrown the desire to "be your best friend" because they want to be like you. Janet Harrison, who works for a nonprofit organization in Washington, D.C., has been blessed with a good metabolism: She can eat what she wants without gaining weight or pounding the Stairmaster. At five feet six inches, she wears a size 2. "Within minutes of meeting women they have asked me how much I weigh, what size jeans I wear, things that are somewhat offensive to me because I don't ask them those questions. And they're like, 'Oh my God, I can't believe you can eat that' or 'Do you have to do anything to keep your figure?' I'm not Ally McBeal, even though people call me that jokingly. And you know what's funny? A lot of these comments come from tiny girls themselves. I think they're jealous of the fact that I don't have to work at it, that I'm having an appetizer and a big sandwich while they're having a salad. It's a sickness. These women look fine yet they'll go out drinking one night and the next day they're like, 'Oh, I gained five pounds. *You* wouldn't understand.'"

We have been socially conditioned to place one another on a thin/fat continuum and categorize one another accordingly. Thus, a thin friend is, in our imagination, pretty, successful, and disciplined while an overweight friend is plain, ploddish, and lacking in control—regardless of their actual attributes. When a friend who had always been fat loses weight, she wreaks havoc with the entire schema. "Weight is like a role you play," according to Susan Head, Ph.D., a clinical psychologist and consultant at Duke University's Rice Diet Program. "You're the fat friend, the fat wife or girlfriend, the one who listens to problems, who's not threatening, who doesn't have a social life," she told *Elle* magazine. "Some part of the identity of people close to you is based on your weight, so when you throw off that role, you upset the whole balance of things."[53]

I meet Laura, a twenty-nine-year-old graduate student, at an intimate sandwich-and-salad restaurant. The only evidence that she is on a diet is her chain-drinking of Diet Coke and constant gum-chewing. Otherwise, there is no hint that over the last year, she has lost fifty pounds through Weight Watchers. Laura is attractive, with shoulder-length light brown hair and brown eyes behind funky, small, oval eyeglasses. "Your life changes," she says dramatically of her weight loss, and she's right. "You're treated differently by guys. You're treated differently by women. But I'm still me— I'm still wacky and funny and crazy, you know what I'm saying? But I also feel like a different person because of how people treat me. Before, if I had a crush on a guy, I knew he would never call me. Now I'll get an email from him two days after meeting him. Guys come up to me and start conversations. It's craziness. It's disturbing, because I'm still me."

But it's her relationships with women that have really devolved to "craziness." Laura now is forced to categorize her friends into two camps: those who are happy with their own bodies and those who are not. "When I'm talking about guys or clothes, I pay attention to whom I'm talking and what their comfort level with their own body is." Laura speaks with a lot of nervous energy, the words tumbling out of her at a breakneck pace. "You know, buying clothes never used to be exciting for me. I was either a 16 or a 14. I'm not saying that there's anything wrong with those sizes. But now I'm in the single digits, and for me, that's exciting. But there aren't that many people I can say that to without their taking it the wrong way. So in terms of women, I censor a lot of what I say." She worries about alienating two close friends, who happen to be heavy.

One of them, Jessica, was in Laura's apartment the week before and spied a pair of jeans dangling over the bedroom chair. She grabbed them to check out the size, which embarrassed Laura. She wants me to know that she did not leave the jeans out on purpose; they were there because she was getting ready to wear them that night. "I watch every word so that I don't come across as 'I'm so great' and I don't want to make her feel bad about herself. Or with my other friend, I might mention one date I'm having, but not mention that I've got three other dates that week, because I don't want her to think, 'I've got nothing going on, and look at you, you're this whole other person.'"

"I'm so scared of being like one of those girls I've always hated," she continues, banging on the table with her finger, "who would brag and who would have lots of guys, who would make you feel bad about yourself. You know, you can be pegged a certain way. It's insane. I can control my weight because I can control what I eat and how much I exercise, but I can't control how others perceive me. You get control over one part of your life, and then you lose control over another part."

What would Laura's life have been like if we didn't have a "thin is beautiful" mythology? Most probably, her "wacky and funny and crazy" self would have shone through to everyone who has known her, not only to other heavy women (her primary friends during her overweight years). She would have felt sure of herself without having to lose weight. Today she would not be drinking so many caffeinated, Aspartame-laced soft drinks, which might possibly do more damage to her health than her old extra weight. She would not feel the need to conform physically to an ideal that, now that it's been reached, she will struggle to maintain for the rest of her life. Even if Laura is "lucky" to remain at her ideal number of pounds, no doubt the pressure to maintain it will be an unbearable burden.

EATING DISORDERS

Why do women, even close friends, compete with each other over their jeans size? Another person's genetics, metabolism, and appetite are unique to her, and therefore not an appropriate platform on which to judge oneself. Yet the narrow beauty ideal fosters the oppressive mythology that one body shape, though unnatural for most women, can fit all. The key to achieving that shape, we are told, is self-control.

Laura's use of the word control is thus entirely apt, since that is what dieting, as with every other aspect of beauty competition, is really about. So many of us feel that our lives are beyond our control, especially given the impossible beauty standards we're supposed to meet. (Teenage girls in particular tend to regard their lives as chaotic, given that their bodies are blossoming, their family life may be changing, and they are contemplating life after high school.) Counting calories and weighing ounces of chicken breast is an accessible way to feel a sense of mastery and control over one's life. Throwing up after a meal is also a way to feel in control over forces that seem uncertain. Studies from the American Anorexia Bulimia Association have found that one-third of preadolescent girls (twelve and thirteen years old) are trying to lose weight by dieting, vomiting, taking diet pills, or using laxatives.[54]

But even the most disciplined diet can spiral out of control and develop into an eating disorder. Diets and eating disorders differ in degree, though not in kind: They are on a continuum. And once a girl or woman falls prey to an eating disorder, she can do quite a bit of damage to the body she is trying so hard to perfect. Roughly seven million American girls and women, and one million boys and men, struggle with eating disorders, according to the National Association of Anorexia Nervosa and Associated Disorders. Over 10 percent of anorexics die from their disorder. The rest may suffer from bone abnormalities, hypotension, heart palpitations, or cardiac arrhythmias. Bulimics can develop a reduced metabolic rate, nervous-system dysfunction, kidney trouble, dental problems, arrhythmias, and tearing of the esophagus. A woman who once had an eating disorder but now eats properly is forever crippled by shrunken bone density. Even diet aids used to lose just a few pounds can cause irreparable bodily harm. The diet drug fen-phen was pulled from the U.S. market in 1997 after a study linked it to heart-valve damage, and the herbal stimulant ephedra, used for weight loss, has been tied to strokes and heart attacks.[55]

Magazines routinely run tragic stories of women who go too far in their quest for the perfect body. A *People* article tells a typical tale: Nineteen-year-old Merrick Ryan, from Alpharetta, Georgia, became obsessed with her weight after spending the summer of 1999 with relatives in New York City. "She'd call and tell us about the women in Manhattan who were all size 2 or 4, and how she felt so fat walking down the sidewalk," said her father. An accompanying photo shows a beautiful woman with long, auburn hair, clad in jeans and a shirt, who does not appear at all overweight. No matter: Merrick Ryan started losing weight and couldn't stop. In several months, she dropped down to eighty-eight pounds on her five-foot-seven frame. She then revealed that while in New York, she had been the victim of a date rape. In recounting the trauma to her mother, she cried, "Didn't he think I was pretty enough?" Shortly after, Merrick Ryan overdosed on antidepressants. While she was at the hospital and slipping in and out of consciousness, she said to her mother, "I don't want to be fat. I want to die."[56]

Most American women know about the fate of Merrick Ryans—yet we continue to diet excessively anyway. A common goal women aspire to, rarely acknowledged, is to diet to the point where we *look* as if we have anorexia without actually having it. (Once again, we see that dieting is really all about maintaining control and feeling accepted.) In fact, many women are spurred to diet after learning the tricks of anorexics and bulimics through documentaries or magazine articles warning against eating disorders. An educational program at Stanford University in the 1990s, designed to prevent eating disorders by letting students hear firsthand about their hazards, backfired: The students became more likely to imitate the behaviors they were supposed to avoid. The program featured two young woman, one a recovered anorexic and the other a recovered bulimic, who made a presentation to a psychology class. There was one problem: The women were attractive, slim, healthy looking, and poised—precisely the kind of women the other students would want to emulate. "They made it look too easy, as if you could get anorexia, get over it and then be thin and a leader like them," said Dr. Traci Mann, who analyzed the program. "The presentation separated the behavior from its mental illness aspect."[57]

Black women suffer from eating disorders as much as white women do, although they are more accepting than whites of full-figured women. But the thin ideal is omnipresent, and blacks are not immune to it. Seventy-one percent of respondents to an *Essence* survey, in which more than two thousand women participated, reported being preoccupied with the desire to be thinner. Hundreds of readers sent in letters along with their surveys; the magazine reprinted a number of poignant excerpts. All of the letters express ways that dieting affects their relationships with other women. One reader revealed that she can't stop throwing up after eating because now that she's thin, she's "in love" with the compliments she gets. Another was worried because she's bulimic and doesn't want her thirteen-year-old sister to mimic her. Another confessed that she has gained thirty pounds over the last two years, and that her husband told her he "hates fat women" and "doesn't want a fat woman and he will not make love to a fat woman…. He went out and got a small woman, and he is never at home anymore. Now I really wish I could lose thirty-five pounds. I know I would look and feel better and win my husband back."[58] Black or white, it makes no difference: In our culture, being overweight makes us victims of our lifestyles.

Essence attributed black women's weight anxieties to their living in predominantly white areas and studying or working mostly with whites. "The overpowering devaluation of African-American racial and ethnic identity—our physical features, foods, rituals, manners—by the dominant culture has made us ashamed of who we are, how we behave, and how we look." Again, readers wrote in, expressing the pain they carry around with them every day. "Pressure to fit in with my white counterparts throws me again into a tailspin," wrote one woman. Another wrote, "When I first started practicing bulimic behavior, I was very much influenced by white beauty standards…. People treat you better when you lose weight and look beautiful." Women with a strong black identity, by contrast, were less concerned about losing weight.[59] They were not greatly influenced by the white thin ideal. But, evidently, they are in the minority.

DIETING MOTHERS, DIETING DAUGHTERS

We know that the thin ideal eventually ensnares and oppresses most women living in this country. We also know that it tends to be perpetuated by women themselves. But what is really disconcerting is that well-intentioned mothers trying to raise happy, healthy daughters often unwittingly create an environment that breeds body insecurity and shame. On a continual quest to lose weight themselves, they transmit messages to their daughters that good-tasting food is an enemy, that denying oneself food is part of a woman's lot, and that being thin is a sign of being a real woman. This is what they themselves believe, and this is what their daughters grow up believing. (Fathers, passively or actively, are often also complicit in passing on these messages because they benefit from having daughters who conform to the narrow beauty ideal: daughters, like wives, are often likened to possessions.)

"You are your daughter's first female role model and mentor. She is looking to you for validation of her female body," explains Debra Waterhouse, author of *Like Mother, Like Daughter*, a guide to mothers to break free of their own unhealthy eating behaviors and thereby serve as better examples for their daughters. "If you are constantly looking for a diet to battle your body fat, she will learn that women are supposed to be at war with their bodies." Indeed, 80 percent of teenage daughters of dieting mothers also diet, and 80 percent of daughters of mothers who practice severe weight-loss attempts (vomiting, fasting, using laxatives, skipping meals) copy their mothers.[60] Even if a mother doesn't actively diet, comments such as "I hate my thighs" or "Honey, which outfit makes me look thinner?" strongly influence her daughter. A mother's body image becomes the daughter's body image.

A *Glamour* survey of four thousand readers concluded that there is a "strong connection between their mothers' behavior around food and their own. We tend to do as our mothers do and we carry maternal messages with us always." One reader wrote in:

> My mother didn't hold a gun to my head and force me to binge and overeat. No, I did that. But her feelings about food and weight colored my self-esteem and colored my life. In my mother's mind, if you ate "good food" and were thin, you were a "good person." I always felt that any success I achieved was minimized in her eyes because of my weight.

This reader's mother weighs ninety-five pounds at age sixty; the reader, age thirty-four and five feet tall, chose not to reveal her weight but wrote that she is now "obese."[61]

A friend of mine, Lisa, was a "borderline anorexic in high school, like everybody else I know," she says with a wry laugh. For breakfast she would have tea with Sweet 'N Low. Lunch would be lettuce and a piece of bread with a tiny bit of peanut butter. Dinner, in front of her parents, would be the smallest portion of whatever was being served that Lisa could get away with. She was exhausted all the time. "I would go to school and then either soccer practice or swim practice. I would come home, fall asleep, eat dinner, do my homework, and fall asleep again." Lisa's mother, who struggled with diets herself, was "totally supportive" of Lisa's diet. "She would say things like, 'Oh, you're so good, you have so much willpower.' I always got so much praise for having willpower. Or she would make all these great meals and then say to me, 'You don't really want another serving, do you?' And she would go through phases where she would decide that she was only going to cook no-fat meals all the time, like cutlets with mustard seeds pressed into them seared in a nonstick pan."

Today, in her thirties, Lisa vows never to diet ever again. She says that she is "bigger than I've ever been," and though she weighs twenty or thirty pounds above what Weight Watchers would assign her as a "goal weight," she appears comfortable with her body—and isn't that the real goal? "I'm so tired of dealing with the whole body image issue; I mean, when is it going to end? I just wish it would go away."

Many mothers actively monitor their daughters' weight. They say, "Are you sure you want that cookie?" or "I think you're putting on some weight, dear" or "You know, sweetie, boys prefer thin girls." These mothers are not evil or ill intentioned. By and large, they truly want what is best for their daughters and mistakenly believe that a little maternal pressure to lose weight will make their daughters happier, more popular, and more successful later in life. But this ploy nearly always backfires. A 1997 University of Minnesota study suggests that girls with mothers who make comments about their daughters' weight are more likely to be unhappy with themselves and go on diets.[62]

Eleven-year-old Lori Gottlieb initiated the diet that became anorexia when her mother began telling her to save the just-baked cookies for her brother and father and making fun of chubby women at restaurants who ordered extra syrup for their pancakes and sausage. Whenever Lori accompanied her mother to the supermarket, and her mother would throw "something fattening into the cart like ice cream or cookies," she would say, "'Dad will love this' or 'David loves these,' just so whoever might be listening in the grocery aisle won't think Mom's buying the food for herself. She doesn't think it's very ladylike to buy fattening foods for yourself. The only thing Mom buys for herself are cottage cheese and tomatoes."[63]

Lori began mimicking her mother's public eating behavior by eating less and less, but unlike her mother, she actually lost weight. Lori's mother, you see, secretely ate chocolate cake late at night, over the kitchen sink; Lori didn't sneak food, so the pounds melted away and she soon had to be hospitalized. Lori's diary perfectly illustrates the hypocrisy of diets and femininity. A woman must eat little to nothing in public, though obviously she must eat something substantive in private; otherwise, she wouldn't be able to thrive. When young Lori follows her mother's public example, she is punished. She hasn't yet learned that dieting is really a sham, that dieters are quite sneaky about the food they actually intake, and that dieting is, above all else, a competition to show who can eat the least yet pretend the most that she really isn't hungry anyway.

Maternal pressure to diet is a losing battle. One twenty-three-year-old woman recalled to *Glamour* a painful adolescent episode. Her mother had promised her a car if she lost twenty-five pounds. "I lost twenty-four and she didn't get the car for me. I was so angry—I ate and ate—just to get back at her."[64] This daughter overate consciously, out of anger, out of revenge. Other daughters with similarly controlling mothers overeat because they have lost touch with their bodies' signals. Waterhouse persuasively argues that if a mother exerts external control on how much and when her daughter can eat, the daughter will become unable to recognize her body's internal hunger and fullness cues.[65] Early dieting, ironically, is one of the causes of early obesity—which explains why Americans are simultaneously so diet-conscious and yet so fat. The younger a daughter is when she first began dieting, the higher her current weight is now. The *Glamour* survey showed that when women started dieting in their teen years, their average adult weight was 146 pounds. But when they started in childhood, their average adult weight was 163 pounds.[66] These women would be healthier and lighter had they never dieted at all.

The quest to look better than the way we now look or better than the way another woman looks is necessarily doomed. Only a small minority of women will ever fit the American beauty ideal, and even they won't fit it their entire lives. The overwhelming majority of us continue to hurt ourselves—physically and psychically—in an effort to win the tacit beauty contest that infuses our daily lives. Besides, even the women who do conform to the beauty ideal are not immune from life's ills. Even women who wear a size 2 experience divorce, disease, disaster, and discrimination. And just as being wealthy does not necessarily make a person happy, there is only a marginal connection between attractiveness and life satisfaction—as was shown by a recent study at the University of Illinois. However, the study's psychologists did find evidence that one's subjective well-being influenced how one judged her own level of attractiveness. The happier the subject, the more likely that she perceived herself as attractive.[67]

CHAPTER THREE
DATING

The overwhelming majority of people in American society believe in the imperative to find a partner to love, live with, marry, and grow old with. "It is not good for the human to be alone; I will make a fitting helper for him," says the second chapter of the Bible.[1] However, today the pressure to marry is more firmly applied to women than to men. Only women compete with each other for a mate. An unmarried man, a bachelor, can live the good life without stigma, while an unmarried woman is berated as defective, a spinster. She is described as homely, masculine, too picky, or too desperate. Confronting this sexist double standard, if you're a single woman, is difficult enough. In addition there always exists the Other Woman, who allegedly has much more to offer than you do. She is desirable, and if you're not, are you really a woman? At the same time, she provides an instant excuse for your "failures" in love and marriage. If she didn't exist, wouldn't you be in a perfect relationship? Get rid of her, and couldn't you live care-free?

Most commonly, the Other Woman refers to a "mistress" involved in a clandestine relationship. But she lurks outside adulterous relationships, too. She is any woman whom you fear might divert your love interest's attention or otherwise cause him to become disenchanted with you. *Glamour* magazine draws out this fear with terrifying clarity in a chart posing as an article, "How to

Deal with the Other Women in Your Man's Life." There are columns for your man's mother, sister, ex-girlfriend, female friend, and boss. (Is there any woman in his life who's *not* an Other Woman?) The advice regarding his female friend is typical: "Face the music" if she is "the first person he calls when he wants to celebrate his raise or commiserate about his father's illness."[2]

Women compete with each other over men because we have been subjected to a relentless message that a woman can only be fulfilled through a romantic coupling with a man. In her book *Here Comes the Bride*, Jaclyn Geller exhaustively chronicles the centuries-old celebration of romantic love at the expense of platonic relationships. "The belief in erotic love as the wellspring of personal happiness and the equation of long-term amorous relationships with maturity and mental health are ideas that now saturate every corner of American culture," she writes. Since every woman is "assigned the role of the husband hunter, while the man [is] the object of hot pursuit," it's no wonder that friendships among women get short shrift: finding a husband is always supposed to take precedence.[3]

But, at least in some parts of the country, particularly urban areas, men tend to feel less pressure to marry; there are fewer men than women; and there are more gay men than straight men. As a result, there is a percentage of women who do not walk down the proverbial aisle. This increases the sense of competition between women and permits the concept of the Other Woman to assume too much power. If we saw women as allies rather than rivals, would we spend more time developing platonic friendships and less pursuing romantic ones? Would romantic love continue to be the

be-all and end-all of a woman's aspirations if there were no competitive pursuit (real or imaginary) involved?

I recently attended a singles' party to reacquaint myself with the
sizing up that goes on between women and women among the look-
ing-for-love set. The event was limited to men and women twenty
to forty, and most had never been married. (While the dynamic of
women competing over a love interest is also present among lesbians and the divorced and widowed, I focus here on never-married
heterosexuals.) I removed my wedding ring before I headed down-
town. From the moment I entered the club, I was nervous. Even
though I hadn't come to flirt, I didn't want to be a wallflower,
either. I was checked out by both men and women, but differently.
The men first looked me in the eye. Their gaze swept at my body
and then returned to my face, sometimes with a tentative smile. The
women began their scan with my shoes, working their eyes up to
my face, but never meeting my eyes. Nor did they smile.

It was a Thursday night, and half the partygoers were dressed in
work attire. The rest of the men and about a quarter of the women
were dressed casually (the men in khakis and striped or plaid shirts,
the women in black pants with a sweater). The remaining women
had dressed up for a party. They wore short skirts with knee-high
boots, sleeveless black dresses, or leather pants. These women
received extra scrutiny from the other women. I chatted with several men (I told them I was married; the pressure of making a good
impression lifted, they loosened up tremendously). Many of the
men were socially awkward. Many didn't know how to mingle or
initiate small talk; their faces looked doleful and doubtful. Only a
handful of men appeared confident, and those were the ones most

of the women had their eyes on. I sat at a banquette. Near me were three individual women who had paired up with a man and each was sitting at a mini-table for two.

I tried to imagine what it felt like to be an unattached woman who had come with hope but had failed to meet any men. Frankly, the atmosphere for these women was lousy. If she didn't meet a man she liked, she also found it difficult to meet a woman she could spend time with. Only those women who had come to the party together had someone to talk to. Of course, this was a *singles'* party; the women had come to meet men, not other women. Still, the atmosphere would have shot up to a warmer level if the women had been able to exchange friendliness.

At this singles' event, the problem of the Other Woman appeared real because so many women went home alone. Yet, in reality, the Other Woman as an obstacle to finding the right man was nonexistent. Although many men went home alone, too, they were not, I suspect, haunted by anxieties over the Other Man. When men do not find love, they rarely blame it on other men.

When two women compete over a man, the situation can sometimes unite them in their realization that no man is worth making fools of themselves, and the two of them may even have more in common with each other. Cynthia Eng, a twenty-nine-year-old advertising executive in Los Angeles, recalls a boy in high school whom she dated a few times. She had a huge crush on him, but he was interested in another girl. He bought the other girl flowers and talked about her all the time. "I was sick with envy. I really hated her, though I had never spoken to her in my entire life," says Cynthia, her soft voice expressing a hint of amusement over her roller-coaster adolescent emotional life. One day, she continues, she and the girl ended up in the ladies' room together and introduced themselves. "And we ended up becoming really good friends soon after that conversation. She didn't date him very long, and he gave us something to bond over."

But competition with another female can also solidify romantic interest in the man. Cynthia talks about Jeff, whom she dated in college but wasn't sure she wanted to commit to; she was trying to decide whether to break up with him. Then another woman, an acquaintance of Cynthia's, expressed interest in Jeff. The effect was to cement her feelings. "We stayed together another two years. Were it not for the other girl, I wonder if I would have broken up with him earlier. In retrospect they probably made a better couple than we did. It's really too bad for Jeff. I guess I felt threatened enough that I had to stake out my little territory."

THE OTHER WOMAN IN LITERATURE

The character of the evil Other Woman has sparked imaginations for centuries. The Cinderella folk tale, to take perhaps the most famous example of a story involving Other Women, has been discovered to have hundreds of versions; the oldest variant is from ninth-century China. In addition to the European version, recorded by the French Charles Perrault in 1697 and later adapted by the German Grimm brothers and then by Walt Disney, there are also numerous African, Arabic, and Indian versions, all containing the motifs of a persecuted heroine, a cruel stepmother and jealous stepsisters, magic help, a meeting with a prince, proof of identity, and marriage with the prince.[4]

The Cinderella story presents an unambiguous picture of the way women and men are imagined to be: A woman wants to be rescued by a rich, handsome, powerful man, who in turn wants a beautiful woman. Some women are so evil they're like devils, and others are so good they're like angels, with beautiful faces to match. An evil woman (an Other Woman) thwarts the efforts of a good woman to find a man. A rich, handsome, powerful man will discover the good woman and bring her into his powerful world. You see, evil women possess a kind of power, but it is no match with the real power that rich, aristocratic men hold. If a woman is good (i.e., beautiful), she will share in the riches of the powerful man who picks her. To summarize: To get the prince, a woman must (a) be beautiful and (b) compete with evil Other Women.

For most of Western history, men wed women whose families provided dowries, and women wed men who could support them financially (in exchange for sex, children, and housekeeping). Before modernity, when marriages were largely arranged and no one expected the bride and groom to be in love with each other, there was no need for women to compete over the affections and attentions of men. For peasants in medieval Europe, marriage occurred when a man and woman forged an economic arrangement that allowed the two to share resources for joint survival. The nobility, meanwhile, were motivated by concerns for property, inheritance, and alliance. Medieval literature involved knights who worshiped pedestaled ladies in courtly love. Troubadour poets desired and elevated women they could never have, since they inevitably pined for the wife of their lord. In the literature of the Middle Ages, men did experience competition with men for the affections of unattainable beloved ladies.

From 1500 to 1700, however, the status of women changed; no longer were they idealized. Catholicism gave way to Protestantism, and wedlock became glorified. In Europe, there was an increased emphasis on choosing a mate for love, friendship, compatibility, and shared interests. This ideal spread to our shores following the American Revolution, and in the fifty years following the founding of the country, love became the primary factor in choosing a spouse. The nineteenth century ushered in the big wedding with the bride dressed in white gown and veil, the bridal procession, the throwing of rice, and the honeymoon. "Giving away a bride adorned in virginal white, hosting a family reception, and sending the couple off on an exclusive honeymoon," writes Jaclyn Geller, "enshrined the Victorian's romantic notions of female purity, conjugal love, and the nuclear family. This was the era in which marriage reached its apotheosis as an ideal."[5]

Marriage remained a union in which the wife was financially dependent on her husband. Women needed an economic provider while men did not, which put men at an advantage. The woman had to attract the man—not an easy accomplishment. In eighteenth-century England in particular, there was a disproportionate number of eligible women, allowing men to be very choosy when selecting a bride.[6] The literature from then on (particularly when written by women) featured women competing with each other for male suitors. In eighteenth-, nineteenth-, and twentieth-century literature, the plot of a woman competing with another woman for a man became obsessive and the concept of the Other Woman was born.

A number of popular novels written by women during that period showcased the modern courtship narrative from the point of view of a young, unmarried woman without financial resources. Many of these novels involved at least one Other Woman as a key offender. Jane Austen's *Sense and Sensibility* (1811) and *Pride and Prejudice* (1813), Charlotte Brontë's *Jane Eyre* (1847), and Edith Wharton's *The House of Mirth* (1905), for example, present marriage as an antidote to financial insecurity. Indeed, the single woman in nineteenth-century England and America had few options for her life. She was denied a formal education; she was denied entry to the professions. If she was middle-class or upper-middle-class, she was dependent on the charity of relatives unless she married. If she needed to support herself, she would work as a governess or teacher. Women of the working classes, whether or not they married, supported themselves through menial forms of employment.

In each of the above novels, the Other Woman attempts to sabotage the efforts of the heroine to marry the man of her dreams. In each case, the Other Woman feels threatened by the heroine's beauty or other attributes and by the male attention she receives. The Other Woman always possesses some defect: She is selfish, or vain, or scheming, or irritating, or unbalanced. In Austen and Brontë's tales, which conclude with Cinderella-like endings, the Other Women are unsuccessful. In Wharton's tragic story, however, the Other Woman gets the best of the heroine.

The story of Jane Eyre is instructive. Jane Eyre is a poor orphan in rural England, abandoned by the landowning relatives who had taken care of her as a girl, and left to languish in a strict, heartless orphanage. At eighteen, she leaves to work as a governess for a little girl, the ward of Mr. Rochester, who just happens to be a wealthy and powerful man and owner of the Thornfield estate. Jane, the heroine, is not beautiful. Nevertheless, Rochester falls in love with her and she with him.

The first Other Woman to spoil the romance is Lady Blanche Ingram, a beautiful woman of fortune. It is rumored that Rochester is going to propose to Blanche, and Jane is devastated. Haughty and mean, Blanche openly sneers at Jane. Blanche comments that she and her mother have employed at least a dozen governesses in their day, "half of them detestable and the rest ridiculous, and all incubi." Regarding Jane in particular: "I noticed her; I am a judge of physiognomy, and in hers I see all the faults of her class."[7]

Jane can at least console herself over the fact that Blanche is not nearly as refined as she likes people to think.

> Miss Ingram was a mark beneath jealousy: she was too inferior to excite the feeling. Pardon the seeming paradox: I mean what I say. She was very showy, but she was not genuine: she had a fine person, many brilliant attainments; but her mind was poor, her heart barren by nature; nothing bloomed spontaneously on that soil; no unforced natural fruit delighted by its freshness. She was not good; she was not original; she used to repeat sounding phrases from books; she never offered, nor had, an opinion of her own.[8]

Rochester, however, is not interested in Blanche and has no designs to marry her. He is in love with Jane and wants to marry her instead. Thrilled, she agrees; their wedding is planned. But at the ceremony, it is revealed that Rochester already has a wife, Bertha Mason, Other Woman number two. Rochester had married Bertha, a Creole from Jamaica, fifteen years before, because she was beautiful and came from a family of fortune; unbenownst to him, madness ran in her family and Bertha soon became mad herself. She had been secretly living at Thornfield. Although unable to marry Jane, Rochester begs her to run away with him, but she refuses to live in an adulterous relationship and leaves him. Brontë tells us that

> Jane Eyre, who had been an ardent, expectant woman—almost a bride—was a cold, solitary girl again: her life was pale; her prospects were desolate. A Christmas frost had come at mid-summer; a white December storm had whirled over June; ice glazed the ripe apples, drifts crushed the blowing roses....[9]

Jane soon discovers that an uncle she never knew about has died and left her a huge inheritance. She returns to Thornfield some time later to discover that Bertha had set fire to the estate, killing herself. Rochester is blinded and living on a desolate farm. Jane finds him, and although she is now independently wealthy, they marry.

Bertha Mason, it has been said by feminist literary critics, can be understood to represent a part of Jane. The two characters mirror each other and may be regarded as two sides of the same person. Bertha was beautiful and fine before she married; now she is a large, ugly, disheveled monster with a "demonic" laugh. Brontë apparently felt comfortable likening Bertha to a monster because of her race, which stands in contrast to Jane's whiteness. Jane, meanwhile, is a small, plain, tidy, virginal, weak young thing with tightly braided hair and repressed appetites. Bertha represents all the passion that Jane possesses but can't get herself to release. As Sandra Gilbert and Susan Gubar wrote in their groundbreaking work, *The Madwoman in the Attic*, Jane "has repressed her own share of madness and rage, [and] there is a potential monster beneath her angelic exterior."[10] Jane must absorb Bertha (the Other Woman) into herself, to achieve an appropriate balance of power and passion, before she can become independent and self-confident—and only then is she ready to marry Rochester. If Jane had married Rochester as a simple, repressed orphan girl, she might very well have become mad herself.

It is possible to suggest, then, that the Other Woman is a reflection of our own anxieties and repressions. She gets away with behavior that we cannot. She represents everything that we wish we could be, all that we wish we could attain. Perhaps we project a part of ourselves—the part that we wish to disavow—so that we can conveniently create a dichotomy between the virtuous heroine (ourself) and the villainess (the Other Woman). Instead of vilifying her, shouldn't we try to understand her?

Moreover, the Other Woman would not exist if not for the secretiveness of men. Rochester first keeps silent about the very existence of Bertha and then provides dubious details about the development of her madness. The sought-after man holds the cards of power by withholding information from the woman who fancies him. So isn't the Other Woman innocent? Isn't *he* at fault? And hasn't he created the situation in which two women are rivals in the first place?

DOLLARS AND DEPENDENCE

The heroines of Brontë, Austen, and Wharton novels lived in a different era. Nevertheless, even today, women have economic reasons for marrying, particularly if they want children, which can also mean halting, slowing, or sidetracking their careers. Many women understand that it's nearly impossible to be financially independent while raising a family. Competing with other women for the attention of a man with a salary may actually be practical.

By the early twentieth century, American men could earn a "family wage," a salary intended to support an entire family (though only skilled or professional men actually earned enough to adequately support their families). "The family wage system," notes social historian and cultural critic Barbara Ehrenreich, "guarantees that, at least for economic reasons, women will have a greater interest in marrying and in marrying 'well,' and a greater financial stake in their marriages than men do."[11] Because of this imbalance, men have feared the "gold-digging woman." In fact, points out Ehrenreich, the very first issue of *Playboy* magazine, in December 1953, contained a contemptuous article titled "Miss Gold-Digger of 1953." *Playboy*, according to Ehrenreich, was one signal of a male revolt from "the bondage of breadwinning."[12] Soon after, the family wage system collapsed. Many men began to earn less than enough to support a family. To make ends meet, or to reach a middle-class lifestyle, many more wives went to work outside the home.

Now, at the beginning of the twenty-first century, many women are economically independent. Most women work; women and men go "dutch" on dates. But are women today less inclined to compete with one another over the attentions of men? Yes and no. Women with careers are not in economic need of men the way they once were. Nevertheless, many women continue to earn significantly less than men. Sure, there are more high-profile women than ever before in law, medicine, management, business, and politics; and women in the top fifth of the labor force have made significant gains.[13] True, women under the age of twenty-five earn 91 percent of what men their age earn, according to the U.S. Department of Labor. But in their thirties their earnings slip behind men's. Families are started and women assume most, if not all, parenting responsibilities and are forced to slow down or halt their careers. When they reach the forty-five-to-fifty-four age group, women earn 70.5 percent of what men earn, but that drops to 68.2 percent among women fifty-five to sixty-four.[14]

Regardless of age or parental status, workers in female-dominated "pink ghetto" occupations (such as sales, teaching, and secretarial work, in which 70 percent or more are women) are paid roughly 18 percent less than male-dominated or mixed-gender occupations.[15] Women tend to gravitate into the pink ghetto because they have been educated and socialized to strive no higher, or because taking time off from a pink ghetto job to raise a child is easier at some level. It's often impossible to take an extended leave if you're running your own business or working round-the-clock in law or medicine. Single women who want to marry and raise a family often need to choose an occupation that allows scheduling flexibility.

Anthropologists Dorothy Holland and Margaret Eisenhart have found that women in college—even bright, ambitious women filled with shimmery dreams of climbing to top-notch careers—are sidetracked into the pursuit of an engagement ring. Their career ambitions and their relationships with women friends are compromised. Holland and Eisenhart followed twelve black women at a black Southern college and eleven white women at a predominantly white Southern college over a period of eight years. All had strong academic backgrounds in high school, and all entered college expecting to pursue a career after graduation; half had said they would major in a math- or science-related field. But once they entered college, they became more and more concerned with who was more attractive to men and how they could meet men. Even women who had never before cared about dating developed an interest. On both campuses, women spent more time going to bars, pools, and fraternity parties where they hoped to meet men than they did on academic work or career-related activities.

To become romantically involved, the women were willing to scale down their career ambitions. After graduation, most married and worked in low-status, low-paying jobs that were meant to supplement their husbands' paychecks. The black women were better prepared to support themselves independently, but both the black and white women ended up with lower academic achievement and lesser credentials than they had originally expected.[16]

Equally disturbing, their relationships with women were also considered expendable. Women friends were important only because they were useful for attracting men. "Women friends tended to be turned into a support group for orchestrating the main activities— activities with men," write Holland and Eisenhart. "Women often sought out one another's company, but their activities together were frequently directed toward being with male romantic partners."[17] While both the black and the white women elevated boyfriends at the expense of girlfriends, the two groups used different methods. The white women relied on their female friends as support to find dates, and once a boyfriend was found, the female friends were given short shrift. The black women, on the other hand, thought it most strategic to not be too revealing about their personal business with their female friends, for fear that such information could be used against them and could damage their reputations. The result for both groups was the same: a weak sense of solidarity with other women.[18]

The "civic religion of romance," comments cultural critic Andrew Sullivan, can do more harm than good: it whips up false expectations. "For a lucky few," he writes, "infatuation sometimes does lead to lasting love, and love to family, and family to all the other virtues our preachers and politicians regularly celebrate. For the other 99 percent of us, relationships are, at best, useful economic bargains and, if we're lucky, successful sexual transactions— better than the alternative, which has long been close to social death."[19] "Bargains." "Transactions." Sullivan strips the romantic relationship to its barest essence: an economic union. This doesn't mean that lovers who get lost in each other's eyes are faking their amorousness, but love alone does not maintain the foundation of most lasting relationships, especially if there is poverty. Of course, finances are far from the only motivation to marry; after all, most women with money also seek husbands. But even women with money tend to look for men with better finances than they have.

"The fantasy of a man who pays the bills, who works when you want to take time off to be with your kids or read *War and Peace*, who is in the end responsible, is one that many women have but fairly few admit to," writes Katie Roiphe. "It is one of those fantasies, like rape fantasies, that have been forbidden to us by our politics. But it's also deeply ingrained in our imaginations."[20] Though she naïvely equates the hard work of raising children with reading literature for pleasure, Roiphe is absolutely right that many women today cling to the 1950s-era dream of marrying a provider. Of course, except among the affluent such a provider is hard to come by. But the dream endures across class lines because it is rooted in the very real situation women face: Most simply don't earn enough by themselves to lead the lives they want or should be able to lead.

If there is any doubt that single American women continue to compete with each other over the affections of a man who earns a good salary, the Fox TV show *Who Wants to Marry a Multi-Millionaire?*, broadcast in February 2000, laid it to rest. Fifty women vied for a man they knew nothing about, not even what he looked like, but who was supposed to have a net worth of at least two million dollars. I was one of the nearly 23 million viewers who tuned in to watch the two-hour special, with growing disbelief and revulsion. But I was gratified to witness such an honest portrayal of marriage among the upwardly mobile. Despite the media spectacle, the marriage that resulted from the show was about as conventional as you can get, right down to the communication gap we later learned about (the groom failing to inform the bride that he had a history of girlfriend abuse, that he was a longtime comic performer, and that he wasn't even worth all that much money) and to the inevitable divorce.

For those who either identify with or aspire to the upper middle class, the Fox show demonstrated, marriage is essentially an exchange of money for beauty. Men are valued, after all, primarily for their financial worth, while women are measured primarily for their looks (even if they are independently successful). These realities unfairly stymie and burden both sexes, but let's face it: Men still have more potential for real power than women do. Beauty inevitably fades, while a wisely invested portfolio grows in wealth. Real power is money, not looks—which is why on the show, Rick

Rockwell (né Richard Balkey) got to choose the bride, Darva Conger, and not the other way around. (In 2002, a similar show, *The Bachelor*, pitted twenty-five women against each other in a humiliating competition for the attention of a successful and an attractive Harvard graduate. The show played up the women's attractiveness as their primary asset, since by and large they did not share the "bachelor's" upper-middle-class status or degree from an esteemed university.)

Of course, women don't marry simply for money. Most of us choose mates we fall in love with and desire as a lifelong companion, often despite a lack of financial resources. But financial security is a basic part of the package that a marriageable man has to offer—the vase that holds the flowers. Our cultural script tells us to look for a provider, and our wage system makes more than one salary necessary to raise a family. It is not surprising that a woman may take a man's salary into account when she is deciding on a lifelong partnership. Unfortunately, choosing a husband based on his income serves to reinforce traditional sex roles in an endless, vicious cycle. The sex roles (man as provider; woman as homemaker, mother, or trophy wife) remain intact, and deep income disparities between men and women also remain intact.

THE NEW SINGLES CULTURE

Despite the continuing heavy social and economic pressures to marry, 43 million women in the United States are currently single. That's more than 40 percent of all adult females. Four decades ago, in 1963, 83 percent of women twenty-five to fifty-five were married; by 1997, that figure had plummeted to 65 percent.[21] The

National Marriage Project of Rutgers University believes these trends are a result of "today's singles mating culture [which] is not oriented to marriage, as the mating culture was in the past." It is instead a "low-commitment culture."[22] The authors of the Project's 2000 study, David Popenoe and Barbara Dafoe Whitehead, lament this trend, which is reflected by the national decline in the percentage of all adults who are married. Some demographers today predict that fewer than 85 percent of current young adults will ever marry (compared with 94 percent in 1960).[23]

Popenoe and Whitehead conducted a small survey of blue-collar heterosexual men and women in their twenties in five major metropolitan areas. Most worked full-time in service, sales, and technical jobs, with incomes in the $10,000 to $30,000 range. The women, the authors found, put the goal of achieving financial and residential independence before the goal of marriage. "Indeed," the authors report, "compared to their male peers, these noncollege women are even more fiercely determined to 'take care of myself.' They cite the high rate of divorce, their past experience of failed relationships, and their desire to avoid the same mistakes their mothers made, as reasons why they are intent on independence." However, once single women approach their late twenties, they do become intent on finding a suitable marriage partner. Yet the late-twenties women in this study voiced pessimism about the likelihood of finding a husband. They complained that the "men aren't there," that "they're not on the same page," or that they aren't mature enough.[24]

Pessimism about their marital future begins in high school. Fewer than a third of girls in their senior year agreed that "most people will have fuller and happier lives if they choose legal marriage rather than staying single or just living with someone."[25] Nearly 75 percent of teenage girls told CBS–*New York Times* pollsters that they think they could be unmarried and happy (compared with only 61 percent of the boys).[26]

According to Marcelle Clements, author of the book *The Improvised Woman: Single Women Reinventing Single Life*, these statistics are hardly cause for hand-wringing. She spent seven years interviewing more than a hundred unmarried women, from their twenties to their nineties. She found that for many women, remaining single is a choice, not the default status of someone who can't marry. Today, she says, being single "seems to many women like the most reasonable option."[27] And it must be true, because *Time* magazine devoted a cover story to it. The August 28, 2000, issue featured the four stars of the HBO show *Sex and the City* on its cover with the headline, "Who Needs a Husband? More Women Are Saying No to Marriage and Embracing the Single Life. Are They Happy?" The pages inside answer the question with a resounding "yes." Single women today are "more confident, more self-sufficient, and more choosy than ever," and "no longer see marriage as a matter of survival and acceptance. They feel free to start and end relationships at will—more like, say, men." A photo captures a dozen laughing thirtysomething Houston women, attractive and stylish, playing a dice game around a coffee table. They are clearly enjoying their own company to the fullest. *Time* attributes this new attitude to women's new freedoms and to single women's determination not to enter into a marriage that is doomed to fail, as 50 percent do. The overwhelming majority of single women and men would like to meet the perfect partner and get married, but if Mr.

Right doesn't come, only 33 percent of women would marry some- one less than right (compared with 41 percent of the men).[28]

Will the rising percentage of singles lead to increased or decreased competition? It appears that many single women are searching for a happy medium. They are satisfied with their lives but still seek an eligible man. Dahlia Rosenberg, a twenty-nine-year-old comparative literature graduate student, confirms the new attitude. She concedes that all her high school friends are married, which puts pressure on her to follow their lead. "But I don't like any of their marriages so much, so I'm glad I haven't made a mistake. Most of the single women in my circle are desperate to get married. I definitely feel a little weird about not being married, but I'm also kind of proud."

Television and pop fiction validate the choice to remain single. *Sex and the City* showcases four incredibly stylish white professional women in their thirties and forties who enjoy all the cultural riches Manhattan has to offer. Three are single, one married and contem- plating divorce. These women are far from losers: They are at the top of their professions; they never run out of cute and witty men to date; they somehow always find time to get together for girls- only brunches and happy hours. Meanwhile, a glut of white single- gal novels in the mid- and late 1990s followed equally hip, urbane, upwardly mobile twenty- and thirtysomethings. The heroines are constantly on the lookout for eligible men, yet they also enjoy the company of other women and have forged a warm community with them.

Despite the bravura of unmarried women turning to sperm donors for childbearing, hurtful stereotypes continue. A single woman is still regarded as vulnerable without the "protection" of a husband. Indeed, the best-selling, man-snagging guidebook *The Rules* encourages women to pretend they're passive, fragile things who need a strong, muscled man to take control of their lives. "In a relationship," caution authors Ellen Fein and Sherrie Schneider, "the man must take charge. He must propose. We are not making this up—biologically, he's the aggressor." They continue, "Don't tell sarcastic jokes. Don't be a loud, knee-slapping, hysterically funny girl. This is okay when you're alone with your girlfriends. But when you're with a man you like, be quiet and mysterious, act ladylike, cross your legs and smile. Don't talk so much." And finally: "Remember, let him take the lead. He declares love first, just as he picks most of the movies, the restaurants, and the concerts the two of you go to."[29] (Take note: co-author Fein has divorced since publication of *The Rules*.)

The same fictional characters of media land who legitimate singlehood simultaneously perpetuate the conflicting idea that a single woman pushing thirty or older is fragile and pathetic. The message seems to be that while it is perfectly acceptable for a woman to forgo marriage, she can't expect to get away without paying some social cost. To wit: Ally McBeal's insecurities about her love life formed her show's central pivot. (Ally had actually gone to law school and entered the law profession not out of a desire to fight injustice or even to make good money, but in order to follow Billy, an ex-boyfriend who ended up marrying another woman.) The women of *Sex and the City* may have accumulated their own brand of power, but all ultimately feel incomplete without a man, whether he is marriage material or just a one-night stand.

And then, of course, there is Bridget Jones. Helen Fielding's novel, *Bridget Jones's Diary*, was first published in Britain in 1996. *Bridget Jones's Diary* has been a commercial sensation both in Britain and the United States, where it was published in 1998; it was followed by a sequel, *The Edge of Reason*; it was made into a movie starring Renée Zellweger in 2001; and it has triggered a steady stream of similar novels with young unmarried protagonists who can't wait to sign up for the bridal registry. Bridget Jones, a London television programmer, is a Singleton, a thirtysomething woman who desperately wants to flee her single status. Yet she also measures more than a smidgen of scorn on the self-satisfied married people she knows: She refers to them as Smug Marrieds and disparages their awful social skills (they love to observe that "All the decent chaps have been snapped up" and that "Time's running out"). In *The Edge of Reason*, she approves when her friend Jude promises at her wedding "never to torment any Singletons in the world by asking them why they're still not married, or ever say, 'How's your love life?' Instead, I will always respect that this is as much their private business as whether I am still having sex with my husband."[30] Still, it is abundantly clear that Bridget will go to wacky lengths to find and marry Mr. Right.

Both Bridget Jones novels take the form of a diary, in which Bridget notes each day her weight, the number of cigarettes smoked, and the number of calories ingested and alcoholic drinks consumed. She is unable to get dressed in the morning, arrive at work, or cook a simple meal without screwing everything up. She spends hours gazing at the telephone. Even though she weighs 130 pounds, a completely acceptable weight for a grown woman, she moans and whines about how fat and unattractive she is. The only literature she reads are faux feminism advice books on codependency and men and women living on separate planets, and she doesn't follow the news. Yet incredibly, a rich, tall human rights lawyer named Mark Darcy, à la *Pride and Prejudice*, falls in love with her, saves her and her family from various legal troubles, and rescues her from dreaded spinsterhood (in the first diary's most famous line, Bridget fears dying "all alone, half-eaten by an Alsatian."[31]) "It's the humor of the pathetic," says Marcelle Clements. "It's as if as women become more successful and powerful, they need to be punished for defying the old laws.... They have to be made to look ridiculous and pitiful."[32]

Bridget happens to be shallow, self-absorbed, and not terribly intelligent. But she also has an endearing quality that sneaks up on you (particularly in the film version—Zellweger made a very appealing Bridget). She is so honest about her flaws and insecurities that you can't help but sigh with relief that she, like most of us, single or not, is learning how to be a capable adult as she goes along. Plus, she's funny (though not intentionally): Even when her life is in danger, as in the sequel when she finds herself in a Thai prison facing ten years of hard time (don't ask), she makes the most of it by teaching the other inmates Madonna lyrics while she dances in a Wonderbra and sarong.

The Bridget Jones books have struck a chord. Single women clearly identify with Bridget and her insecurities. We may be living in a time when women are more self-sufficient than ever before, but being a self-sufficient woman is still not considered entirely acceptable. Unmarried women are sick and tired of being instructed that being single is synonymous with being deviant, that a woman who remains unpartnered is not part of "normal" society. And yet, and yet…so many do buy into the belief that marriage equals salvation. This ambivalence is represented in the slew of other single-gal novels; it is expressed perhaps best by Suzanne Finnamore in her offering *Otherwise Engaged*, about a thirty-six-year-old woman who manipulates her boyfriend into proposing by offering him the classic ultimatum that they either get hitched or he takes a hike. "It is primal, furtive; my ovaries cracking cheap champagne. I win," says Eve after Michael capitulates. "Those two words; that's exactly how I feel. Happy, but not in an I Knew It All Along way. Definitely in a Contestant Who Has Won in the Final Round Despite Major Setbacks way."[33]

Today's stereotypes about single women are truly convoluted. Even though they are deemed vulnerable, unmarried women are also supposedly tough, like men. Notes a perplexed Clements: If women are presumed to be needy and husbands are supposed to be strong, then women without husbands are automatically assumed to be strong and capable—too strong and too capable, even—rendering them unfeminine. By "sheer virtue of surviving," they are "therefore often said to be hard, unsexy, too cranky, too demanding, too—in a word—male."[34] Two of the characters on *Sex and the City*, Miranda and Samantha, fit this mold. Miranda is a hard-edged corporate lawyer who puts her own needs first. Her relationships fail because she refuses to engage in the give-and-take compromising that all successful relationships require. She is a single mother, but her mothering capabilities are suspect. Samantha is the show's slut, a woman who uses men for sex and discards them the next morning. She is the epitome of a proud, strong single gal of the twenty-first century. When she does fall hard for one man, it is a surprise to everyone, even to herself. But as one woman told Clements, "I get irritated when someone tells me for the umpteenth time how strong I am." Another confided, "Married women get to break down. I'm not allowed to break down."[35]

These clashing stereotypes serve to keep single women divided from one another. After all, would *you* befriend a needy, pathetic, yet ballbusting woman? She sounds terrifying—to men and women alike. No wonder the Bridget Jones novels and *Sex and the City* have been so commercially successful: The heroines may be tiring in their obsessions over men, but they also come across as women you would want to befriend—which is more than you can say about most media representations of single women.

THE OTHER WOMAN TODAY

The conflicting demands to act weak and be strong, to desperately search for a man and contentedly live a life filled with carefree sex, take their toll on the single woman. Anyone who has to negotiate this impossible terrain will find it difficult and look for a scapegoat: other unmarried women. The latter are painful reminders of what being single and female represents in our culture.

Competition doesn't necessarily end once a woman enters a serious relationship with a man. She may resent her boyfriend's former loves. In Jonathan Tropper's hilarious novel about coming to terms with turning thirty, *Plan B*, the protagonist, Ben, recognizes that his wife doesn't like his ex-girlfriend. He chalks it up to "retroactive jealousy." Ben's ex admits that the feeling is reciprocated: "Most women would like to see their ex-boyfriends dead and buried before they see them with someone else," she says.[36] Essayist Meghan Daum confessed to *Vogue* that she is obsessed with her boyfriend's ex-wife, Julie. Daum pores through Julie and Frank's wedding album, decreeing the big dress and pastel color scheme "nothing I'd want." Still, Julie's "persona consumes me as though she were a villainous character in a novel I read again and again simply to hear her dialogue."[37]

At least for Daum, the ex is far away and rarely in contact with her boyfriend (since they don't have any children or other entanglements). Janet Harrison, who works for a not-for-profit organization in Washington, D.C., relates what happened to her recently. She went to a bar with her boyfriend; his ex, whom he's still friendly with, happened to be there. Janet decided to initiate a conversation with her "because I feel like if I can be friendly with this person and know her as a person, then I'm less likely to stereotype her as an ex. So I did talk to her a little bit and she was friendly enough." But a while later, the ex went over to Janet's boyfriend and sat on his lap. "He got her off very quickly," she assures me. "But I just couldn't understand it. I'd just had a conversation with her!" Janet laughs wryly, then adds, "I don't know that she wanted him as much as she wanted to have some attention at that moment."

What we have here is competition as proprietorship. Single-gal novels devote pages and pages to encounters such as this. In Melissa Bank's much-hyped collection of short stories, *The Girls' Guide to Hunting and Fishing*, narrator Jane Rosenal comes face-to-face with her boyfriend's ex-girlfriend from college. Bella is French; she is "turn-and-stare gorgeous—big dark eyes, long dark hair, smooth dark skin."[38] *Otherwise Engaged*, likewise, is devoted almost entirely to Eve's coming to terms with her fiancé's ex-wife, Grace, and ex-girlfriend, Gabrielle. "If only I could eliminate Gabrielle. I took a sip of wine and backed a steamroller over her in my mind."[39] Gabrielle "had long curly hair the color of redwood, and the thinnest waist I have ever seen. Green eyes, high Parisian accent, the entire catastrophe."[40] When Eve meets and has lunch with Grace, "We played a little game.... Each time I said something, she made no response. This, I saw early on, would be the sport. To see who could reveal the least to each other. Yet we had revealed everything by choosing the same man. I, of course, would lose. She knew that, which is why she had chosen the game."[41] Eve understands the source of her resentment: She is forever a replacement, and there is nothing she can ever do to change that fact.

> I wish he had never been married before, because he's already done everything with his first wife, Grace. He was thirty-one when they went on their honeymoon in Spain. I resent him being thirty-one with someone else. Deeply. Somehow he should have known, and saved himself for me. If he really loved me, he would have.
>
> First wife, second wife. I will always be second. Even if his first wife dies, I don't move up the ladder. It's not like being an understudy. [42]

An ex is just that: a former flame. As troubling as her existence may be, a woman can console herself that the ex is of the past while she is in the present. A woman who dates your boyfriend *while you are dating him*, on the other hand, is an entirely different matter. The boyfriend has the responsibility to remain faithful, of course, but many women hold his new love interest accountable for the liaison.

This type of Other Woman plays a crucial role in all contemporary single-gal novels. Austen, Brontë, and Wharton's heroines confronted Other Women who had designs on the men they wanted. In today's tales, Other Women ignore the fact that the men they want already have girlfriends. In Anna Maxted's book *Getting Over It*, Helen, a single woman living in London, is involved with men who are always being shadowed by other women who will do anything to capture them. One Other Woman is a "sly witch"; another guards Helen's love interest "like a hyena guards an antelope carcass"; still another has "hair as big as a barn."[43]

The modern crop of novels may be fun reads, but they are also very irritating: Their protagonists are mostly pathetic rehashes of our canonical heroines. Austen, Brontë, and Wharton's heroines faced very real consequences if they remained unmarried, and yet they maintained an inner strength. They did not attach themselves to any man who might rescue them. They never compromised their own principles to get a man. In *Sense and Sensibility*, Elinor Dashwood refused to subvert Lucy Steele's manipulations in snagging Edward Ferrars. Jane Eyre resigned herself to her fate as a spinster rather than live adulterously with Rochester. And Lily Bart refused to lower herself to the moral level of Bertha Dorset, the Other Woman in *House of Mirth*, who instigates Lily's social downfall (leading to her death). These heroines are defined by a strong sense of morality, an allegiance to things bigger and more important than themselves and their marriage prospects. Contemporary heroines, by contrast, just seem desperate.

However, the modern fictional narratives seem to mirror the stories and attitudes that women share with me about women they regard as competition. Crystal, twenty-nine, is involved in the San Francisco punk-music scene and has purple hair, piercings above and below her lips, and a tattoo on her upper arm. When she was twenty-six, she dated a twenty-eight-year-old musician. One day she discovered the love letters of an eighteen-year-old girl inside one of her record sleeves. "Instead of realizing that she was eighteen and I was twenty-six and that I should just cut my losses, I got real competitive with her." The girl went to all of Crystal's boyfriend's concerts. At one show the girl was up by the stage area, singing all the words, and Crystal's boyfriend put the mike near her mouth. Crystal pushed her away from the microphone and called her a "slut." "I had never done anything like that before and it really scared me," says Crystal softly, "because it was something I never thought I would resort to."

Single black women in particular may be likely to regard each other as potential Other Women because, as they related to me repeatedly, they face a supply and demand problem: There aren't enough marriageable black men to go around. "If you're a professional black woman," says Clare Mason, a successful thirty-year-old executive, "you unfortunately limit yourself to who you're going to date. We limit ourselves to professional men. So now we're dealing with a very small pool. A lot of black men are in jail, and there are gay men, and we have age limits. We put restrictions on ourselves, so there end up being more women than men."

It may be tempting for black men who are in demand to take advantage of their desirability, pitting women against each other. Denene Millner, author of *The Sistahs' Rules*, a black takeoff on the white-oriented get-him guide, admonishes black women not to reward black men who "say they can afford to be 'picky' and 'playas'—that is, date a host of women at the same time—because society's taught them that their education, career title, salary, and 401(k) plan place them squarely in the 'in serious demand' category."[44] Millner implores her readers to rearrange their priorities so that they don't miss out on all the great men who are not college educated or six-figure earners. Plus she reminds her readers who don't have men to "leave the blocking to the football players. Just because you don't have one doesn't mean your girlfriend can't have one."[45]

Aisha Price, thirty-six, gets right to the point: "I don't know how it is in white America, but in black America, if you get a man and he's ten percent worth having, everybody else wants him." Married and divorced twice, Aisha tells me that her first husband left her for one of her best friends. Another friend has gone after every man Aisha's had. The friend would buy Aisha's boyfriends Christmas gifts. After Aisha broke up with one guy, the friend bought him a cellular phone. Did she ever confront this friend? "This is the thing with most black women," she tells me. "Even if you don't have a confrontation, we know they're there, we know what they're about, and we know to keep our men away from them." But we're discussing her *friends*; does she have to keep her men away from them, too? "Well, it kinda makes you think: Are they really my friends?"

For a black woman looking for a black man, the issue of looking attractive is especially loaded because black women live in a beauty culture dictated by white men and women. I ask Clare Mason how she reacts when a black man dates a white woman.

The honest answer is that if he's good-looking, smart—what you consider a catch—then it's a stab in the back. We take it personally. We feel, 'What's wrong with us?' And black women have always dealt with the issue of 'Are we beautiful by society's standards?' And the answer has been no, at least until very recently, because you didn't used to see black women as symbols of beauty. Yes, that's changing, but it's an issue that we still deal with. So if you're not considered a symbol of beauty, and the only people who might find you beautiful are your own men, and then they turn around and reject you for a white woman, that hurts. And there's resentment because there are so many white men who love white women, so white women have a big pool of men, [and yet they go into] our very small pool.

WHEN THE OTHER WOMAN IS YOUR FRIEND

What happens when two friends are each other's Other Woman? There is a code among girlfriends of all backgrounds that one friend does not date the ex of another friend unless she has obtained permission to do so. This is probably because monitoring a friend's relationships is one arena in which an unattached woman knows she can exert some control within her own life, which may not be going quite as planned. But the details of the code—whether you must request permission right at the beginning of a relationship or only when it gets serious; whether permission is mandatory even when the friend's breakup occurred over five or even ten years ago; whether you are obliged to stop seeing your friend's ex if she asks you to—are fuzzy. "There are so many situations, and stuff can come up," explains Megan Silver, thirty. "I think that as a general rule, you should not date someone's ex without checking in. But it depends. What if you're being set up on a blind date with him, or you met him at a party, and had no idea that he was an ex of a friend? The point is that you shouldn't do it knowingly." And what if you check in with your friend and she says, "No way"? "In theory, you don't do it. But it's very situational. What if the guy is *the* guy? It's so complicated."

"Of course, you *never* date somebody your best friend dated," exclaims Janet, twenty-nine, "unless you're willing to ruin the friendship. It's an unspoken rule." Janet, a lesbian, recounts a recent incident at a dinner party "where there was a woman who she knew was an ex-girlfriend of her friend Amy. They had dated over ten years ago. Janet started flirting with Amy's ex. Then she went into the kitchen to ask another friend if she thought Amy would mind. "Are you kidding?" the friend said. "Amy would kill you!" Janet was rather surprised, since the relationship had ended so long ago. "I think ten years is a fair amount of time. And if I can't go out with someone she's ever slept with, then there's going to be nobody in the world for me to date, because Amy's gotten around. I don't mean that she's slutty"—she laughs—"but it is a small gene pool. Inevitably there's going to be some recycling."

Genuine friendship is a noble attachment. Think of the Bible's Jonathan and David; consider the Roman Empire's Caesar and Brutus. These relationships from antiquity are between men in cultures based on loyalty oaths, yet even today, even among women, there is an unspoken code that friendship is sacred. Romantic relationships may take precedence, but a platonic relationship between girlfriends is also a very special thing. Women's friendships are comforting and supportive. When a friend then dates your ex, it feels like a betrayal. If their relationship turns out to be stronger than the one you had, it can have consequences for the friendship. Both friends will judge themselves, and each other, according to their successes and failures with the same man.

When a boyfriend cheats on a woman with her best friend, she loses her two closest allies in the world. It's a betrayal that stings for many, many years. Erica Snyderman meets me at a bar near her office and begins her story: When she was a senior in college, three years ago, her boyfriend broke up with her and immediately took up with her best friend, Jennifer—and it turned out that the two of them had been sleeping together for several months. "It was the worst experience of my entire life. I fell into a depression. I was on antidepressants. I couldn't sleep, couldn't eat—I lost about thirty pounds in four months. I did psycho things, trying to hurt myself. One night I broke a mirror. I would drive really fast without a seat belt because I didn't care." Jennifer and Erica had been the closest of friends for three years. They had lived across the street from each other and spent all their time together. How could Jennifer betray her like this? "I think she wanted to prove something to herself. In college, she hadn't had a single boyfriend. She slept around, but she never had a significant relationship. No one wanted her. And here I was, dating Dwight and spending all my time with him. She was jealous of my relationship and jealous that someone wanted to be with me."

As Erica suggests, for a woman to go after a man who's spoken for is often a cheap and easy pick-me-up, like a narcotic. It proves to the world and, most importantly, to herself, that she is a desirable woman. She is so irresistible that she can sway even a committed man. Maria, a thirty-two-year-old journalist who was raised in Colombia, admits to stealing her cousin's boyfriend when they were teenagers. She explains her behavior in part because "that was the way we were all trained in Colombia. It was terrible. All the women were like: 'Get the best, and get 'em fast.'" But Maria also acknowledges that she "went after him just to prove that I could get him. Well, I got the guy but I ruined my relationship with my cousin. When I look back, I realize it wasn't worth it. I wouldn't even say hello to the guy now."

Cynthia Eng likewise had something to prove to herself. She was "awkward" from the age of eight until fourteen—"you know, braces, glasses, the whole works. When I turned fourteen and guys started noticing me, I liked it, and I wanted to see where I could go with it." One of her closest girlfriends was seeing a guy, and they were a "consistent couple," but she let him "fool around with whomever he wanted to fool around with. 'Fooling around' back then"—this was the mid-1980s—"meant just messing around; it didn't mean having sex like it does today. At one point, he and I fooled around a couple of times. We didn't keep it a secret. We didn't lie about it or anything."

Okay, so Cynthia didn't have intercourse with the guy, she was honest about the liaison, and besides, he had been given *carte blanche* to play around. Still, her behavior was clearly a betrayal. Why did she do it?

> I think it was like a contest to see how many guys you could get to be interested in you, though you realize later on that it doesn't take much to get a guy to want to fool around with you. It's partially a contest with yourself and partially a contest with other girls. It was a way of showing each other how attractive we were to guys. And I guess because I had felt so ugly for so long, this was fun for me. I had always thought that my friend was prettier and that the guys considered her smarter and wittier and more inter-

esting, so I guess [long pause] by nailing this guy, not literally though [small laugh], who was so enthralled with her, it was kind of a score for my ego. That I could kiss him if I wanted to.

When a woman looks for a boyfriend or husband, she seeks much more than companionship, romance, a shared life, and sex. Being partnered, as a woman, means one has attained a measure of power. Or so our heterosexual- and marriage-minded culture tells us. When a woman poaches another woman's man—particularly a friend's—she may experience a double dose of power. She has "proof" of being not only desirable, but irresistible. When a woman is satisfied with who she is, as well as with the life she is living, she will not need a man to feel complete, and will not need to push other women aside to search for one. Society conditions us to believe that two halves (man and woman) make a whole and that we cannot feel complete otherwise. Society benefits from this conditioning because it needs us to procreate. However, in a better world men and women would be able to relate to each other as two complete people. Desperation would disappear or at least be diminished, as would competitive feelings.

HERE COMES THE BRIDE

A woman planning a wedding enters a subculture filled with magazines, menu tastings, dress fittings, appallingly high prices of fresh flowers, and the rules of invitation etiquette. This is a whole new arena in which to be judged and to judge others. The marriage ceremony itself is a public declaration of a couple's commitment to one another—a public spectacle, if you will. It therefore invites comparisons, compliments, and competition. Envy over what other couples can afford often leads to a concern with one-upmanship.

"When a girl has a really big diamond," says Hanni, a twenty-three-year-old graduate from Barnard College, "other girls will say, 'Uch, why is she carrying a mountain on her hand?' Everybody views that as ostentatious. But maybe when girls make those comments, it is somewhat of a jealousy issue because the other girl has this big, expensive piece of jewelry." When a woman announces she's engaged, it is *de rigueur* to ask to see her ring, inspect it carefully, and then tell her that the stone and setting are beautiful and that her fiancé has impeccable taste. But one woman, married, wearing a diamond ring, admits to me that she checks out other women's rings even when they aren't offered for inspection, even long after the women in question have been married. Valerie, thirty-one, a researcher at a not-for-profit organization, admits the ring is status. I ask her if she wishes her diamond were bigger. "Maybe a little bit. Or I think that I'd like to get another one to add on to it. You want to make sure that you're keeping up with the Joneses."

Listening to Valerie, I am reminded of the celebrity-obsessed media's reaction to the diamond ring that Jerry Seinfeld bought for his bride, Jessica Sklar, in 1999. Apparently, insiders at Tiffany were "horrified" that he'd bought only a two-carat ring. "Couldn't he afford more? Really," said one employee to *The New York Times*.[46] Likewise, Valerie tells me that she is "judgmental of a man who is able to just have his mother's or grandmother's ring [to give to his fiancée]. I respect the guy who saved his money and went out and bought a new ring." Magazines like *In Style* don't help: In the "Celebrity Weddings" issue of February 2001, a three-page spread on diamond rings told readers that Madonna has an Edwardian platinum ring, Sharon Stone has three emerald-cut diamonds totaling

4.5 carats (which "symbolize the couple's past, present, and future together"), and that Kate Hudson has a "glamorous Asher-cut diamond of approximately 5 carats set in a streamlined art deco mounting" (whatever that means).[47]

The wedding party is another opportunity for competition. Good taste is expensive. Christina Pappas, an event planner in Los Angeles, plans weddings for affluent brides, usually aged thirty to thirty-five, willing to spend between $150,000 and several million dollars for a wedding. (In many cases their families are footing the bill.) Pappas is accustomed to having brides approach her with ideas culled from *Martha Stewart Weddings* magazine and websites like www.theknot.com. They tell her, "I need to do something different." "I want it to be special." "I don't want something cookie-cutter." "God, don't give me that because it looks tacky." "Make sure there's no stock"—a floral filler—"in my floral arrangements; it looks cheap." "Oh God, I'm so sick of looking at white linens. I need something special." On a personal level, when she attends weddings, Pappas is used to hearing asides from friends or family members like, "Oh my God, look at her dress" or "I heard they spent this much on the flowers, and look at them" or "Oh God, salmon *again?*"

The first thing Pappas always tells her clients is that the most important ingredient in a wedding party is a good attitude. "The bottom line is that what you spend doesn't really matter"—refreshing words from someone who earns a living off the big sums her clients are willing to spend. "Your guests will pick up on how you feel. Your guests will have a good time if you're having a good time, whether you're serving fish and chips or lobster." Many brides, however, don't quite see it that way. "A friend of mine who is getting married in a few months was at a wedding of another friend with me," says one New Yorker in her mid-twenties, wincing at the recent memory. "She spent the whole time criticizing everything, saying that things were not as classy as she would have it. She even took pictures of the centerpieces so that she could show her florist what not to do. She commented on the bride's gown and said it was too shiny and there was no waist, and that [the bride] looked like 'a big shiny piece of metal.' It was so inappropriate. It was a beautiful wedding and I don't know what she was talking about. I hope that her wedding will be beautiful, but I can't imagine that it will be absolutely perfect."

While it is true that there may be more women than men who wish to marry, it is also true that competition for men is not a result of raw numbers. For women, it is the result of the cultural idealization of marriage over all other types of relationships. Women are taught they must marry (and have children) in order to be happy and fulfilled. Yet many people are not suited for lifelong monogamy, as the 50 percent divorce rate reveals.

If platonic friendships were valued as much as romantic ones, many people would still form attachments and marry, since marriage can meet the needs of many. Women would not need to compete for men because men would not be regarded as a scarce commodity or as the ticket to fulfillment. For all their flaws and obsession over landing a man, even Bridget Jones and the heroines of *Sex and the City* recognize that girlfriends come first. If neurotic, self-absorbed fictional characters are capable of this achievement, surely we are as well.

CHAPTER FOUR
WORK

"I'd rather work for a man than a woman."

Many professional women, particularly in fields traditionally dominated by men, confess they prefer male rather than female supervisors. They complain that women at work refuse to share power, or withhold information, or are too concerned about receiving credit for every little thing they accomplish, or are cold toward underlings (male and female alike). In such complaints, they use the word "bitch" a lot. They also claim that men in positions of authority appear more comfortable, are more laid-back—that counter to what you might expect, men feel less threatened by women and therefore give them more opportunities to advance than other women do. Many such confessors are women who in all other areas of their lives enjoy the company of women. But not at work. They feel guilty about it, as if they are betraying a feminist cause—and yet, they feel betrayed by female bosses.

☛ Christine, twenty-nine, works in publishing. Several years ago, she had a boss who felt imperiled by younger women in the industry. "It was her job to mentor me, but she never let me acquire books," says Christine. "She never let me pursue authors. She felt threatened every time I was friendly to any of her authors—which was my *job*. She didn't give me a single raise the entire time I worked for her—two years. I was making $25,000 a year. So I got a new job at [another publishing house]. When I told her, she was infuriated and said, 'Well, aren't *you* ambitious.' She couldn't mask her fury. I gave her the news on a Wednesday, and she told me she wanted me gone by the end of the week."

☞ Jane, a legal assistant in a small law firm, has worked in law offices since 1980, providing her with a wealth of experience and knowledge. She is often assumed to be the lawyer, not the assistant. This does not always sit well with other women. Jane tells me about a twenty-eight-year-old fellow legal assistant in her office who went to law school at night and earned her J.D. This woman "always reminds me that I'm not an attorney and that I don't have the degree." Why on earth does this colleague, who is younger than Jane's children, seem so threatened by Jane, who, after all, can never take her job from her? Jane speculates: "I know a lot and she knows that the other lawyers turn to me for a lot of answers. No, I can't do their cases, but they often come to me, and she doesn't like that."

☞ Diana, a thirty-year-old freelance writer and researcher, compares working with women versus men as "the personal versus the professional." She says, "I enjoy working with men a hundred times more and I don't feel apologetic for saying it. Men love writing things down. They embrace contracts; they embrace memos. I love that! When I have to do contracts with women, they never want the agreement written down. They worry that one party isn't trusting the other. But I don't care if someone is worried. Let's write it down and have the contract as a safety net. Men get this and move on."

These stories—and there are scores more—are not meant to suggest that all women prefer working with men. Judy Hecker, a curator at the Museum of Modern Art in Manhattan, works in a female-dominated department that she loves. "It's a very supportive environment," she says. Her boss, a woman, "is incredibly inclusive and likes to see her underlings grow." Judy has a colleague with the same title, but who has not been at the institution as long; their boss is very clear about assigning responsibilities in line with the two employees' level of seniority, and therefore there is no room or reason for competition.

And of course, even when female colleagues do go head-to-head, it does not always translate into negative feelings. Charlotte Baker works in a not-for-profit international exchange organization; most of the employees, except those at the highest level, are women. She tells me about a colleague who "promotes herself very well": She is excessive in sending "cc" emails to the boss, just to make sure he always knows what she's doing; she always puts her name first on projects she has worked on collaboratively with Charlotte; in meetings, she always manages to bring the discussion to the projects she's working on. "She is just so concerned about getting credit," says Charlotte, "and making sure that everyone knows what she's doing. It is truly amazing. And you know"—Charlotte pauses and looks me in the eye—"you really have to admire it. She is professional and energetic and well-spoken. She eggs me on, which challenges me to do better work."

Countless female bosses nurture and mentor younger and less experienced women; numerous female employees challenge their female colleagues in a positive way. Women can be very supportive of other women. Christina Pappas, a thirty-five-year-old Los Angeles event planner, is frequently approached by young women thinking of entering the field who want to ask her questions about getting a foot in the door. "I always say, 'Come to the office and I'll show you my books.' You know why? Because I got my start from another event planner. I went to her and asked for information, and she took a liking to me and said, 'Come on in.' There is so much work out there that I don't have to feel competitive with younger women."

I myself am lucky to have been adopted as a protégé by author and consumer health activist Barbara Seaman, who has served as my informal mentor since 1994. Barbara has selflessly introduced me to just about everyone in her vast Rolodex, reads my work and offers incisive criticisms, and is always available by phone or in person when I need advice about contract negotiations or just to gossip and have a cup of coffee. I would still be a writer even if Barbara hadn't entered my life, but her presence smooths my path because she validates my work and makes me realize that, as she has done, I can use my writing to trigger debate about important cultural issues. Unfortunately, not all of us are fortunate to have a Barbara in our lives or to work in an office with supportive women stimulating us to be ambitious.

Are complaints about other women in the workplace always true? Do many working women really act like "bitches"? By and large, I believe that countless working women have an "attitude" that is expressed most sharply around other women. However, this attitude has nothing to do with female chromosomes. That is, working women often behave in a "difficult" manner because of the pressures in the workplace imposed on women. There is sex discrimination. There is the erroneous belief that a woman is less capable than a man. And when a woman wants to have children and continue working, she is up against the glass ceiling. (The phrase describes invisible barriers, such as being paid less than men, being denied promotions, and generally being held back from advancing to the top echelons of the corporate structure.) There are no blueprints for how women should get ahead in corporate America because their mothers, aunts, and older sisters never were allowed to try. And when they did, they remained in low-paying, repetitive jobs where the only time they saw senior management was at a Christmas party.

Why do we vent our frustrations on other women? Because, as is often the case whenever anyone feels powerless, it seems more expedient to lash out at others in the same powerless position than it is to fight the people with real power. Besides, when a woman challenges the inner circle of men, she runs the risk of being left on the periphery. Joining with other women to fight for better working conditions (such as flex-time and on-site child care) is time-consuming, tiring, and risky. But if a woman belittles other women, she can prove her superiority among women—and is one step closer to the inner circle of men.

Over the past century, women workers in the United States have increased steadily. In 1900, only 5 million women worked outside the home, representing 18 percent of the labor force; in 1950, the number of working women was 18.4 million, occupying 30 percent of the labor force. Today, there are 64 million women in the civilian work force. Forty-seven percent of all workers are women, 60 percent of all women work for pay, and ninety-nine out of every one hundred women will work for pay at some point in their lives.[1] According to the numbers, women are deeply entrenched in the workplace. They have furthered their education to increase their earnings. They have pursued work in occupations traditionally held only by men. They play a vital role in the workings of the economy. And yet, many working women don't feel the psychological sense of security that should, by all rights, come with such strong representation in the labor force. Instead, women feel beleaguered, as if they were still fighting to prove they can work as effectively as men, as if they were still struggling to be accepted as worthy employees.

SEX DISCRIMINATION: YES, IT STILL EXISTS

In fact, women do have reasons to feel under attack. Despite numbers and efficacy, women are still fighting the same old fight for equity and respect. Only a very few women possess real power in the workplace. Millions of women earn a decent salary. Yes, many women hold positions of authority as physicians, attorneys, editors, supervisors, managers, vice presidents, and presidents of companies. But the real power—that comes with the title of department chair, partner, publisher, and chief executive—still resides overwhelmingly with men. No matter how high a woman rises, you can be sure that (with few exceptions) she ultimately has to answer to a man. Female doctors are more likely than their male peers to teach at medical schools but are far less likely to be promoted to senior faculty positions, according to a study in the *New England Journal of Medicine*.[2] "How many of your female classmates have become law partners?" Judge Shirley Abrahamson, the first woman to serve on the Wisconsin Supreme Court, asks lawyer and Harvard professor Susan Estrich. Estrich relates that she can count the number of women on one hand, compared to dozens of men, "ratios that bore

no relation to the composition of my law school class," she says.[3]
There are only six female chief executives at Fortune 500 companies—Carleton ("Carly") Fiorina of Hewlett-Packard, Marce Fuller
of Mirant, Andrea Jung of Avon, Anne Mulcahy of Xerox, Patricia
Russo of Lucent, and Marion Sandler of Golden West Financial—
and women occupy only one out of every ten seats on the boards of
those companies, according to Catalyst, a research group devoted
to advancing the role of women in business.[4]

Women hold a mere 6.8 percent of "line-officer" jobs—positions
with profit-and loss-responsibility that lead to promotions to senior
management—in America's five hundred largest companies, according to Catalyst. The women in those companies most likely work in
"staff" jobs in human relations and public relations.[5] The women who
do move ahead are almost always white. Three quarters of the Fortune
500 have some sort of policy in place to encourage racial diversity, but
most are negligibly effective since they are not coupled with mentor-
ships or the chance to network informally with colleagues.[6]

A majority of working women in the United States hold low-
paying jobs in fields traditionally dominated by women. Ninety-
eight percent of secretaries, typists, kindergarten teachers, regis-
tered nurses, speech therapists, and billing clerks—positions, in
other words, that lack high salaries—are women. Nearly 60 percent of women work in clerical, sales, and service occupations, which
typically pay one-half to two-thirds of the wages in blue-collar craft
work.[7] Women don't so much choose to work in these fields as
these fields choose them. These are professions in which women
can easily get hired and can return after a hiatus to raise children.
Jobs with better salaries tend not to offer these advantages.

In 1998, women earned 76 percent of what men earned. That translated into median weekly earnings for women working full time of $456 compared with $598 for men, a difference of $7,384 a year.[8] Employers get away with wage discrimination by arguing that women are not providers for their families, so they don't really need their income the way men do. But according to the Bureau of Labor Statistics, working mothers contribute income in two-thirds of all families with children under the age of eighteen. In 19 percent of these families only the mother works, either because she is a single parent or because her partner does not work, while in 47 percent the mother is part of a dual-earning couple in which the father also works and both incomes are necessary.[9]

According to a survey sponsored by the AFL-CIO, 60 percent of working women and 67 percent of those with children under eighteen say they work at least forty hours a week, with 15 percent reporting that they work more than forty hours a week. Twenty-nine percent do not have paid sick leave, and more than half have no paid leave to care for a child or ill family member. One-third has no flexibility at all over their work hours.[10]

Even breadwinning women who outearn their husbands can get the short end of the stick. Nearly one in three working wives nationwide is paid more than her husband—a trend that is particularly evident among very highly educated women. When wives earn more, do their husbands do more chores? Not necessarily, according to University of Washington sociologist Julie Brines. She has found that when a woman disrupts the traditional female role by surpassing her husband's income, the couple becomes more likely to cling to traditional roles within the home, with the husband helping less and less with household work as his wife earns more and more.[11] In addition, although a vast majority of male chief executives have stay-at-home wives who care for their homes and children, travel with them, appear with them in public, and entertain clients and colleagues, female executives usually are stuck with the "wife" chores as well, which can hurt their careers or compromise the well-being of their families.[12]

When Carly Fiorina became the president and chief executive officer of computer giant Hewlett-Packard in July 1999, she worked hard to downplay the significance of her gender. "I truly hope that we are at the point where everyone has figured out that the accomplishments of women across industry demonstrate that there is not a glass ceiling," she said at a news conference.[13] "My gender is interesting," she told reporters, "but really not the subject of the story here."[14]

Fiorina was wrong. Far from being an aw-shucks, nothing-special Everywoman, Fiorina possesses an unusual amount of corporate power. It is unusual precisely because of the widespread existence of sex discrimination in our country's labor force. In recent years, Mitsubishi Motors and the drugmaker Astra USA have agreed to pay tens of millions of dollars to female employees after the Equal Employment Opportunity Commission found evidence of widespread discrimination. The EEOC also recently determined that the Wall Street investment bank Morgan Stanley Dean Witter had discriminated against women employed in its institutional stocks division. That case stemmed from a complaint filed in 1998 by Allison K. Schieffelin, a Morgan Stanley trader who was repeatedly passed over for promotions while less-deserving men were elevated to the top rank of managing director. She was also excluded from male-only events, such as golf outings and visits to Manhattan strip clubs, which hurt her chances of mingling with top executives.[15] Catalyst conducted more than five hundred exit interviews with women managers who left more than twenty companies in the 1990s. The vast majority of the women said initially that they were leaving to spend more time with their families. But six months after they left, only 15 percent were still at home. So what was the real reason for their resignations? Nearly three-quarters of the women told Catalyst that there was a lack of opportunity for advancement at their old job.[16] In a separate survey, two-thirds of the women who work at the seven major securities firms on Wall Street told Catalyst that they must work harder than men for the same rewards. A third reported a hostile environment where crude or sexist comments were tolerated, they were treated unfairly, or they were subject to unwanted sexual attention.[17]

Most invisibly—and therefore most insidiously—the structure of the workplace itself, intended for workers who devote long hours and many uninterrupted years, creates a glass ceiling. "Most professions are not organized to accommodate a woman's biological clock," explains Susan Estrich in her fine exposé and analysis of discrimination against women, *Sex and Power*. "The periods of most intense work are often just when it's time to have kids."[18] In medicine, for instance, the age at which female doctors tend to have children is also the time when they must aggressively pursue grants and complete significant research if their careers are to advance. In law, the age at which female attorneys tend to have children is also the time when they must work punishing hours round the clock to prove how devoted they are to their clients and how worthy they are of being made partner. Only women, of course, bear children; women nearly always also take on the primary responsibility to care for their children, whether or not they work for pay. Sums up Debra Meyerson, a professor at Simmons Graduate School of Management and an expert on the glass ceiling, "It's not the ceiling that's holding women back; it's the whole structure of the organizations in which we work: the foundation, the beams, the walls, the very air."[19]

And what does all of the above have to do with women and competition? Everything. If women were allowed to have and earn a big chunk of the pie, they wouldn't have to compete with each other for the crumbs. Women are more than 50 percent of the population. They are nowhere near 50 percent of the power holders.

JOB INSECURITY

"A woman does not walk into the room with the same status as an equivalent man, because she is less likely than a man to be viewed as a serious professional," reports psychologist Virginia Valian. "A woman who aspires to success needs to worry about being ignored; each time it happens she loses prestige and the people around her become less inclined to take her seriously."[20] A woman is regarded as "slightly unsuited" to the professional world; she is routinely undervalued and assumed to lack competence, while men are presumed to be good in their professions. Sixty-three percent of female lawyers surveyed in Massachusetts reported that court workers had asked them, "Are you an attorney?" (as opposed to a legal assistant). This was more than double the proportion of men who were asked the same question.[21] A classic experiment had subjects read essays they were told were written either by John T. McKay, J. T. McKay, or Joan McKay. The essays were identical, but Joan's was evaluated as the least intelligent and persuasive, by both men and women.[22]

A successful man is skilled and intelligent; a successful woman got lucky. One thirty-three-year-old account executive tells me about an opening in her division for a manager. Rather than hire or promote one person, upper management, composed of all men, divided the responsibilities between two senior women. According to the account executive, "The division [of responsibilities] has been very destructive" for the department and for the careers of the two women. "It was almost as though they couldn't decide between the two of them," she muses. "You just know that they would never do this with men. They would have made a decision. They would not have two men sharing power. One of the men in senior management, who played a role in this decision, told one of my colleagues, 'We're coconut-ing them.' It means banging them together to see which one breaks."

Women, like men, are apt to stereotype women as inherently unsuited for their responsibilities. A thirty-two-year-old tire sales expert is used to having "men come in and demand to speak with a man. Women aren't as blunt but they have been very dubious about my abilities until I tell them, 'Look, I've been doing this for three years. I'm not going to sell you the wrong thing.' The whole bonding thing of 'you go, girl' that you would think would happen is not there."

Jennifer, a thirty-year-old financial planner, tells me that clients are often hesitant about having a woman manage their money—and female clients happen to be the most uncomfortable. On an average day, she sits down with five or six people who are considering working with her. Right away, she knows the signs of a woman who will never become a client. "She may look uncomfortable or shift in her chair or reads the brochures on my desk. She's not paying attention to me, as she should. Or she's looking at me, but I can see that her expression is blank—that the lights are on but no one's home. Yet she is clearly interested in having someone manage her money. Finally she says, 'Well, I have to think about this more,' and then never gets back to me. I don't get that with men. Some people might say it's because I'm cute, so I can keep their attention more. But I don't think so. If someone doesn't want to listen to you or feels threatened by you, she just shuts down." Echoing the tire salesperson, Jennifer says, "It's very curious, because you would think the opposite. You would expect a certain camaraderie."

Women legitimately worry about not being taken seriously. They are also concerned they will be handicapped in their career development if they take advantage of family-friendly policies such as maternity leave, flexible scheduling, job sharing, and telecommuting.[23] A study of the Boston Bar Association found that while 93 percent of Boston-area law firms offered reduced-hour options, only 6 percent of lawyers took advantage of them—because they worried that there would be strings attached.[24] And guess what: They would be right. One of the reasons men earn more and are promoted more than women is that men are assumed to be more devoted to their careers, while women are assumed to be less ambitious and more concerned with their families. Yet in 1998, the majority of new mothers returned to work within one year after childbirth.[25]

In 1993, Congress signed the Family and Medical Leave Act, which requires companies with more than fifty employees to provide up to twelve weeks of unpaid leave for new parents. (The law's scope is appallingly limited when compared with the parental-leave policies of most European countries, which offer at least ten months of universal paid parental leave.) Although fathers have just as much legal right as mothers do to take family leave, it is mothers who predominantly take it. "Men are terrified to take parental leave," observes Suzanne Braun Levine, author of *Father Courage: What Happens When Men Put Family First*. "While their organizations may profess to be family-friendly, their bosses are giving them the message that men who take leave are not very manly, or are somehow letting down the team."[26]

Yet women who take maternity leave also get the message that they are somehow letting down the team. "Since I came back from maternity leave, I get the work of a paralegal," complains one Boston lawyer. "I want to say, look, I had a baby, not a lobotomy." At a hearing of the American Bar Association's Commission on Women, Barbara P. Billauer, president of the Women's Trial Board, testified that "every single woman that I have spoken to without exception, partner or associate, has experienced rampant hostility and prejudice upon her return [from maternity leave]. There is a sentiment that pregnancy and motherhood [have] softened her, that she is not going to work as hard."[27]

The "mommy track"—a lower and slower track for parents who want to devote time to their families—has serious penalities.

Working part-time in the legal profession is seen as "an automatic career breaker," according to Rosalind C. Barnett, a senior scientist at Brandeis University and senior fellow at Harvard University. The Institute for Women's Policy Research found that part-time work almost always involves enormous sacrifices of pay and benefits. If you work half the hours, you don't get paid half the salary. Managers earning $800 a week for full-time work can earn as little as $200 or $300 for a twenty-hour week.[28] Well-paid, flexible jobs are hard to come by. A 1997 study of three thousand workers found that 63 percent of them wanted to work fewer hours; of those who worked fifty or more hours a week, 80 percent wanted a shorter work week.[29]

Women who work part-time temporarily, so that they can spend a few hours a day with their children in their youngest years, are penalized permanently. A 1993 study of graduates of the University of Michigan Law School found a significant earning gap between men and women who started out with similar qualifications. The single largest factor explaining the gap was a period of part-time work, which had an impact on salary even years later, after the women had returned to full-time work.[30] Young women in law, the American Bar Association has found, look at the sacrifices made by Baby Boom women to make partner and increasingly they reject them. As Estrich puts it,

> [T]hey "understand" that a choice must be made between success at work and family life, and they are willing to make it, in favor of family. The problem is not that they are making the wrong choice, but that they see it as inevitable, and the provision of options like "of counsel" [an in-house legal position with man-

ageable hours but a lower salary than one could earn as a partner at a law firm] makes it even easier to opt out of the rat race.
Unfortunately, that decision tends to have lasting consequences.[31]

What about having children early, before a woman has
embarked on a career, as conservative author Danielle Crittenden
advises in *What Our Mothers Didn't Tell Us*? This course of action is
highly unrealistic. For one thing, most of us have not found a life
mate by the age of twenty-two. Besides, "becoming a part-time
manager is easier if you're already a manager," observes Estrich
dryly, dismissing Crittenden's censure of working mothers in a
powerful slam-dunk. Tellingly, Crittenden does not offer the same
advice to men: She takes it as self-evident that women are better
parents than men, that women prefer to be primary parents, and
that this gendered division of labor is natural and inevitable.

Successful men don't have to worry about when and if to
become parents. Successful women do. The more successful the
woman, the less likely she is to have children. In her book *Creating
a Life: Professional Women and the Quest for Children*, Sylvia Ann
Hewlett notes that 42 percent of women in corporate America are
childless, with half of the most powerful career women also without children. According to Hewlett, only a fraction—14 percent—
of these women actively chose childlessness. The overwhelming
majority stumbled into childlessness because they concentrated on
their careers in their thirties—as any driven employee in corporate
America is pressured to do—bypassing their fertile years. Men
don't have to choose between success and parenthood. Indeed, "The
more successful the man, the more likely he is to be married with

children," she writes. "One pair of figures from corporate America says it all: 49 percent of 40-year-old women executives earning $100,000 or more a year are childless while only 10 percent of 40-year-old male executives in an equivalent earnings bracket do not have children."[32]

So you will have to excuse women, whether they work in white- or blue-collar jobs, if they feel more than just a tad defensive. Madelyn Jennings, a former vice-president of personnel at Gannett, the international media corporation, and former vice-president of human resources at General Electric, recalls a statement made by Charles Schultz, the creator of *Peanuts*. "He said that every morning, when he worked on his cartoon strip, he felt that he had to prove himself, even though he'd already proven himself. I think [that his mind-set] is typical of the way women feel. That kind of anxiety makes for a more brittle relationship with others. You're a little more tense than the guys are, and it can be felt." To deal with this tension, women develop coping mechanisms. Unfortunately, these coping mechanisms often serve to distance themselves from other women (and often from men as well). Instead of directing their frustrations toward the individuals who can do something about their situation—that is, the men who run the corporations and make the ultimate decisions about promotions, work schedules, and corporate lifestyle—working women vent in the presence of those who, like themselves, clutch petty power: other women.

Consider the tension that can exist between mothers and child-less women in the workplace. The mother envies her childless colleagues' flexibility and mobility. The colleagues rumble with resentment if the mother needs to arrive late or leave early because her child is ill or is in a school play. Fathers usually don't take this kind of time off as often as mothers do. The mother is caught in a sharp-edged double bind. If she puts work first, she is appallingly ambitious. If she puts her family first, she is castigated for not caring about work. She's either a bad mother or a bad worker—or a bad mother and a bad worker.

One thirty-year-old woman, Risa, an associate at a law firm (married but no children), complains about a colleague who is senior to her, who is about to go on her second maternity leave in two years. The colleague was instructed by her doctor to work at home during her ninth month. "I'm working on most of her cases," sighs Risa, "and she is giving me absolutely *no guidance*. None. There is no transition whatsoever." Her voice rises. "It's driving me crazy, plus she's hostile to me. I wish she would tell me what she knows [about the pending assignments], and I'll finish the work on my end. But the problem is that she keeps everything very close to her chest, and then I have to recreate the wheel, and then she calls me stupid because I don't know everything that she knows. I think she just doesn't want to give up her power."

I sympathize with Risa, but I also ask her to look at the situation from the point of view of her colleague, who is feeling insecure and concerned that once she cedes power, it may remain forever beyond her grasp. No doubt the colleague is worried not only about how to juggle work and family but also how to raise two children at the same time. Shouldn't Risa talk to her and acknowledge these anxieties? Perhaps the colleague would relax her grip on the assignments if she feels that Risa is sympathetic to her situation. But Risa says, "There's only so much sympathy I can have for her about feel-

ing insecure about not being able to do things, when I'm here trying to do them. If I told her, 'Look, I'm too busy to help you out,'
then I would understand. But I'm trying to make things easier for
her and she's not cooperating."

A mother may feel particularly insecure because she spends
many, many hours away from the office doing "invisible" work—the
work of parenting. Unlike workplace work, parenting usually goes
unrecognized. There simply is no glory of the type you have at least
a shot at in the public world of work. Even if you know you've done
a stellar job, it always feels good when others acknowledge it. Who
doesn't want confirmation that she isn't screwing up? Who doesn't
sometimes feel like a fraud unless she's received a pat on the back?

And women can be especially sensitive about receiving public
recognition. "If you ask a salesperson what drives them," says Jennifer,
the financial planner, the answer is "two things: money and recognition. For women especially, it's recognition. I find that a lot of women
in my field go nuts when they don't get the recognition they deserve,
or if they are slighted in any way. A man is more likely to say 'so
what?' if he doesn't get a plaque or an award. He's more interested
in the money. Women want the money too, but the recognition
holds a lot of weight." Jennifer wrote up the internal newsletter for
a company she used to work for. She recalls that employees enjoyed
seeing their names in print when she described projects they had
initiated or were working on. "But the ladies I worked with got very
excited. Maybe they just showed it more. They really liked being
distinguished."

Madelyn Jennings points out that "When you're the new person
on the team"—and in an historical sense, all women are new on the

team—"you feel the need to get applause in order to substantiate your existence. And it hurts if you don't get it. Often women really haven't gotten the credit they deserve. Very often a woman states an idea in a meeting, and no one hears it until some guy says the same idea five minutes later, and then the reaction is, 'Oh, what a wonderful idea.'"

TOUGH AS NAILS

For a number of years, I have worked part time as an editor in a not-for-profit organization run entirely by women. There are some men on staff, but the highest echelon of power is female. There is a feeling of warmth. People smile at each other in the elevators; colleagues kiss each other hello and seem genuinely interested when they inquire about family, vacations, the health of one's children, and the health of one's aging parents. Frivolous small talk centers not upon men's sports but upon women's basketball or soccer, diets, exercise routines, fashion, hot flashes.

At the same time, there is coldness. A woman from a different department, with whom I once worked closely on a project, never says hello to me. I must have done something during our collaboration that irked her, but she never told me what it was. I heard another colleague instruct a subordinate never to wear short skirts because her big calves made them unflattering. Everyone gossips. When one colleague took a month off from work because of a critically ill family member, another colleague rudely questioned the need for her absence. Mid- and high-level employees are overly concerned with hierarchies and status. Lower-level employees fear backstabbing. A number of the women in leadership positions jockey for the best office space and are indignant if they don't get what they think they deserve. People steal each other's ideas and pass them off as their own, and are loath to share credit. On memos, it is common to see five, even ten names on the "cc" line because God forbid if someone is excluded from a courtesy notice about a ten-minute meeting scheduled to take place in two months.

This contradictory behavior is a result of the colliding presumptions we have about women and work. Women are regarded as deferential and lacking in authority. But *working* women are expected to be aggressive and masculine. It's no wonder that many of us have no idea where to begin defying these stereotypes. What is the "right" way to behave as a successful worker? As a woman? It's no wonder that many of us feel perplexed, precarious, even paralyzed.

Worried about being perceived as a mediocre or incompetent worker, many women go out of their way to prove they are not too emotional or passive, and can be more aggressive and demanding than any man. In politics, female candidates regularly adopt "tough" stances on issues such as criminal punishment to prove that constituents won't be shortchanged by a timid female representative. But for women, there is a fine line between appearing masculine and being inappropriate. If a female candidate is too tough, voters will reject her on the grounds that she's not feminine (read: normal) enough. Writing about Hillary Clinton during her 2000 Senate campaign, author and columnist Anne Roiphe observed that "Women should be nice. Hillary is not nice. This makes her the kind of woman men don't like, the kind other women fear, run miles from, don't want to be mistaken for. Thirty-five years into this feminist wave we are still confused: What is female? What is male?

Hillary's hairstyles reflect her own anxiety: What kind of woman am I? Is my ambition well enough disguised?"[33]

Hillary Clinton won the election in 2000. But her case is unusual, since she is the first woman ever to win higher office in New York State. (In her victory speech, she unwittingly reminded supporters that she is a woman in masculine drag by describing her androgynous political uniform: "Sixty-two counties, sixteen months, three debates, two opponents, and six black pantsuits later—here we are!"[34]) Geraldine Ferraro ran for the Senate twice and never got past the primaries. Elizabeth Holtzman also lost twice in her bid for the Senate. Betsy McCaughey ran for governor and lost. Karen Burstein ran for attorney general and lost to an unknown, Dennis Vacco. Bella Abzug ran for the Senate in 1976 and lost to Daniel Patrick Moynihan.[35] In 2002, only five women occupy the governor's office in the fifty states.[36] Seventy-two women serve in the U.S. Congress—thirteen in the Senate and fifty-nine in the House—compared with 463 men. By and large, voters regard men as better political leaders, since men are presumed to be better able to handle the tough crises that arise in political life.

The same rule applies in business. In 1999, *The New York Times* ran a surprisingly harsh profile of Jill Barad, then the chief executive of Mattel, the world's largest maker of toys, including Barbie dolls. The article, which appeared on the front page of the Sunday Business section, highlighted characteristics of Barad that just so happen to be stereotypical of a woman with power. At the time the article appeared, the company was undergoing financial losses, attributed to Barad's "management style." Barad, one of only a handful of women occupying the position of chief executive of a major corporation, had built Barbie from $250 million in annual sales in the mid-1980s to $1.7 billion in 1998. "Ms. Barad's flaws are exacerbated," wrote reporter Gretchen Morgenson, "by the way she jealously guards her power." As a result, according to several former colleagues and customers, "she has driven away many effective managers who might now make up for her shortcomings and help Mattel out of its mess." Another factor weakening the company, according to a senior manager, was the 'Jill Factor,' a cryptic reference to her volatile management style."[37]

A similar article appeared in the same place, the front page of the Sunday Business section of the *Times*, a year and a half later. This time Linda Wachner, then the chief executive of Warnaco, a major lingerie company with licenses to make Calvin Klein jeans and underwear and Speedo swimsuits, was the woman under attack. Warnaco, the paper reported, was almost $2 billion in debt; additionally, two groups of shareholders had filed class-action lawsuits contending that the company and its executives artificially inflated the price of the company's stock. The Securities and Exchange Commission was investigating possible violations of securities laws. What was the cause of Warnaco's downfall? "Mrs. Wachner's management style," which "has hurt and perhaps even killed the company." Reporter Leslie Kaufman addressed at length the reputation Wachner had developed for being "abusive and unprofessional" and "for demoralizing employees by publicly dressing them down for missing sales and profit goals or for simply displeasing her. Often, many former employees said, the attacks were personal rather than professional, and not infrequently laced with crude references to sex, race, or ethnicity—an accusation that Mrs. Wachner flatly denies."[38]

I don't doubt these characterizations of Barad's and Wachner's leadership styles; both reporters collected enough damning quotations and evidence to make their cases. I do know, however, that you just don't read articles so personally inflammatory in the *Times* business section about male chief executives. It seems likely that both reporters, consciously or not, were influenced by the gender of their subjects and characterized them accordingly. And, let's face it, these character assassinations are titillating precisely because they support the belief that women should be kind and gentle and definitely not chief executives of big companies— which means, conversely, that any woman who does hold the chief executive position of a major company must possess a tough, mean, even crude personality. Barad, it must be noted, sought to represent herself first as a woman and second as a chief executive: The posed photograph that accompanied the article about her depicted Barad in a bright, Barbie-inspired, bubble-gum-pink pantsuit. This image did not help her—or Wachner. By late 2001, both women had been ousted from their jobs.

THE POWERFUL WOMAN

There are notorious examples of powerful women who are considered "difficult" to work with. In Hollywood, studio chief Dawn Steel, who died in 1997, was regarded as "the ultimate ballbuster" known for "yelling, screaming, controlling, demanding fealty and obeisance from all who came into her purview."[39] Senator Barbara Mikulski of Maryland has been ranked the number-one "meanest" senator by *Washingtonian* magazine. A former Mikulski staff member told *The Washington Post* that "the way people got yelled at was brutal. It could be humiliating.... It was an atmosphere of fear."[40] At *Vogue* magazine, junior staffers know not to speak to editor-in-chief Anna Wintour unless she speaks to them first. A *New York* reporter experienced riding in an elevator with Wintour: Young female staffers who joined them on different floors were so afraid of making illegal eye contact with their boss that they silently bowed their heads "like schoolgirls before a headmistress."[41]

A haughty manner is not limited to female bosses with high profiles. Female domestic workers (usually women of color) are widely mistreated by the women (usually white) who employ them. (The men in these households typically choose not to intervene.) One nanny I know works for a family with a three-and-a-half-year-old who calls her "stupid"; from where do you think the child learned this name-calling? This woman—sweet, gentle, affectionate with children—is a "live-in" and works from seven A.M. to midnight (in addition to taking care of the kids, she's also responsible for housework), often on weekends as well, is not allowed to eat dinner until her work is done, and is paid $18,000 a year. She deals exclusively with the mother and rarely sees the father. She would like to find another employer, but doesn't have the time to search for one. Another live-in nanny, Mina Zayas, from Paraguay, told *The New York Times* that her female employer confiscated her passport and paid her $200 a week for five days of work (an annual salary of $10,400). When Zayas complained, her employer threatened to call the immigration authorities, since Zayas lacked a resident foreigner's green card.[42] A private Catholic university in Texas, the University of the

Incarnate Word in San Antonio, recently agreed to pay $2.4 million to eighteen former housekeepers who were routinely called "dumb Mexicans" by their supervisor, a nun. The supervisor also hit them, pulled their hair and ears, and ordered the Spanish-speaking employees to speak only English, even during their breaks and at lunch.[43]

The difference in power between a boss and her employee can be demoralizing for anyone holding the subordinate position. When the boss is white and the subordinate is a woman of color, the difference in power (in more ways than one) can be corruptive. Varsha, a thirty-year-old lawyer who works for a legal advocacy organization in Los Angeles, has had it with the white women who run the organization. She senses that the white supervisors are competitive with the women of color who report to them because the latter possess crucial skills and talents that the former lack—and how dare women of color be more skilled than white women? Says Varsha:

> They congratulate themselves on hiring women of color, and they always use P.C. language, but then their actions belie them. They are pissed off when there are women of color who have the nerve to think that we can get to where they are. When I interviewed for the job, they told me that if I were interested in a project, I would be given the chance to work on it. But instead, everything has been a major power struggle and I'm not given the chance to move ahead. My boss feels threatened by me because she's never practiced law. Plus, she's patronizing. When she introduces me to someone she says, 'Varsha has *much* better legal skills than I do'—as if I require an explanation that I am a worthy person to work with. You know, I could be making a hundred thousand dollars a year if I wanted to. I've taken a major pay cut to do the work I love, and also because it's work I believe

> in. Part of the contract in working for low pay in a social justice
> organization is that I get treated with respect. And when I don't
> get it, it drives me crazy. Because why am I making so little
> money if I'm going to be treated like shit?

Clearly there are women, just as there are men, who lack a fully developed sense of the ethical or proper way to treat other human beings. But women are not inherently competitive, they can feel comfortable with power, and they can treat subordinates with respect. Unfortunately, many working women believe they have to prove their worth and show everyone they are deserving of their position. When you're worried about being judged, it's exhausting and difficult to be generous with praise, kindness, and warmth.

Given the impossible standards that women in authority are expected to uphold, it is not difficult to feel schizophrenic. Having to maintain their femininity with male colleagues, they can be tart with female colleagues. Yet perversely, when women compete with each other in the work force, they effectively maintain the status quo—meaning their own status does not change. A woman may think that "keeping down" a female subordinate helps her own cause, but in reality she collaborates with a system that favors men anyway.

Psychologists Graham Staines, Carol Tavris, and Toby Epstein Jayaratne coined the term *Queen Bee* and analyzed her behavior in the January 1974 issue of *Psychology Today*, based on the results of a questionnaire that had drawn twenty thousand responses. Their groundbreaking research, though nearly thirty years old, largely continues to hold up. (The title *Queen Bee*, which referred to a token high-level woman, soon entered the vocabulary, although today people tend to use it to refer to any "difficult" female boss.) "The

Queen Bee who is successful in a male-dominated field feels little animosity toward the system that has permitted her to reach the top," they wrote, "and little animosity toward the men who praise her for being so unique. She identifies with the specific male colleagues who are her reference group, rather than with the diffuse concept of women as a class.... The Queen Bee thereby disassociates herself from the fundamental issues of equality for women, while reassuring her male colleagues that she is not of that militant ilk."[44] The irony, of course, is that the Queen Bee is perfectly positioned to help women because she has unusual access to power and male favor, yet she declines to support women as a group.

Golda Meir, prime minister of Israel from 1969 to 1974, has often been invoked as the quintessential Queen Bee. She was elected leader of Israel at the age of seventy, after decades of proving her worth. Though she recognized the existence of sex discrimination—she told *Ms.* magazine that "to be successful, a woman has to be much better at her job than a man"—she also decried, "I have never suffered for being a woman because of men. Certainly I've been lucky. Certainly, not all women have had the same experience; however, my personal experience doesn't prove those crazy women [feminists of the late 1960s and '70s] are right."[45] Likewise, Hollywood reporter Rachel Abramowitz has documented the individualist rhetoric that powerful women in the film industry have used to distance themselves from less powerful women in the business. Elaine May, the only woman to direct a studio movie between 1966 and 1979, told *Time* magazine, after directing the hit *The Heartbreak Kid*, "I don't know if it's important if you're a man, woman, or chair. I found no sexism in getting the first job." Sherry Lansing, head of Paramount Pictures, is famously chummy with the men working in Hollywood but standoffish with the women. She has vigorously denied ever facing discrimination or prejudice.[46]

Of course women are not obligated to mentor every single woman who requests guidance. Being a proper mentor is time-consuming. Lisa Hanock-Jasie, forty-six, a public relations executive in New York, is a proud mentor to a number of younger women. But there are limits. "There are women in the generation ahead of me and women in my generation who work very hard to make inroads for women," she says. "But I feel that many younger women today want instant gratification and therefore do not feel obligated to pay their dues. They don't realize it took a lot of us a long time to get where we are and that all of us had to pay ours." There is value in "paying your dues," and a younger woman can't expect to rise quickly within an organization just because she's smart and impatient. A more experienced colleague who recognizes that the younger woman needs more training before being promoted, then, can't just be written off as a Queen Bee. A more experienced colleague who is threatened by the younger woman and makes no attempt to create a hospitable environment for her, however, is a problem: She is a gatekeeper to the glass ceiling.

Among all the generations, female denial about gender bias—an underlying cause of Queen Bee behavior—persists. When Judy Rosener, author of *America's Competitive Secret*, questioned female entrepreneurs about their reasons for leaving the male-dominated corporations where they had previously worked, 80 percent said that they "had to work harder than males to be advanced at the same rate,"

50 percent observed that "women in my firm had less credibility than males," and another 51 percent thought that "men were uncomfortable working with women." A mere 7 percent believed that "men and women were treated the same." Yet only 11 percent of the same group of women reported leaving their former positions because of "sex discrimination" or "a hostile environment." (Almost half explained that they wanted to make more money, and another 47 percent said that they wanted "to have more control over my life.")[47]

Obviously, not all women who hold positions of authority are Queen Bees. However, many are automatically perceived to be. Women with less authority often presume that women with more authority will be hostile to them. Solomon Cytrynbaum, Ph.D., professor of psychiatry and behavioral sciences at Northwestern University who has studied gender and authority for more than twenty-five years, has witnessed the ways women react to female authority figures as opposed to male authority figures. Cytrynbaum studies what are called group relations conferences—three- to ten-day living laboratories intended to be microcosms of organizational life. Members of a conference take on different roles, delegate authority, and participate in a group—while simultaneously describing and discussing the events and processes as they occur. Participants apply what they have learned about authority and working together to their real-life organization back home.

Women in positions of leadership are nearly always devalued, Cytrynbaum has found, by both male and female participants. In contrast, men in positions of leadership are viewed as caring and engaged. In one all-female group conference, members refused to allow anyone to differentiate herself as a leader or to compete openly for a leadership role. "This was so extreme," Cytrynbaum reports, "that members at one point physically extruded the female director of the conference from one of the events. They also reported fantasies of violence being done by women to one another." In co-ed groups led by women, female leaders are perceived as "unfeminine," "cold," and "unfeeling" and are described as "plotting against" male members. In co-ed groups led by men, on the other hand, "women avoided active competition for leadership; rather, in a 'ladylike' manner, they competed for favorite status position in relation to the male [leader], reflecting a traditional framework."[48]

Cytrynbaum attributes men's and women's behavior to the power of negative stereotypes of women. Stereotypes influence not only the way that people regard members of the stereotyped group, they also affect the behavior of the targets of the stereotype. Being aware that one is stereotyped often leads a person to act in a way that confirms the stereotype. Cytrynbaum writes, "[M]en and women have become socialized to internalize a powerful stereotype of females as having legitimate authority only when performing nurturant tasks. When women attempt to exercise authority in areas deemed culturally inappropriate to the traditional stereotypic sex-role, and behave in nontraditional 'unfeminine' ways, they run into difficulty because subordinates experience disruptive feelings." A stereotype, then, can become a self-fulfilling prophecy. "The differences in members' reactions to male and female [leaders]," Cytrynbaum continues, "are due in part to the actual differences between female and male gender role behavior and gender-based styles of leadership."[49]

THE FEMALE ADVANTAGE

There is a school of thought that elevates the role of women in today's work force based on their supposed softer side. An entire literature of advice to women in business promotes the idea that women in authority are kinder and gentler than men in authority. "Female" qualities, these proponents tell us, are an asset in the world of business.

In bookstore business sections, there are books written specifically for women: *The 7 Greatest Truths About Highly Successful Women* by Marion Luna Brem; *Success On Our Terms: Tales of Extraordinary Business Women* by Virginia O'Brien; *Why Good Girls Don't Get Ahead...But Gutsy Girls Do: 9 Secrets Every Working Woman Must Know* by Kate White; and *Hardball for Women: Winning at the Game of Business* by Pat Heim. These books provide common-sensical advice about finding a mentor and promoting yourself without stepping on anyone's toes. But there are many other books with titles like *The Female Advantage: Women's Ways of Leadership* by Sally Helgesen; *America's Competitive Secret: Women Managers* by Judy B. Rosener; and *Why the Best Man for the Job Is a Woman: The Unique Female Qualities of Leadership* by Esther Wachs Book. According to these authors, women are uniquely beneficial to the workplace because they are more caring than men, which makes them superior managers and employees. Sally Helgesen, for instance, writes in her enormously popular book that the values of female executives

> include an attention to process instead of a focus on the bottom line; a willingness to look at how an action will affect other people instead of simply asking, "What's in it for me?"; a concern for the wider needs of the community; a disposition to draw on per-

sonal, private sphere experience when dealing in the public realm; an appreciation of diversity; an outsider's impatience with rituals and symbols of status that divide people who work together and so reinforce hierarchies.[50]

Helgesen followed four female executives for a few days and was impressed by their focus on relationships with others and their willingness to share information. She also observed that they were not very concerned about hierarchy and ranking and were likely to express concern for the welfare of their employees. She cites the examples of the executive who keeps fruit around her office "in order both to encourage healthy eating and to provide spontaneous opportunities for interaction," and the executive director of a large not-for-profit whose phone has a speaker attachment, though "she doesn't use that impersonal device unless she's sharing the conversation with someone in her office." Helgesen explains that women in leadership roles are particularly inclusive and caring because of their experiences as mothers. Motherhood, she writes, is "an excellent school for managers, demanding many of the same skills: organization, pacing, the balancing of conflicting claims, teaching, guiding, leading, monitoring, handling disturbances, imparting information."[51]

It should be obvious, however, that not all female managers are mothers; not all mothers are inclusive and caring (or good parents); and that fathers can be inclusive and caring too. Some women can be more "relational" than some men, but the reverse is also true. Perhaps the four executives who allowed Helgesen to shadow them are, as described, dream bosses who truly care about and want to advance the people who work for them. We just do not have evidence that women as a group are more humane in the workplace than men. *The Female Advantage* is designed to make women feel good about themselves and to convince male executives that women should be admitted to the top echelons of business. These are admirable goals, but in trying to achieve them Helgesen reinforces the stereotype of women as super-nice people who cannot (and should not) be tough, aggressive, or ambitious. To my mind, as long as one is respectful of others, there is nothing wrong with being tough, aggressive, or ambitious.

Judy B. Rosener's book *America's Competitive Secret* similarly makes the case that organizations should turn over their management to women because women make better managers than men. Rosener's much-discussed article, "Ways Women Lead," published in the *Harvard Business Review* in 1990, formed the basis of this oft-cited book.[52] *Interactive* is the word she uses to describe women's "leadership style." Men use a "command-and-control" model in which decisions are made from the top down and there are clear lines of authority. The "interactive" model, by contrast, favored by women, emphasizes the sharing of power and information and the building of consensus. Although Rosener claims that neither style is "better or worse than the other," she also writes that the "interactive" model is "increasingly recognized as critical to fast-changing, service-oriented, entrepreneurial, international organizations—the types of organizations best equipped to compete in the new global environment." As examples of women who share power, Rosener refers to Susan J. Inseley, the highest-ranking woman in the U.S. auto manufacturing industry in 1992, who told Rosener that she spent a lot of time on the Honda engine plant factory floor "listening hard to the real experts," as she referred to the company's workers and suppliers. Rosener also describes Charlotte Beers, a top executive at the advertising agency Ogilvy & Mathers Worldwide, who likes to compliment lower-level staff members to clients.[53]

Like Helgesen, Rosener attributes women's "interactive" skills to their experiences as mothers:

> Over time, women develop a particular set of skills and values shaped by their life experiences. For example, they are comfortable with ambiguity because their lives are full of uncertainty. They are good at juggling and completing many tasks simultaneously because that is the story of their daily existence. It isn't strange to see a woman feeding a baby, watching the news on TV, listening to her husband, and thinking about how to solve a problem at work, all at the same time. Not so with men, who more often than not have the luxury of focusing on one or two things at a time. It is not strange for women to change plans and moods as often as sheets, because household chores and family responsibilities are not easily scheduled and women rarely have others to take care of their schedules for them.... Consequently, they develop negotiating skills that are often different from those of men.[54]

Rosener's argument does not convince me because she makes many unwarranted assumptions. Like Helgesen, she assumes that all women are mothers, and that all mothers have young children. She assumes that mothers are necessarily busier and juggle more tasks than non-mothers do. She assumes that all mothers are good at what they do. She assumes that because a mother's home life is filled with constant interruptions, she will tolerate or even welcome constant interruptions at work. (To the contrary, I find that because my life at home with my children is so chaotic, I crave consistency when I work away from home and have little tolerance for interruptions and juggling multiple tasks.) Rosener's comparison of women with men—that is, mothers with fathers—is insulting to fathers: Even though most mothers take on a far greater share of the burden of domestic responsibilities, fathers today are not exactly sitting in lounge chairs eating bonbons. Middle-class fathers, like mothers, race around the playground or baseball field with their children, a briefcase or laptop or cell phone brought along for the sake of a few stolen minutes of work, and then make a pit stop at the supermarket on the way home to pick up groceries for dinner. Working-class fathers are even more likely to have a stressful, demanding schedule, and possibly are holding down more than one job.

The myth that women are apt to disavow hierarchy in favor of inclusive power-sharing is so entrenched that it was stated as fact in a recent *New York Times* news article about women in the legal profession. Women make up approximately half of all law school students (up from 10 percent in 1970 and 4 percent in 1960); according to the front page of the *Times*, this "trend will affect the way schools operate—perhaps making classes more teamlike and less adversarial, for instance—and change somewhat the way law firms operate."[55] Social psychologist Carol Tavris offers a different viewpoint. "When I was growing up, I heard [some feminists say,] 'We want women in law because they'll humanize the law. The law will become warm and compassionate.' That's bull. What happened was, [women who entered the profession] became lawyers. So you get women behaving like lawyers, not behaving like women. It's the environment, the job, that determines [a person's behavior], not her physiology." As anyone who either works in the legal profession or knows someone who does knows, the increasing number of women entering the law has not translated into a warmer work atmosphere, nor has it affected the glass ceiling. In New York, for example, women represent more than 41 percent of the associates at law firms, but fewer than 14 percent of the partners are women. Of 655 federal district court judges, only 136 are women. Women make up only about 20 percent of full law school professors.[56]

There is a problem with the mind-set that women possess unique traits that are valuable in the work force. This is not to dispute that women may have a different style of management, but to dispute the ways in which the mind-set can be used against women. Hiring and promoting a few women then takes the place of dismantling a work environment that privileges men.

SOFT AS SILK

Just as some women go out of their way to show how "tough" they can be, others want everyone to know how nice and accommodating they are. Afraid of coming across as masculine, they overcompensate by being ultra-feminine. Most people, in the spirit of Helgesen and Rosener, think that women are supposed to be agreeable and cooperative—isn't that what it means to be a woman?—and many of us find it difficult to violate that expectation.

The most popular girl in my high school class was blond, slender, and wealthy. I think her queenly social ranking came not only from the dumb luck of her genes and inheritance but from the behavior that she cultivated: niceness. She was one of those all-around-nice types who never had a bad word to say about anyone; she never rocked the boat by doing anything outlandish or controversial. She was a leader of centrism, a conformist who inspired further conformity within the satellite group of girls and boys who looked up to her.

Niceness, of course, can serve a person well. People like to be near you. You don't alienate people because you rarely contradict them. You are eternally bouncy and chipper and content and respectful. But in being nice, you have to walk a very fine line. Niceness can work for you or against you, and unless you are loaded with charisma, consistent niceness can spell disaster. For to be truly nice, you must veil what you really think and feel. Since being nice is really about seeking the approval of others, you slide into the habit of being deferential. You give in on things rather than put up a fight. Niceness may sound nice, but it actually can create serious consequences.

I vividly remember the interview for my first job out of college, as an author's assistant. I felt relaxed because I'd already received another job offer, so the outcome of this interview wouldn't make or break me. And everything was going well: The author was talking about "when" I would be working for her, not "if." Then my potential boss told me the salary. It was a very low figure—an amount hard to live on in New York City—and she paused to gauge my reaction. I would love to tell you that I made a pointed comment and asked for more. Instead, I said, "That's very generous. Thank you." The author smiled and asked when I could start. A few weeks into the job, I stumbled upon a file containing the salary of my predecessor. She had earned $10,000 more.

I was so eager to please, to be cooperative and respectful. At one level, my "niceness" worked: I got the job. But on another, it didn't: I sacrificed my ability to earn more—and in doing so, I implicitly told my boss that I couldn't or wouldn't stand up for myself. Was it a coincidence that she piled on the work to such an extent that I was regularly in the office until midnight?

Another woman tells a similar story of nice negotiating gone awry, but from the other side—as the employer. Shari, a thirty-two-year-old New Yorker, was looking to hire a nanny for ten hours a week to care for her newborn daughter. She found the perfect woman. But, as with me, there was a disjunction between what Shari wanted to say and what she did say. She didn't know quite how to set the terms she wanted because the cloak of authority felt strange and uncomfortable. So she ended up telling her interviewee that she needed her for twenty hours rather than ten. "I felt guilty asking for such a small amount of time from her," she explains. "Already I am regretting the arrangement that I've made with her. It was entirely because I was trying to be nice." By granting a concession before negotiations had even begun, Shari must part with extra money and deal with an employee she can't help but resent.

Shari and I, like most women, learned the hard way that being "nice" has a habit of sliding into being deferential. Being nice feels piously good in the short term, but it can create long-term liabilities. Many women fall into a familiar pattern of self-sacrifice: We say "I'm sorry" when we have nothing to be sorry about; we give in to our kids' demands against our better judgment; we buy something we don't really need or want because it's easier to say yes than no to a friendly salesperson; we do favors for others at our own expense; we give credit to someone else even when we are the one who deserves recognition; we ask our assistant, "Could you please do this?" or "If it's not a problem, could you do this?" instead of saying, "Please do this"; we feel hesitant to ask our partners for sexual pleasure. In essence, we allow others to take advantage of us. And many of us feel compelled to do it again and again. After all, as we know, people don't like women who aren't nice.

In 1969, psychologist Matina Horner reported on anxiety about success that she called "motive to avoid success" or "fear of success" among smart, high-achieving college women. She proposed that girls are raised to regard ambition as unfeminine and, as a result, become anxious at the prospect of attaining achievement. To measure the phenomenon, she had 178 University of Michigan undergraduates, male and female, complete a story that began, "After first-term finals, Anne (John) finds herself (himself) at the top of her (his) medical school class." Females wrote about Anne while the males wrote about John.

Nearly all of the males wrote stories expressing happiness and satisfaction over John's achievement. ("John is a conscientious young man who has worked hard. He is pleased with himself. John has always wanted to go into medicine and is very dedicated.... John continues working hard and eventually graduates at the top of his class.") By contrast, 65 percent of the females wrote bizarre stories with negative imagery. ("Anne starts proclaiming her surprise and joy. Her fellow classmates are so disgusted with her behavior that they jump on her in a body and beat her. She is maimed for life.") Another story began, "Anne is sitting in a chair with a smile on her face." Females low in "fear of success" anxiety wrote continuations like, "Anne is happy—she's happy with the world because it is so beautiful. It's snowing and nice outside—she's happy to be alive and this gives her a good, warm feeling. Well, Anne did well on one of her tests." Females filled with anxiety about success wrote entries like this: "She is sitting in a chair smiling smugly because she has just achieved great satisfaction from the fact that she hurt somebody's feelings." Horner explained that excellence in women was associated with the loss of femininity, which meant social rejection and personal destruction—that is, no man would ever want to marry a high-achieving woman. It's not that so many women want to fail, Horner stressed, but simply that they recognize the high price of success.

Horner's results attracted wide media attention and her research was soon under attack. Critics said that Anne's success was in a "gender-inappropriate" field, medicine, and that the females might not have reacted so bizarrely had her success come from something more "appropriate" (like teaching). They pointed out that women were responding to the success of another woman, not themselves, in writing the stories, and perhaps they would not have felt so anxious about their own success. Finally, they noted that if men had written about Anne, perhaps they, too, would have expressed hostile feelings.[57]

The critics raised valid points. Had the tests been designed differently, no doubt the results would have been quite different. Perhaps women truly are more anxious about the prospect of competing with other women than about achieving success themselves. Nevertheless, Horner's basic thesis does ring true. A female at the top of her medical school class today is commonplace, while in 1969 it was unusual; but even today, success in a field traditionally male-dominated continues to raise issues for women about their suitability for the job and about their ability to take on the job's responsibilities while simultaneously fulfilling the requirements of the feminine role (raising children). Today women tend to face the career/motherhood disjuncture later than women in the 1960s did, so it is probable that today's female undergrads (ages eighteen to twenty-two) face zero or little "fear of success." But high-achieving women in their late twenties and thirties certainly do. I don't need more research reported in a peer-reviewed professional journal to confirm this. My peers and I live it.

In this context, being too-nice is a defense mechanism—a way to have your cake and eat it too. You can be ambitious, but hide your ambition beneath a veneer of accommodation and deference. It is a way of reassuring yourself that even if you are at the top of your medical school class, you are still feminine, and no one can take that away from you.

Psychoanalyst Joan Riviere, who worked closely with Melanie Klein in the 1930s and '40s, wrote a fascinating article in 1929 in the *International Journal of Psycho-Analysis* about this very conundrum. One of Riviere's patients was a wife and mother who was also engaged in professional work. In the course of her work, she often had to speak publicly. As Riviere reports it, the woman became severely anxious after each speaking event and would compulsively flirt with the men present, who were father figures. She was seeking reassurance that her performance was good, and more important, that she was still sexually attractive. Riviere wrote that the compulsion to flirt was, in a way, a reversal of her intellectual performance; it was the feminine erasing of her masculine achievement.

> Womanliness therefore could be assumed and worn as a mask, both to hide the possession of masculinity and to avert the reprisals expected if she was found to possess it—much as a thief will turn out his pockets and ask to be searched to prove that he has not the stolen goods. The reader may now ask how I define womanliness or where I draw the line between genuine womanliness and the "masquerade." My suggestion is not, however, that there is any such difference; whether radical or superficial, they are the same thing.[58]

Femininity, then, "is a mask which can be worn or removed," in the words of film theorist Mary Ann Doane.[59] "Normal" femininity is a charade; in the case of Riviere's patient, that charade is pathological. Riviere makes clear that adopting exaggerated, stereotypical feminine behavior is a method of distancing oneself from supposed masculinity. Being "nice" and deferential and sweet in circumstances when such behavior is counterproductive is a common strategy used by many women who, consciously or not, are anxious to please and not to be regarded as masculine.

Indeed, a program in California, Bully Broads, encourages women in leadership positions to soften their style and behave more like, well, the way women are "supposed" to. Bully Broads is targeted to take-charge executive women who have been criticized by their colleagues for being too "oppositional" (that is, opinionated, brash, straightforward—qualities that people tend to admire in male executives). Blue-chip companies such as Sun Microsystems and

Hewlett-Packard pay Jean Hollands, the founder and director of the program, about $15,000 to advise their female troublemakers on how to "smile, soften their voices, alter their walks, and employ 'vulnerability actions,' including self-deprecation and stammering." One very accomplished woman enrolled in Bully Broads praised the program to *Elle* magazine because it has taught her "the strategic value of self-abnegation."[60] Self-abnegation is apparently popular among many high-level women. A survey of 240 executives at big companies by The Leader's Edge, a management training company, found that a smaller percentage of women (69 percent) than men (82 percent) in top positions were comfortable challenging other people's ideas. Nearly all of the senior executive women (95 percent) were concerned about people's perceptions of them, while only 68 percent of their male counterparts felt the same way.[61]

Being nice often backfires. Rose Davis Green, an obstetrician-gynecologist, relates that she prefers to remain silent rather than challenge members of the health care team she supervises when their work is substandard. "I tolerate a certain amount of dissatisfaction with the way things are done before I confront anyone about it," she admits. "I'm more likely to just go and correct the problem myself and stew about it. And that has served me badly because by the time I do have to address it, it's already gotten farther out of hand. Or things build up inside me and I have all these pent-up feelings, so I end up letting loose and overreacting to a small problem."

Many women, like Green, are nice by default. We hold back our true feelings rather than assert what's on our minds. But some women use niceness in a manipulative manner. Wendy Schneider, a thirty-two-year-old television producer in San Francisco, confides that she lives the adage "You get more out of honey than out of vine-gar." At the TV studio, an incredibly pressured environment, she always acts sweet to the production crew. As she explains, "My expectation is that I will get more out of people if I've offered up some congeniality or something to make them feel good." In her personal life, too, she dotes on others. She drives people to the air-port—friends, acquaintances, even neighbors—because, she explains sheepishly, she wants them to like and appreciate her and, if she's lucky, do favors for her when her time comes.

Schneider's niceness is a seductive *trompe l'oeil*. It draws people to believe she really cares about them. Schneider uses niceness as a strategy, like staying late at the office not because one is overworked but to show everyone how hardworking she is, which enables her to get ahead. It's a strategy that is also inefficient. Says Schneider, "Being nice slows me down and creates a lot of extra baggage. I have to worry about not hurting people's feelings. I'm fearful of calling people on things because then they won't like me anymore and won't perform for me." Inevitably, Schneider's niceness backfires. After all, she is entering others into a contract they don't even know they're entering. So when they don't respond the way she thinks they should, she becomes resentful and ultimately hostile. In her personal life, for instance, she often lets phone messages pile up without returning the calls from her "friends" because she can't handle the responsibility of friendship.

Intimacy can also be used manipulatively. Naomi relates that when she was employed as a paralegal for a big law firm, she worked with another female paralegal who was four months senior to her but who felt entitled to boss her around. Working late one night, the colleague came out to her as a lesbian. First the colleague quizzed her on her views about homosexuality and led her into a conversation about the issue. Then she said that she had a "secret" and made Naomi promise not to tell anyone. Naomi found the confession manipulative. "It was her way of saying, 'How could you be mad at me? I've opened up to you.'"

CAUTION: WOMEN AT WORK

Some women who find it difficult to toughen up may be more likely than men to cry at work. Crying "is one surefire way to make others uncomfortable in the workplace," warns Catalyst president Sheila Wellington. "Keep your cool; emotionalism makes you look unreliable and unsteady and reinforces the stereotypes about women that men already hold."[62] Gail Evans, executive vice-president of CNN, observes that when former U.S. senator from North Carolina Lauch Faircloth lost his reelection bid, he cried at his press conference—and the media ate it up, calling it "a powerful display of emotion." But when "former congresswoman and then-presidential candidate Pat Schroeder cried on television, men smirked. Just like a woman, they said."[63]

Gloria Steinem has admitted that she cries when she gets angry. "Not only do I find this humiliating, but it also lessens my ability to explain what I'm angry about, leading to more anger and an even bigger lump in my throat."[64] When we need to, of course, we can inhibit the impulse to cry; but Steinem worries that, ironically, *not* crying makes us enslaved to the stereotype that women do often cry—that is, being aware of, and embarrassed by, the stereotype makes us force ourselves to hold crying in even when we really need to release stress and anger. We are damned if we do, damned if we don't. Yes, it is hard to keep control when anger bubbles up. And at home, in one's private life, it's usually fine to release tears. But at work, keeping control is wiser. As Evans points out, when a powerful man cries, people think he must have an excellent reason. But "women are expected to cry. And when we do, men think it's because we're giving in to a natural instinct or worse, they think we're using tears as a game prop, a tool to manipulate them into feeling guilt."[65]

Indeed, while tears at work are often genuine, they can also be manipulative. Jennifer, a financial planner, recalls an incident several years ago that occurred when she was supremely busy. Her assistant was out to lunch and her phone was ringing constantly. A colleague, who was working on a project that didn't need to be completed for several days, came to her while she was on the phone and said, "Jennifer, I need you to help me with this." Jennifer whispered, "Come back later, okay?" But the colleague continued standing in front of her and said, "It's never going to get done. Can't you just spend a minute with me?" Jennifer became furious. She put her client on hold and harshly told her colleague, "Don't you ever interrupt me like that again. I told you that you can come back later, and you can." The colleague turned and walked away. Jennifer returned to her caller and forgot about the exchange.

The next morning, Jennifer went to the colleague and said, "Okay, do you want to work on that project now?" According to Jennifer, the colleague's eyes "watered up. She said that she was very hurt by the way I had acted the day before and that sometimes I can be very mean. The tears were coming down by this point. I apologized, because I really had never wanted to hurt her feelings, and explained that she had to be respectful of my time. I think that she intended to make me feel bad."

Varsha and some of her fellow colleagues, all women of color, told the white women they worked with they were being treated inequitably because of their race. How did the white women react? They started crying. Varsha had no patience. "When you cry," she says, "it makes you the victim, so you're the one who now needs to be taken care of. It completely shifts the dynamic. This is one way that women exert control over each other: through guilt." And an important conversation about racism never took place.

Women at work often gossip about each other; often the gossip centers on alleged sexual behavior. One book editor speaks about a senior colleague whom everyone believed was promoted because she was sleeping with the boss. It turned out that he *wanted* to sleep with her, and had sexually harassed her, but they had never actually had a sexual liaison. "And it wasn't the guys who spread the rumor," the editor tells me. "It was the girls." One reason sexual gossip spreads so quickly is that a woman in a position of authority is suspect. That is, it seems inconceivable that she earned her power legitimately.

Not uncommonly, however, women do flirt with the men they work with. Many women admit to using sexual allure to distinguish themselves from their colleagues in the eyes of a male supervisor. "In a lot of workplaces," one lesbian magazine editor says candidly, "your sexual energy plays a part in your interactions with your co-workers. It's like we're competing for the flirtatious attention of our boss, even though none of us wants to date our boss or have sexual relations with him at all. I mean, God help us. But I wonder if [a colleague I feel competitive with] is smarter than me, more talented than me, is she a better editor, is she a better worker—and is she also cuter than me? Do men find her more attractive? Certainly I do think about whether men find me attractive. Just because I'm not trying to get a boyfriend doesn't mean that I'm immune to the attentions of men or the validation of men."

"I will use whatever I have to use, and at times it is the physical nature of being a woman," declares a thirty-four-year-old publicity director who works with women but reports to a man. "If I can look attractive while looking professional, I will do that, so that I have something extra. I have this additional thing that I can use if I want to." Diana, a freelance writer and researcher, tells me about a meeting she had recently with several men to go over a contract for work with a new company. She was the only woman present. "I wore trousers and a blue cashmere sweater and my lavender pashmina scarf," she reports. "My hair was down. I looked like a woman, but I didn't play it up. There was no cooing or smiling or any of that. So even if they initially thought I was attractive, I don't think they were thinking about that the whole time." Why did she choose to wear a pretty sweater instead of a blazer? "Because I'm feminine and I like to look attractive and that's how I feel best when I'm giving a presentation. I don't want to hide that I'm a woman."

I don't want to hide that I'm a woman. We want to do our best work, we want to go as far as our ambition and talent will take us, but we want to remind ourselves and the people we work with that no matter how far we go, we are still women. As we have seen, this can be a double-edged sword, since whether we behave in a manner associated with men or in a manner associated with women, we still have to prove our worth.

It's no wonder that some women are fed up and opt out of the whole game. Diana recalls that when she was a junior in college, she was nominated to be editor-in-chief of the literary magazine, even though she hadn't sought the position and frankly didn't care much about it. There was a classmate who had pined for the editorship since freshman year and who "was busting up like Sylvia Plath in the bell jar." So Diana told her that she could be co-editor and relinquished half her job to her. "I only did it because I felt bad for her. Well, it turned out to be a terrible decision. I realized belatedly that I actually *wanted* to be the leader and so I became resentful of her. It wasn't to my benefit. Maybe I felt uncomfortable with my success because I got it so easily and I wondered if I really deserved it."

In a more troubling incident of running away from competition, a thirty-two-year-old graduate student in literature, Amy, tells about an adviser who is also a member of her dissertation committee, and who therefore has the power to grant or deny Amy the Ph.D. she has been working toward for seven years. Amy had shown her adviser a paper she was interested in getting published in order to elicit her advice: was it indeed worthy of publication? The adviser had a curious reaction. She admitted to Amy she felt competitive with her, because they were pursuing similar work. Despite being aware of her feelings, she did not try to overcome them. Instead, the adviser accused Amy of stealing ideas she had presented in a class in which Amy had participated and of not giving her proper credit for her research. She told Amy that the paper was not ready for publication in any event.

Amy admits that of course she was influenced by the class she took with the adviser, but she had already done much of the work for the paper beforehand. So she solicited advice from another professor—a man who is a competitor of the adviser. He was far more encouraging. Nevertheless, Amy decided not to pursue publication because she did not want to offend her adviser. "This adviser is very important to me and I don't want to ruin our relationship," she explains.

I ask Amy why she thinks her adviser is so overprotective of her work. "She is at the top of her field. She is tenured, very smart, extremely ambitious, and very well known. But still she doesn't get the same level of recognition that the male professors get. She reacts to what she feels is a disrespect of her own work. So I can understand her. I absolutely know where her behavior is coming from. It's a shame that her reaction is directed against me. If I were a male student, who knows? A male student might not even ask her about the paper, and might be off on his own, and she wouldn't even have a chance to say anything."

Business consultant Carolyn Duff once asked a group of women attending a conference on women and leadership how many of them had ever refused, or hesitated to pursue, a promotion that would have placed them above the women they worked with. At least half raised their hands. "It just wouldn't feel right," they said. "I just didn't think I could handle it." Those who withdrew from competition admitted that they ended up resenting their co-workers. Several women told

Duff that when they wanted to move ahead, they switched companies rather than face the prospect of becoming a boss over former colleagues.[66]

I don't want to hide that I'm a woman. We are never going to get beyond the impasse we face until we define what it means to be "a woman" at work. To me, it means being whatever the circumstances require without losing our self-respect or the respect of others. If we develop confidence in our abilities, we will treat people with the respect they deserve, and receive the respect we deserve.

CHAPTER FIVE
MOTHERHOOD

An infant creates an easy bond between women, particularly mothers. Carrying a newborn infant in a sling or pushing him or her in a stroller is an instant conversation starter. Women from different cultures and social classes, as well as women from the same background, want to know: How old is your baby? Boy or girl? What's the name? What was the birth weight? How long was your labor? People are fascinated by newborns. Women, thinking they too might one day give birth, or remembering their birthing experiences, feel compelled to make a connection with a new mother.

On the other hand, for every friendly inquiry, there is a competitive one. Are you breast-feeding? Are you *still* breast-feeding? Are you going back to work soon? Isn't it time you went back to work? Motherhood does not automatically unify women. Other mothers look at a new mother and compare her parenting skills with their own.

There is an unspoken competition over who is a "better" mother. Who is more willing to efface her own desires and needs for the sake of her child? Whose parenting style is going to produce the smarter child? Who is, in sum, most qualified for this job? Fathers benefit from this competition. With mothers under constant scrutiny, fathers, by and large, escape judgment of any kind. After the birth of a child, most fathers continue lives not altogether different from their childless days. To be sure, most—if not all—fathers give up evening or weekend leisure time and/or remain in jobs they may be dissatisfied with for the sake of health insurance. But the lives of mothers change completely. They assume most of the responsibility and alone tend to be defined by their parental skills. (Thus, baby products are often touted as "mother-approved," as if fathers did not buy and use them too. A fabric cleaner for spit-up is named Mother's Little Miracle. Mylicon Drops for infant gas "are so safe and effective, mothers have made them #1 for 30 years.")

All mothers, and especially first-time mothers and mothers of young children, experience mother-against-mother competition. And it's not only mothers who judge mothers "good" or "bad": these pronouncements are made every day in the news and in popular culture. Over the last two decades, the common media-generated image of the "bad" mother has been an overweight, unmarried woman of color, living on welfare with six children from as many fathers. This stereotype has served to make middle-class mothers of all races feel smug. Today there is a new, contrasting stereotype—the emaciated white Park Avenue wife, affluent and with no job (just "charity work"), with one child but no time for her—that serves the same function. She is characterized in the best-selling book *The Nanny Diaries*, a satiric novel about wealthy Manhattan mothers and the nannies who care for—and raise—their children. The novel's Mrs. X is unambiguously a "bad" mother whose son is, in her eyes, a failed status symbol since he wasn't accepted into the prestigious private-school kindergarten of her choice. She does not play with him, let him touch her (lest his grimy four-year-old hands soil her minks and cashmeres), or console him during illness or nightmare. Mrs. X leaves all those crucial aspects of parenting (and more) to the "help"—the nanny. While the welfare-mother stereotype has serious and disturbing policy implications, resulting in mandated workfare for millions, the Park Avenue mother stereotype is just a ridiculous laughingstock. Thus, she actually represents progress. After all, no politician is going to force her (a potential campaign contributor) to get a job or surrender her Bergdorf's charge card.

The overwhelming commercial success of *The Nanny Diaries* is evidence of mothers' competitiveness. Of course, the novel owes much of its popularity to the voyeuristic thrill of seeing how the other half lives—how affluent stay-at-home mothers with full-time nannies and housekeepers sleep in pressed sheets, casually cast off $400 shoes they've lost interest in, maintain studio apartments in the same building as their three-bedrooms so they can spend time alone and away from their children, and force their children to have meals of kale and soy milk instead of peanut-butter-and-jelly sandwiches. But mothers like me have devoured it mostly because it validates our own mothering. The mothers in the novel are so negligent and self-centered that we real-life mothers know, without a sliver of doubt, we shine in comparison. Sleep-deprived, anxious, and unsure about the validity of every contemporary parenting concept from "nipple confusion" to "timeout," we need all the solace we can get. As long as mothers alone are held responsible for raising well-adjusted children, we will feel insecure and competitive—and stereotypes of deficient mothers will continue to delight us, and divide us.

THE ISOLATION OF NEW MOTHERS

Competition among mothers leads to destructive silence about the realities of childbirth and parenthood. When one feels competitive, she often conceals information in the belief that knowing more than everyone else makes her more powerful. Yet the opposite is true: Sharing information can empower everyone at no one's expense.

The silence surrounding childbirth and parenthood is all the more disturbing because more than at any other time in history, first-time mothers are left on their own. If the father is available, he is expected to return to work soon after the birth. Many women live far away from their own mothers. Many women are giving birth at older ages, making it likely that their own mothers are in ill health or deceased. Or, their mothers live nearby and are in good health, but they're busy with their careers or tending to their own ailing parents. Supportive communities of women have largely eroded, since many are active in the labor force without the time or means to get together for coffee and communication. In the past, when a woman gave birth, she knew she could rely on the expertise and assistance of a bevy of female relatives and friends who would demonstrate breast-feeding techniques, how to bathe a newborn, how to care for the umbilical stump. These women would bring over home-cooked meals, offer to clean the house, and watch the baby for a few hours so that the new mother could go out to get her hair cut or take a much-needed nap. Today, a new mother needs to pay a stranger—a nurse or a doula—for her expertise. If she can't afford the help, and her female friends and relatives are too busy, she's out of luck.

Of course, even if our mothers are unavailable or we lack sisters or aunts, most of us have at least one or two peers who have given birth and who can and should help us prepare by telling us about baby care and, more importantly, how having a baby changes us. But mothers are often quite secretive in these matters with mothers-to-be. "When I gave birth," says novelist Christina Baker Kline, "I felt as I had been granted entrance into a private 'Mothers Only' club of people just like me—and, at the same time, that I had never been more alone in my life."[1] Experienced mothers sugarcoat the truth, emphasizing the wonderful aspects of parenthood and glossing over the hellish ones.

For instance, everyone knows that labor and delivery are excruciatingly painful, but few mothers warn mothers-to-be of the raw physical pain following delivery (caused by a Caesarian section, a perineal tear, or an episiotomy, an incision made in the perineum to widen the birth outlet). Everyone knows that newborns need to be fed around the clock, but few mothers warn pregnant women of the extent to which infants remain awake in the middle of the night and how extremely sleep-deprived their mothers are. For many new mothers, the first ten to twelve weeks postpartum are horrible: they can barely walk or sit comfortably and cannot piece together a coherent thought, let alone feel connected or "bonded" to their child. But most have no idea just how bad it is until they experience it firsthand.

It is estimated that 15 to 20 percent of mothers fall into a serious depression—known clinically as "postpartum depression" (PPD)—within a year of childbirth. Few new mothers who become depressed are willing to speak openly about this experience either. The condition typically appears soon after delivery; it can last months, even years. Women in the first year of motherhood are five times more likely to become mentally ill than at any other time during their life, calculates Susan Maushart, a sociologist and author of *The Mask of Motherhood*; they are sixteen times more likely to develop a serious psychotic illness. "We can deduce," she says, "that it is perfectly normal to experience some degree of 'baby shock'—to feel anxious, depressed, isolated, and overwhelmed—in the early stages of mothering." The very diagnosis of PPD "has proven to be a two-edged sword for women" because it pathologizes the normal range of new-mother experiences and drives "the normal abnormalcy of early motherhood even farther underground."[2] Indeed, in the wake of Andrea Yates's murder of her five children in 2001, many people now associate PPD with brutal murderous tendencies.

Why would an experienced mother remain silent about these realities with a mother-to-be? Why would she perpetuate a gap in knowledge that can so easily be closed? One reason is that she doesn't want to spoil the experience of giving birth for those who haven't yet undergone it. Why take the chance that the messenger will be resented for the message? I also suspect that the experienced mother found taking care of a newborn much harder than she had ever dreamed, and she worries (even years later) that there had been something wrong with her—that she had lacked a certain inborn skill to decipher if her baby had cried because he was hungry, tired, cold, hot, overstimulated, wanted to be held, had a dirty diaper, or just needed to cry for no particular reason at all. Better to keep silent than suggest, as she fears, that she had botched up her child's first few months. If she suffered from depression, she no doubt prefers to keep that her secret, as most people who become depressed worry about the stigma surrounding this condition.

But I believe there is another reason for an experienced mother to dwell only on the "miraculous" and "incredible" facets of birth with inexperienced peers. She is nervous about betraying that she felt and feels ambivalent about parenthood. Ambivalence is a dirty secret among mothers. The "good" mother unconditionally, unequivocally adores her maternal role. If she even hints at the downside, she fears, she will be denigrated for being a "bad" mother, an "abnormal" woman. "To confess to being in conflict about mothering," says Shari Thurer, author of *The Myths of Motherhood*, "is tantamount to being a bad person."[3] Of course, any mother prefers to think of herself as "good" rather than "bad," but the concept of "good" makes sense only when others are "bad." So in order to secure her identity as a "good" mother, she buries her ambivalences and projects to other mothers or mothers-to-be how amazing and gratifying parenthood is. Besides, if she shares her ambivalences with mothers-to-be, the latter may be better equipped than she was to handle this huge transition.

When my second child was nine weeks old, I was introduced to a woman who also had a newborn—as well as a two-year-old and a four-year-old. I myself had only another two-year-old to contend with and couldn't imagine parenting a third young child as well. This mother looked wonderful—well-rested face, makeup, coordinated outfit. I, on the other hand, sported bags beneath my eyes and the only skirt I could squeeze into (and it showed). "Wow, you look so great," I marveled, adding, "I still feel like such a basket case." I received a cool response: "When you have three children, you *can't* be a basket case." I was left thinking that there was something wrong with me, that I was deficient. I could barely handle two, and this woman handled three—with aplomb. Later I realized that this mother was simply hiding her own travails.

Competition over who is a "better" mother leads first-time mothers to make poor decisions at the expense of their own physical and mental health and at the expense of the well-being of their babies. It makes them doubt everything they do. I was terrified of dropping my first baby, of swaddling him too tightly or not tightly enough, of letting anyone who hadn't thoroughly washed her hands get within five feet of him. Why didn't I leap up immediately to hold him the very second he began crying—did I lack some mommy gene or hormone? I worried I was using too much baby talk, that his toys weren't educational enough, that I capitulated too quickly in giving him his favorite foods rather than the vegetables he refused to eat. Did he really need to wear shoes when he wasn't walking yet? Come to think of it, why *wasn't* he walking yet? All new parents harbor similar anxieties, but when you believe that you're on your own, these anxieties can become magnified to the point of obsession. And the only benchmark you have of what "normal" parenting is and what a "normal" child does is from other parents and their children.

If a mother feels insecure about her parenting, and sees another mother doing things differently, it would be reasonable to want to learn from the second mother. But that is not what happens. Instead, feelings of insecurity are transformed into a sense of self-righteousness. We go on the defensive: Our way becomes the right way. Other mothers are quick to tell you *their* way is the right way. Mothers feel defensive because the deck is stacked against us. We bear the brunt of parenting anxieties individually. No matter how involved a father is, it is the mother who is judged by her child's behavior and accomplishments. If the child is well behaved and precocious, the mother takes the credit. If he bites and scratches other children and knows only ten words while they know thirty, the mother is to blame. Thus, despite the common ground that two new mothers share, it can be difficult for them to feel comfortable with each other.

A clinician at a department of psychiatry at a prestigious school of medicine told me about her involvement in both individual and group treatment for women suffering from PPD. She had presumed that because women with PPD feel isolated and fearful, they would be comforted by the presence of other women experiencing the same symptoms, and that group treatment would be more efficacious than individual therapy. Surprisingly, the opposite was true. Those who participated in individual therapy fared better. She explains: "Much of the group seemed to become derailed in terms of value judgments about life choices: who was staying at home, who was working, what those choices said about them. [The women in group therapy felt that] if 'I'm a working mom and you're a stay-at-home mom, we really have nothing in common. It doesn't matter that we're both depressed, it doesn't matter that our marital relationships are very similar, it doesn't matter that we might be struggling with the exact same kinds of adjustments to a new child.'" The women in the group therapy did not get better. Every woman in individual therapy, meanwhile, recovered from her depression.

Although the organizers of the group went out of their way to create a supportive and loving environment—including a chance for mothers and babies to interact together—"the mothers struggled with feelings of fantasies of criticism. They felt they were being looked at and judged, and they had tremendous anxieties. [They felt] that 'if my baby is tired and not smiling, and the other babies are smiling, are you going to think this is because I'm a bad mom?'" When a mother voiced her concern about being judged in front of the group, the other mothers did not try to console her. They never said, for example, "That's funny, because I noticed how *good* you are with Joshua" or "I'd like to do with Amy what I saw you do with Nicholas." According to the clinician, "The nonclinical word [to describe their behavior] is cold."

Ironically, the plethora of books published each year trumpeting expert advice about taking care of babies, getting them to sleep through the night, and raising well-behaved, independent children can cause more confusion than reassurance. There are so many books with so many different parenting philosophies that even if you're getting six straight hours of sleep, you are sure to get a headache flipping through these works.

Parenting guides began to proliferate in the late 1800s and early 1900s, when Americans found a new faith in the power of science. Doctors and other child care authorities (always male) were presumed to know better than parents how to raise children, and parents—especially mothers—deferred to them. The first popular parenting guru, Luther Emmett Holt, published *The Care and Feeding of Children* in 1894. It was reprinted twelve times over his lifetime. Holt advocated a strict schedule and rigorous discipline for infants—the goal being to rear polite, well-behaved children. In the mid-1900s, however, an entirely different child care philosophy took hold. Dr. Benjamin Spock published *The Common Sense Book of Baby and Child Care* in 1946; since then it has been reprinted hundreds of times and has sold more copies than any other book in American history except for the Bible. Unlike Holt, Spock emphasized the importance of relaxed discipline and the need for mothers to watch their children's cues and fulfill their needs. Mothers had to be present constantly and create a stimulating environment at each developmental stage. Motherhood instantly became a lot more work.

A mother was now responsible for molding happy, healthy children who would grow up free of any psychological distress. If her children were unhappy or in ill mental health in any way, it was her fault. Neither the children's father, nor their friends, nor their culture, nor their inborn temperament was to blame: Mother alone was responsible for their outcome.

The responsibility may have been overwhelming, but all a mother had to do was follow Spock's advice to the letter and be as attentive as she could to her children, right? Not exactly. If she was too attentive, too involved, too loving, she became overbearing—and that was just as destructive. Hurtful jokes about the "Jewish mother"—who pushed her sons to achieve material success ("my son, the doctor") and her daughters to "marry well"—proliferated. The Jewish mother was vilified by Borscht Belt comedians and authors like Philip Roth, whose novel *Portnoy's Complaint* (1969) featured a man ground down by his controlling mother (aided by his passive, constipated father). A mother did not have to be Jewish to worry about stifling her children. In his 1942 book *Generation of Vipers*, Philip Wylie blamed overbearing mothers for corrupting American men and turning them soft and emasculated. "Now mothers were really in a bind," notes Shari Thurer. "Told by Spock to love their baby, they had to be careful not to love too much."[4]

If mothers in the mid-twentieth century were confused about the extent to which they were supposed to dote over their children, mothers today are no less befuddled. Some parenting experts advise letting your infant cry at night for thirty minutes or more so that he learns to fall back to sleep on his own without being coddled. Other experts admonish that you must comfort him right away. Some believe that sharing a bed with your baby is a bad idea because then he will never adjust to sleeping in a crib. Others say that it's the only humane thing to do. Some say you should resume your career so that your children have a role model who is involved in the larger world. Others say that you should stay home to care for them full-time, and that if you don't, you must obviously be selfish and unconcerned about your children's welfare. "The anxiety among mothers to get it right has never been any higher," comments Susan Maushart. "Ironically, the odds of doing so have probably never been lower."[5]

THE SACRIFICIAL MOTHER

When a woman is pregnant, especially for the first time, she is encouraged to nurture herself. Massage therapists who specialize in "maternity massage" offer "an hour of pampering and peace." If she is seen carrying or lifting heavy packages, others scramble to lift her load. She is urged to relax whenever possible. Unless one suffers from an extreme amount of nausea and aches, being pregnant can actually be a fairly pleasant experience. My advice is this: A woman should savor being pregnant, because once she goes into labor, she is transformed from the one who is nurtured to the one who nurtures at her own expense. She may very well never go back.

In her classic work on the binds and ambivalences of motherhood, *Of Woman Born*, Adrienne Rich spells out the unexamined assumption that a "'natural' mother is a person without further identity, one who can find her chief gratification in being all day with small children, living at a pace tuned to theirs." Maternal love "is, and should be, quite literally selfless."[6] A "good" mother elevates her children's needs above her own. She willingly puts aside her own needs. The sacrificial mother is soft and warm and pliant—not unlike children. Women and children are often lumped into one category, which explains the infantilizing language used by baby-product manufacturers even when products are directed to mothers. (A popular nursing pillow, for example, is called My Brest Friend.) Mothers sometimes become accustomed to this patronizing language and begin to say things like "poopy diaper" and "wee-wee" without any irony even when their children aren't in the room with them. The sacrificial mother may be the protector of our nation's future, but she is also condescended to.

When a thirty-four-year-old publicity manager, working in a pressured office atmosphere dominated by women, announced she was pregnant, many colleagues began behaving less harshly. As a mother-to-be, she felt reduced in status. "Women I don't normally have a relationship with now seek me out and ask me how the pregnancy is going, how I'm feeling; they say, 'Oh my God, you're only three weeks away.' On one level, I have found this to be very positive. But a lot of these women want to talk with me because I'm less of a threat now." She is cast as a mother figure and disregarded by her colleagues as a formidable figure.

In exchange for sacrificing her authority in the larger world, a mother is able to invoke moral authority in the domestic sphere, that is, any issue connected with family or safety. Mothers, especially full-time mothers, are widely presumed to be trustworthy and ethical. They are untainted by the dirty world of politics and ambition. Thus, mothers can advocate for controversial social issues like gun control, such as with the Million Mom March on Washington in May 2000, and for raising the national drinking age, such as with Mothers Against Drunk Driving, without fear of much opposition.

Mothers often compete with one another over who is most sacrificial. We compete in the same way that colleagues compete in the workplace. But since there is nowhere to advance to, no promotions to be had, and no end-of-year bonuses or raises to strive for, we compete for social approval from our peers, families, and husbands. Many of the choices mothers make about how to parent are influenced by the desire to be, or appear to be, as devoted as possible.

Sacrifice begins during pregnancy. A pregnant woman is instructed not to consume any alcohol and caffeine, smoke, or take drugs. Although a small amount of caffeine each day and small amounts of alcohol on a regular basis are acceptable, most people react with horror when they see a pregnant woman holding a coffee cup or sipping wine at a restaurant. The very idea of a pregnant woman not making these sacrifices is abhorrent: Her own needs and desires are dismissed as selfish and unimportant, even when they do not affect the health of the fetus.

She must also decide whether to brave the excruciating pain of labor without anesthetic medication (which is best for the baby) or to receive anesthesia (which might have some repercussions on the baby, but will make labor more tolerable for her). In the United States, there is enormous pressure to experience labor drug-free (advocates call it "natural" childbirth). The anesthesia most commonly used in labor is the epidural block, which numbs a woman's pelvic region. (The woman remains completely conscious.) Most of the time, epidurals are safe, though there is always some risk of complications, and the drug is passed through the placenta to the baby. Women have voted overwhelmingly in favor of pain relief: Between 1981 and 1997, the percentage of women who had regional anesthesia during labor in large hospitals tripled, from 22 percent to 66 percent.[7] Natural-childbirth proponents, alarmed by this trend, warn pregnant women that if they choose anesthesia, they are losing the opportunity to experience one of the greatest events of their lives.

When I was in labor with my first child, I requested an epidural block after I had endured much body-splitting pain. The pain of contractions was not erased, just minimized. I will never regret having made this decision. Once I wasn't entirely focused on my pain—as I had been before the epidural—I was fully cognizant of the enormity of the passage from fetus to baby. There was a full-length mirror in the delivery room, and I was able to watch my son wriggle from my body as I pushed him out. Now that was an experience.

Yet advocates shower with praise the women who eschew drugs and make the rest of us feel that we have done something wrong. After writer Margaret Talbot gave birth to her second child, a nurse stopped by her hospital room and asked if she had been given an epidural. When Talbot said no, as recounted in *The New York Times Magazine*, the nurse "was so instantly approving I half-expected her to slap a gold star on my hospital gown. I had been a good girl, it seemed."[8] Responding to Talbot's essay in a letter to the editor, Maria Schneider wrote, "As one who has experienced natural childbirth three times…I feel grateful, proud, and, I admit, morally superior. So what?"[9] Schneider's blithe "So what?" implies that her feeling of moral superiority doesn't hurt anyone. Yet some of us who made a different decision are made to feel selfish or morally inferior. Of course, each woman should make the decision that is best for her.

The rhetoric surrounding breast-feeding is similar. A mother who gives her baby formula (or even, to some purists, breast milk from a bottle) is masculine and career oriented: a woman who selfishly refuses to put her family first. A mother who nurses is regarded as caring, soft, maternal: the epitome of a "good" mother. The "good" mother grins and bears the teeth-rattling pain and inconvenience of breast-feeding because that is what "good" mothers are supposed to do.

Throughout Western history, mothers have often chosen not to breast-feed. Since formula wasn't invented until the twentieth century, the only alternative was to have another lactating woman take on the job. Wet-nursing flourished in Western Europe beginning in antiquity, peaking in the eighteenth century. For hundreds of years, recounts Shari Thurer in *The Myths of Motherhood*, it was confined to the upper classes, but it caught on among the middle and working classes as well beginning in the seventeenth century. Children were sent away from their parents' home for a year and a half to live in the home of the wet nurse, whose own baby might have died or been abandoned as a result.

By today's standards, this practice sounds barbaric. Putting aside the issue of the tragedy of the wet nurse's child, it seems inconceivable that a mother would want to deprive herself of being close to her newborn (assuming it was wanted) for such a long stretch of time, or that she would trust that her child was in good hands without being close enough to see for herself. But, as Thurer points out, today's standards did not apply in previous centuries. For some mothers, sending away their children was a necessity since they were extremely busy with the day-to-day functioning of their household and nursing would have caused economic consequences. For others, it was no doubt a status symbol. For most, the prevailing belief was that there was no harm in sending one's child to a wet nurse and that indeed the country air was beneficial for an infant's health. Thurer also provides another possible explanation: Since fathers (who were very involved in raising their children until the time of the Industrial Revolution) were the ones to broker the transaction with the husband of the wet nurse, she theorizes that men may have been jealous of women's capacity to nurse and therefore sought to devalue the experience of breast-feeding. In any event, wet-nursing became unfashionable through most of Western Europe during the second half of the eighteenth century, though it persisted in France until the late nineteenth century.[10] More and more, mothers decided to nurse their infants themselves.

In the early twentieth century, drug companies began to manufacture infant formula designed to mimic breast milk. In the United States, breast-feeding became unpopular in the 1920s. Most American mothers chose formula until the early 1970s, when the women's health movement encouraged women to feel in control of their bodies and to be skeptical of the motives of drug companies.

Today, once again breast-feeding is in fashion. In 1997, the American Academy of Pediatrics recommended that women nurse their children for a minimum of one year, preferably well into their second year of life. Research has linked breast-feeding with decreased incidents of allergies, respiratory problems, ear infections, sudden infant death syndrome, and diabetes. There are also claims that breast-fed children have slightly higher IQs and a potentially lower risk of heart disease than their formula-fed counterparts. In the United States, only 59 percent of women breast-feed at all (exclusively or in combination with formula) at the time of hospital discharge. Six months later, only 22 percent of mothers are nursing. The United States has one of the lowest breast-feeding rates in the developed world.[11]

> — *"Are you going to breast-feed?"* (a relative)
> — *"I don't know yet. I'll try it, but if it doesn't work out, then I'll stop."*
> — *"But you work at home, so you can do it."*

> — *"Are you going to breast-feed?"* (a friend who was breast-feeding her five-month-old daughter)
> — *"I don't know yet…"*
> — *"Well, you should do what's right for you. But Sarah hasn't gotten sick once, while my friends who don't breast-feed have all seen their babies get sick."*

— *"How much does your son weigh?"* (a family friend when my son
was four months old; she had breast-fed her three children)
— *"Seventeen pounds."*
— *"Well, formula sure does blow them up."*

When I was pregnant with my first child, my obstetrician and
son's pediatrician both urged me to breast-feed. I was asked by family members, friends, even acquaintances and strangers if I planned
to do so, and the expected reply was affirmative. I was willing and
curious to try, since I was aware of the literature that said that breast
milk was better than formula (even cans of formula say on the label,
"Breast milk is recommended"). Breast-feeding is said to build a
special bond between mother and baby. But I was nervous about
being solely responsible for my child's nutrition. I'd heard that it
hurt, and I didn't relish the idea of being unable to leave my apartment 95 percent of the time.

Breast-feeding my first child was technically difficult, painful,
and imprisoning. My first son was unable to properly latch on to the
nipples. For the first four weeks, it took thirty minutes for him to
attach himself to one nipple (during which time he'd wail with frus-
tration), which he would suck for fifteen minutes, and then I had to
repeat the procedure. If he hiccupped, the suction was lost and I'd
have to start over. The pain caused me to suck in my breath. Two and
a half hours later, day or night, I had to go through the whole
process again. And those two and a half hours were the time elapsed
after he had begun feeding, not after he had ended. Between feedings, if latching on went smoothly, I had approximately an hour in
which my baby was not attached to me. In short, I was tethered to

my son. I didn't dare feed him in public, because of the latching-on problem; there was no way I was going to subject strangers in a café or bookstore to his howling. Breast-feeding made my time with my son burdensome. The overromanticized "special bond" did not develop. Instead, I began to resent him. I also began to resent all the mothers who seemingly nursed so easily.

My experience was not unusual. Most mothers suffer some pain with breast-feeding, especially in the first weeks. Some women develop infections with fever and painful lumps. The most true-to-life description of the breast-feeding experience I have found was provided by novelist Cathi Hanauer. Before she became pregnant, Hanauer had imagined that she would dreamily sit in a rocking chair with her baby peacefully attached to her breast.

> Here's the reality: I'm sitting on the spit-up-stained sofa bed trying to balance my wailing three-week-old daughter, Phoebe, atop two pillows on my C-sectioned lap. I'm preparing her, but really I'm more preparing myself, for her ninth or tenth meal of the day. However I hold her, I'm in for some serious pain. First she'll clamp on with a grip astonishing for a person who could fit inside a shoe box. Then she'll suck off the scabs that have formed on my nipples since the last feeding, oh, two hours ago. For a good thirty seconds my milk will "let down"—something the books describe as a mildly tingling sensation but for me feels like having my entire upper body mashed in a vise. Sweat runs down my body, and I clamp the couch, or my husband, and yell, "Shit Shit Shit!" So much for the baby's virginal ears.[12]

After four weeks, I rented an electric breast pump and began giving my son milk pumped into a bottle. At least now my husband could give a bottle if I wanted to take a walk or sleep. But since I was home all day and he was not, and he needed to wake up with a clear mind for work and I did not, I remained responsible for feeding our son the majority of the time. Between the time it took me to pump and the time it took me to feed, there was even less "free" time than before. Two weeks later, I called it quits. I was exhausted and miserable. Breast milk may be best for the baby, but formula was best for this mother. Yet, when I returned the pump to the local drugstore, the woman at the cashier, a mother herself, asked me in dismay, "You're returning it so soon?"

My experience was echoed by Cindy Friedman, a thirty-five-year-old graphic designer in San Francisco. Cindy likes to joke that "breast-feeding sucks" and that she would "rather drink than breast-feed." But breast-feeding was no laughing matter for her. "I did it for three months, but I hated it," she says. "It hurt like hell and I resented [my son] because he was like a little piranha, so I preferred to pump. But it was really hard to pump and feed him; it's like double the work. And you feel like an idiot with a pump on you. I was speaking with a woman who was just starting to wean her one-year-old and she said, 'I had thrush, but I kept doing it. It gets so much easier.' But you know what? I don't care if it would have gotten easier. I didn't want to have a kid stuck to my boob all day; that was the bottom line."

(I have a vision that, several years from now, researchers will discover that breast milk is not really the wonderful stuff it is purported to be. Indeed, it has been reported that over the past twenty-five to thirty years, a number of toxic chemicals, such as PCBs, DDT, and solvents, have been discovered in breast milk.[13])

Since breast-feeding is a challenge for most women, those who do stick it out should be rewarded for their efforts. For the most part, they are praised by the medical establishment, women's health advocates, their peers—and they do not hesitate to praise themselves. However, depending on her peer group, a woman who breast-feeds may not receive social support. One thirty-year-old woman who breast-fed for eight months told me, "None of my friends did it. Nobody. I didn't receive any criticism, but I didn't receive any support. There was no, 'That's great, keep doing it.' It was, 'How long are you going to keep doing it for? You're not going to be one of those mothers whose kid lifts up your shirt in public, are you?' I'd say, "No, I'd never get to that point.' But in the back of my mind I'd think, 'Would that really be the worst thing that could happen?'"This woman stuck with her decision for as long as she could, but a less confident woman might have been pressured to join her friends in giving her child formula before she was ready.

Of course, formula is not poison. Giving up breast-feeding, or choosing not to do it, does not mean a mother is negligent. Playwright Wendy Wasserstein offers a hilarious but disturbing account of her run-in with breast-feeding proponents the morning after she had given birth to a daughter. Wasserstein had been forced to deliver prematurely by C-section because she suffered from a potentially life-threatening case of preeclampsia, a high-blood-pressure condition that can lead to liver and kidney failure.

> The Nipple Nazis attacked the next day at dawn.
> "Are you pumping?" an ultra-thin woman demanded from my doorway.

"Not yet," I answered. "I just had preeclampsia, a Caesarian, and my daughter was born at 27 weeks. I think I need to sleep."

"You must pump every three hours!" she announced. "Or you will dry up."

She wheeled in a breast pump that looked as if it could bail out a battleship. Sternly, she showed me how to pump each breast separately or, if I liked, both together, a sort of duet for mammaries.

Duly intimidated, I tried to sit up and attach two plastic bottles to my now Hindenberg-size breasts. Hurricane Floyd was raging outside, and incision staples were pinching my stomach.[14]

Some breast-feeding proponents can be so zealous in their cause that women who do not nurse are made to feel they are not maternal, feminine, or devoted enough. "Women call me in tears and in pain, asking for permission to stop," says Fern Drillings, a lactation consultant in New York City. "They're having a bad time, but to quit would seem like they failed."[15] Cindy Friedman relates that she loved her lactation counselor who, not coincidentally, was male. "I think the reason he was so great was that he had never breast-fed and never will breast-feed." When she did stop breast-feeding, she "stopped going to mommy-and-me groups because I didn't want to be around a group of breast-feeding women and have them look at me. I didn't want to be judged."

When her son was four weeks old, writer Pamela Gerhardt went to a meeting of the La Leche League, an organization that strongly opposes the use of infant formula and encourages all mothers to nurse for as long as possible. She asked if she could have a glass of wine occasionally. "Total silence," she writes, "as if I had just asked them to help me score some crack." What if she wanted to go to a movie? "One woman with a toddler on each breast said, 'I can't remember the last time I watched a movie with my husband—not even on TV.' Heads nodded. Appreciative murmurs. Another said, 'I don't even see my husband—it's just me and the kids until bedtime.' She smiled."[16]

Similarly, one young mother living in Queens, New York, complains that if she hires a baby-sitter so that she can go out for a few hours, her mother scolds her and warns her not to go out without pumping some milk first. "God forbid, I should give the baby formula. Well, you know what? I'm nursing 24/7. Maybe I don't have enough milk to pump. Maybe I don't have twenty minutes to sit down and pump a bottle. If I do go out, I don't want to stress out if I need to pump or not. When I went out to get a manicure, she said, 'Why did you have to get your nails done?' Maybe because I haven't had them done in a year and I'd like to treat myself. It's relaxing for me. I shouldn't have to explain myself."

No, she shouldn't have to explain herself. But because of the cultural ideal of the sacrificial mother, just about every new mother worries that she is not sacrificial enough, that she is not good enough—and other mothers feel entitled to call her to task for not being so. The new mother finds herself explaining and justifying and defending. The new father faces little pressure to explain his parenting (unless he abandons or abuses his child). When mothers become so involved in judging each other, fathers escape many of the day-to-day responsibilities of parenthood. And even when fathers are involved in their children's lives, they are rarely expected to make the kinds of sacrifices that mothers are.

THE BIGGEST ANTAGONISM

"You can't work and be a good mom. You've got to choose one or the other."
—Comment made in my presence during my second trimester by a stay-at-home mother who knew I planned to continue working. Needless to say, she did not expect my husband to choose between working and being a good dad.

New mothers often judge one another on every meaningless thing from the month their children sit up to the outfits they wear. But of course, the real dealbreaker is the issue of work. Whether or not a woman continues to work for pay outside the home is considered the premier factor of her fitness as a mother. Susan Chira, an editor at *The New York Times*, says,

> When I talked to other women, I felt as if a bomb could explode every time the subject of children came up. A mother at home said she was "too much of a perfectionist" to entrust her children to another woman. A working mother talked of how much she missed her children and how she would quit in a heartbeat if she could afford it.... I wanted to say that for me, it was possible, even exhilarating, to have a job and raise children. At times, out of defensiveness, I think I must have sounded smug. Yet I, too, am prey to guilt and anxiety.[17]

Mothers on both sides of this issue go to great lengths to defend their position. When two mothers disagree, each tries to explain why her choice is best for her. Many times, each goes too far and ends up explaining why her choice is best for every mother.

The issue of working mothers became a matter for public discourse in 1992, when Arkansas governor Bill Clinton was running for president and his opponent, former California governor Jerry Brown, accused him of directing state business to the law firm where his wife worked and thereby personally benefiting financially. Bill Clinton angrily denied the charge, saying it was "insulting" and "unfair." Hillary Clinton responded to reporters that the appearance of impropriety couldn't be avoided, given her choice to work as a lawyer rather than to busy herself solely as the hostess of her governor husband. "I suppose I could have stayed home, baked cookies, and had teas," Hillary Clinton said, "but what I decided was to fulfill my profession, which I entered before my husband was in public life." Twenty minutes later, when few reporters were still around, Hillary Clinton elaborated. "You know, the work that I've done as a professional, as a public advocate, has been aimed in part to assure that women can make the choices that they should make—whether it's full-time career, full-time motherhood, some combination, depending on what stage of life they are at—and I think that is still difficult for people to understand right now, that it is a generational change."[18]

As we all know, it was Hillary Clinton's "cookies and teas" comment that was ferociously covered by the news media; her eloquent plea that people respect whatever choice a mother makes ended up on the cutting-room floor. Stay-at-home mothers were indignant that she was so seemingly disdainful of their choice. A former CPA who quit to raise her children wrote in to *The Washington Post* that she was "deeply offended" by the "cookies and teas" comment. "Let me assure [Hillary Clinton] that I have never worked harder in my life…. All I ask is that the stay-at-home decision of women like myself receives the respect it deserves—at least from a woman who claims to be a children's advocate and whose husband aspires to be president." Another letter-writer, a Yale graduate who worked on Capitol Hill for five years before staying home to raise her children, claimed that "on cold winter afternoons I occasionally pause a few moments for a cup of tea, and I even bake cookies now and then when I have the time. I believe that raising my three young children is extremely important, and what's more, I find it even more fascinating and challenging than my work for Congress."[19] Later in the campaign, Hillary Clinton tried to woo the offended by admitting that, on second thought, she does enjoy baking cookies. She gave Americans her favorite chocolate chip cookie recipe in *Family Circle* and participated in a bake-off against Barbara Bush. Clinton won the bake-off and the position of First Lady.

The debate over which is "better"—to continue working and hire others to care for your children or to raise your children full time—has raged for decades. Those who believe a woman's place is in the home tend to blame feminism for encouraging women to be hard, driven, antifamily, and therefore ruining our country and our future. To conservative critic Danielle Crittenden, hard-edged feminism has even erased the happiness of mothers, who would all prefer to stay at home rather than work: "For in all the ripping down of barriers that have taken place over a generation," she writes in her paean to stay-at-home mothering, *What Our Mothers Didn't Tell Us*, "we may have inadvertently also smashed the foundations necessary for our happiness."[20] Even the radical architects of women's liberation in the late 1960s and early '70s were divided. Those who already had children and stayed home with them were criticized for not stretching beyond housework by women who equated liberation with paid work. Those who stayed home envied the aspirations and accomplishments of the child-free and the mothers who returned to the labor force, yet criticized them as well. Over the last thirty years, feminists have come to recognize that most women who work outside the home must do so to support their families. Besides, those women who work in low-paying, dead-end jobs derive little satisfaction from their work. In Barbara Ehrenreich's exposé of the lives of the millions of working poor, *Nickel and Dimed*, she shows that it's impossible to survive on jobs that pay $6 or $7 an hour unless you work at two jobs, and that if you have children, you don't have a chance.[21] Nevertheless antagonism remains between mothers who stay at home full time and those who work full time.

In Hollywood films, the working mother has been portrayed as negligent and deserving of punishment. In *Mildred Pierce* (1945), Joan Crawford played an independent working mother who successfully runs a chain of restaurants. One of her daughters dies, while the other grows to become an arrogant, competitive, blackmailing young woman who tries to steal away Mildred's second husband. Jump forward a half-century to *Stepmom* (1998), whose narrative is more complicated but whose message that stay-at-home motherhood is best is roughly the same. In this movie, a hardworking photographer, Isabel, played by Julia Roberts, tries to mother the children of her divorced boyfriend. But something about being a professional renders her defective in the mothering department: The kids resent her and worship their mother, Jackie—the perfect, sacrificial, always-there mother played by Susan Sarandon. In this movie it's the stay-at-home mother who is punished: Jackie discovers that she has cancer and dies. But the *role* of the stay-at-home mother triumphs: Isabel quits her job in an effort to emulate Jackie, morphing into the perfect mother the kids can now accept and love.

Julia Roberts has also represented the other side: the heroic working mother. In *Erin Brockovich* (2000), Roberts played the real-life working-class mother of three young children who grapples with the logistics and pain of spending time away from her kids. As an assistant in a law firm, she investigates a suspicious real estate case involving Pacific Gas & Electric Co., which is poisoning residents in the area through illegal dumping. In an unusual move for Hollywood, the Roberts character is applauded for remaining committed to her job despite the hardships of raising children at the same time. Still, the Roberts character is upheld as virtuous because of the nature of her work. If, instead of playing a pivotal role in one of the biggest class action lawsuits in American history against a multibillion-dollar corporation, she had simply typed up tax law correspondence for a living, she may have been vilified as a derelict mother.

In a *Redbook* photo accompanying an article titled "Why Are These Moms at War?" in April 2000, a woman with a tailored dress and a briefcase and another woman wearing jeans and a T-shirt with a diaper bag are going at each other with boxing gloves. In the article itself, six women—three stay-at-home mothers, three not— "duke it out over PTA cliques, the true meaning of quality time, and who's really the better mom." The mothers on both sides come across as self-righteous and disingenuous: It seems that they will say just about anything to make themselves look good as mothers. René Clawson, thirty-six, a licensed architect who stopped working when the first of her two children (now six and two) was born, disparages the "working moms and dads [who] come to the park with their laptops and their cell phones. I wouldn't think of bringing the newspaper, a book, a cell phone, or a laptop to the park with me." But if parents who have to or want to work can find a way to spend time with their kids and be professionally productive at the same time, shouldn't they be rewarded for negotiating this delicate balance?

Meanwhile, another mother, Miriam Bender Birge, M.D., a thirty-eight-year-old pathologist with a ten-year-old and a seven-year-old, is out of the house every weekday, all day. Does she feel that she's lost something? "No, I don't," Birge replied. "I don't feel like my kids lost anything either. We share wonderful moments, but I don't feel I need to be there every time they're upset, or every time they need to share something that happened in preschool.... I think a wonderful thing I've given my kids is their independence. And one of the reasons they have that is because I haven't been there all the time."[22] A mother who works should be supported for leading the most complicated life imaginable, but it is foolish to suggest that neither she nor her children have lost anything by the arrangement—and that, moreover, her children have developed better because of her long work hours. After all, most people would agree that when a father works long hours, both he and his children lose out on precious day-to-day interactions.

Both sides have staked the moral high ground. Instead of continuing an endless round of "I'm right," "No, I'm right," let us put both decisions—to resume in the labor force and to quit one's job to stay home with the children—into some much-needed perspective.

WORKING MOTHERS

What a rare find is a capable wife!
Her worth is far beyond that of rubies.
Her husband puts his confidence in her,
And lacks no good thing....
She looks for wool and flax,
And sets her hand to them with a will.
She is like a merchant fleet,
Bringing her food from afar.
She rises while it is still night,
And supplies provisions for her household,
The daily fare of her maids.
She sets her mind on an estate and acquires it;
She plants a vineyard by her own labors.
She girds herself with strength,
And performs her tasks with vigor.
She sees that her business thrives;
Her lamp never goes out at night.
She sets her hand to the distaff;
Her fingers work the spindle....
She oversees the activities of her household
And never eats the bread of idleness.
Her children declare her happy;
Her husband praises her,
"Many women have done well,
But you surpass them all."
—"A Woman of Valor," Proverbs 31:10–29[23]

Most mothers work for pay. In 2000, more than half (55 percent) of mothers returned to work before their infants celebrated their first birthday, up from 31 percent in 1975.[24] The older and more educated the mother, the likelier she will return to work before her baby can walk: Seventy-seven percent of college-educated women ages thirty to forty-four decide to continue their outside work while they mother their child.[25] Many mothers single-handedly raise their families: More than 7.5 million households are headed by single mothers.[26] But even families with two parents must rely on the income earned by the mother, since two salaries are a necessity for most families today given the skyrocketing costs of real estate, college tuition, and health insurance, as well as the risk that the father will be laid off from his job.

That most mothers work is nothing new. Throughout history, mothers have always performed myriad tasks while they raised their children and while they delegated child care to others. The "woman of valor," glorified in Proverbs as the epitome of the successful wife and mother, worked day and night to attend to the many details of her busy household. She bought real estate, planted vineyards, collected food, and spun fabrics. The idea of "staying home" with her children would have seemed ludicrous to her. From earliest settled life until the growth of industrialization, men, women, and children together were involved in the ceaseless activities of preparing food, producing textiles and clothing, and making soap and candles. Work and home, public and private, were intermingled. Mothers were just as busy as the rest of the family and rarely spent time alone with their children without engaging in other tasks at the same time. Fathers were very involved in raising their children and often took control of their education.

The Industrial Revolution forever changed both the nature of work and the makeup of home life. Settled agrarian life gave way to factory work and a demographic shift to cities. Now there were two separate spheres, public and private. Among married couples, men left the home to go out and earn money in the public sphere, while women remained at home in the private sphere with the children. We see, then, that the man as breadwinner is actually a modern role, cropping up in the 1800s. Mothers remained busy with chores and activities. They continued to be central players in the economic well-being of their households. Many remained active in the manufacturing of goods. As the professions rose, many mothers became involved in teaching, nursing, and social work. Mothers were primarily, but not exclusively, involved in child care.

The concept of the "full-time" mother was invented in the industrialized twentieth century and reached its apex in popularity in that aberrational and short-lived era, the affluent years following World War II. During the war, millions of women moved into the work force. But by the end of the 1940s, most had been fired from industrial jobs. "Rosie the Riveter, the tough, can-do war worker, suddenly vanished from American iconography," write Rosalind Barnett and Caryl Rivers, researchers at the Wellesley College Center for Research on Women. "She was replaced by the smiling mother driving the station wagon, who knew that her place was at home with her children."[27] Although the decade of the 1950s was atypical in its rigid distinction between the sexes—with dad earning enough on his own to support a middle-class lifestyle for his family and mom staying home baking pies and tending to the children—most Americans living today tend to think of that era as normative. That's what the American family is *supposed* to be like.

As historian Stephanie Coontz has pointed out, the decade of the 1950s seems "normal" only because it coincided with the rise of popular television sitcoms designed for the tastes of white, sub-urban, nuclear families.[28] With reruns of *My Three Sons*, *Leave it to Beaver*, and *The Adventures of Ozzie and Harriet* playing endlessly over the last fifty years, it's no wonder that so many Americans equate "family" with "breadwinner dad, stay-at-home mom." This is the family that so many grew up watching on television. It seems hard to believe that by 1960, 19 percent of mothers with children under six were in the labor force, along with 31 percent of those with children between six and seventeen, and that in the 1960s, more and more mothers reentered the work force.[29] From that point, the 1950s-era ideal family continued to live on only in televised images. Nostalgia for the nuclear family as it was depicted in these shows has whipped up anxiety that the traditional nuclear family is the only correct and healthy type of family arrangement: When mothers work, the nostalgic-minded believe, families (and society) suffer. Echoing the prevailing sentiment, an amazon.com reader-reviewer of *What Our Mothers Didn't Tell Us* opines that "There's nothing more selfish than leaving your precious two-year-old at seven A.M. for a full day of work."

But the traditional nuclear family is far from the norm. Only 23.5 percent of U.S. households contain a married man and woman along with their children, and only in a minority of those households is the man the sole breadwinner.[30] Besides, there is ample evidence that two-career families are healthy and thriving. With the help of a million-dollar grant from the National Institutes of Mental Health, Rosalind Barnett and Caryl Rivers conducted a four-year study of the lives of two-earner families. They focused on three hundred mostly white couples from different economic circumstances and with different educational levels living in two communities in the greater Boston area. "On the whole," they write, "the news about the two-career couple today is very good indeed." The researchers found that the two-earner family has been a positive development, not a negative one.

Among their findings, which are presented in their book, *She Works/He Works: How Two-Income Families Are Happy, Healthy, and Thriving*: The fathers in these families are closely involved with all aspects of their children's care; working mothers are in good emotional and physical health overall; the parents' relationships with their children are close and warm; and having two incomes provides the parents with a buffer against swings in the economy.[31] "Women are not selfish careerists, destroying their children and their families and undermining society," write Barnett and Rivers. "The portrait that emerges from our study is one of men and women working together on both the work and home fronts."[32]

When mothers work, fathers are more apt to pitch in with parenting responsibilities. Other research backs up the claim that men want to spend time with their families and eschew the role of primary breadwinner. A nationwide survey of a thousand men in their twenties and thirties, conducted by Harris Interactive in 2000 for the Radcliffe Public Policy Center, found that the overwhelming majority of men view themselves as fathers first and workers second. Their perspective mirrors that of young women, most of whom likewise say that having family time is a priority over any other single career factor.[33] It seems that young men know what's best not only for their families but also for their own health. The fathers in the Wellesley study conducted by Barnett and Rivers who were deeply involved in their children's lives had the fewest health problems, while those with the most troubled relationships with their children had the most health problems.[34]

Meanwhile, despite charges that working women are miserable because of the pressures of their multiple roles and responsibilities, the researchers found the opposite: that working mothers report better physical health and fewer emotional problems than nonemployed mothers. "Work…offers [women] adult companionship, social contacts, and connection with the wider world that they cannot get at home," conclude Barnett and Rivers. "So while [working mothers] often have problems—long hours, too much to do—and don't hesitate to complain about them, that doesn't mean they are basket cases."[35]

Barnett and Rivers found that "working mothers are good mothers"—a fact that has been backed up by other research. Most notably, the National Academy of Sciences put together a distinguished panel of social scientists to review the research on good mothering, and concluded that there were no consistent effects of maternal employment on child development. This is because there are so many other variables that need to be weighed when considering a woman's life and how her children fare—what her income is, her level of education, whether her children are receiving quality child care, and the level of support she receives from her family.[36] Consistent, quality child care, given by one or several people, is the most important thing for children—not necessarily whether it is given solely by the biological mother. It's foolish to suggest that biological mothers are inherently better parents than anyone else. Many mothers are negligent, inattentive, or abusive. Being affectionate, attentive, and caring are far more important attributes than merely being a biological mother—as countless fathers, grandparents, and paid caregivers show with the love and excellent care they shower on the children in their lives.

Barnett and Rivers focused their research on the lives of working parents. Ellen Galinsky, president of the Families and Work Institute, on the other hand, examined how children are affected by double-earner families. For her book, *Ask the Children: What America's Children Really Think About Working Parents*, Galinsky spearheaded a survey that asked a representative group of more than a thousand children, ages eight through eighteen, from all different backgrounds what they think about employed parents. The problem, she discovered is not that mothers (and fathers) work: It is *how* they work. Most children did not express a desire to spend more time with their working parents—but they did say they wished that their parents were less stressed and less tired at the end of the workday. Thirty-two percent of the children reported that they worried about their parents "very often" or "often"; when the "sometimes" response is added, the percentage went up to 65 percent. Yet most children also assessed their parents positively on twelve different parenting skills.

To Galinsky, mothers don't need to quit their jobs. They do need to make their children a priority and to focus their attention on each child when they spend time with them. The best parents, she found, are fulfilled by their work, which affects their mood and energy at the end of the day. This enables them to be attentive to their children and to interact energetically with them when they get home.[37]

Unfortunately, most people experience little job fulfillment and can't help but feel frustrated and tense in the evening. While Galinsky's research is encouraging because it indicates that being a working mother per se is not a problem, it also implicitly suggests that many working mothers (and fathers) are not adequately fulfilling their children's needs. Working mothers (and fathers) need to be honest with themselves: Are they able to fully devote themselves to their children when they are at home? If not, is there anything in their control they can do to be more relaxed and attentive?

It is ironic that while working mothers are often accused of being selfish, they actually work harder than almost anyone else. Ann Crittenden, author of *The Price of Motherhood* (not to be confused with conservative Danielle Crittenden), calculates that on average, working mothers work more than eighty hours a week, counting both their paid job and their unpaid labor at home. In effect, they work the equivalent of two full-time jobs, "forcing them to cut back on everything in their lives *but* paid work and children." (They have drastically reduced the amount of time they spend on housework.)[38] After reading this passage in Crittenden's book, I whipped out my calculator and discovered that I do indeed work 80 hours a week—since I am frantically busy from seven A.M. to eleven P.M. with both tending home and children as well as working for pay—but these eighty hours are confined only to the weekdays. If you factor in my weekends as well, the figure jumps to more than a hundred hours.

On the face of it, part-time work seems like an ideal solution. Children get to spend a good amount of one-on-one time with a parent while both parents can continue to advance in their careers, relax in the intimate knowledge of the details of their children's days, and have the chance to do household chores before nine P.M. In reality, however, part-time work means part-time salary and is economically unfeasible.

Even for those who can afford it, "basically, the picture is bad," says Dr. Wendy Chavkin, editor of the *Journal of the American Medical Women's Association*, regarding the opportunities for women in medicine to practice part time. More and more female doctors are willingly sacrificing higher salaries for a balanced and flexible schedule. They are joining multiphysician practices or working as employees for practices run by managed-care companies. But is the trade-off worth it? There is now a "pink collar" level of medicine: Women are concentrated in the lowest-paying, least prestigious specialties. Very few residents studying surgery, for instance, are women. And while the average male physician in private practice in the United States earns $273,690 a year, the average female physician earns only $155,590. Approximately one-half of female doctors report incomes of less than $100,000, compared with 22 percent of men.[39]

The case of female physicians mirrors the situation of all women who reduce their work hours to accommodate their families. In exchange for a flexible schedule, they give up competitive salaries, benefits, prestige, often job security. Moreover, the health benefit for all working mothers discovered by Barnett and Rivers kicks in only when they work more than twenty hours a week. In fact, part-time work can have a negative impact on a mother's mental health. Researchers Elaine Wethington and Ronald Kessler speculate that women who work fewer than twenty hours a week "operate under the fiction that they can retain full responsibility for child care and home maintenance," which causes them to be even more stressed and pressured than full-time working mothers.[40]

Telling mothers to work part time or not at all, as many stay-at-home mothers and their advocates do, helps no one. What we should do instead, as a nation, is put pressure on our government to subsidize and improve the child care available to working mothers so that they can be assured that even when they're not with their children, their children are well taken care of. In Western Europe, high-quality child care is either provided or subsidized by the government. France in particular boasts a comprehensive network of neighborhood child-care centers throughout the country, staffed by trained teachers and psychologists. Israel has an extensive, high-quality child-care system, with the government subsidizing the cost depending on family size and income. But here in the United States, day-care centers (which roughly three million children attend every day[41]) are of pitifully poor quality and/or exhorbitantly priced, and parents receive little or no help from the government.

Only 9 percent of U.S. child care is excellent, and only 30 percent is rated "good," according to the National Institute of Child Health and Human Development.[42] Most day-care centers are staffed by employees with a high school education. A day-care teacher who works twelve months a year earns $24,606, which, as the AFL-CIO points out, is less than the amount earned by parking lot attendants and animal caretakers.[43] High turnover is common: According to a study that looked at staffing in seventy-five better-than-average California day-care centers serving children ages two and a half through five, three-quarters of the teachers and 40 percent of the directors in 1996 had quit by the year 2000.[44] Quality child-care centers with trained professionals are too expensive for most working families, and nannies or full-time baby-sitters are so expensive that they are available only to the upper middle class and upper class. In many parts of the country, good-quality child care costs between $4,000 and $10,000 a year per child. In my neighborhood, there is a day-care center with a stellar reputation; tuition per child is $12,240, and there is a two-year waiting list. The going rate in New York City for a full-time (forty-five hours), live-out nanny is at least $20,000, plus two weeks of paid vacation.

Rather than work to improve the quality of all day care and the accessibility of the centers that have proven their excellence, researchers are committed to trashing the entire concept of non-mom child care. Dr. Jay Belsky, of the University of London, one of the principal investigators of the nation's largest long-term study of child care, reported to the media in April 2001 that children who spend more than thirty hours a week in care given by anyone other than their mothers are three times more likely to exhibit aggressive behavior in kindergarten than those cared for primarily by their mothers. (Seventeen percent of those in care for more than thirty hours a week exhibited aggression compared with 6 percent of the children in care for less than ten hours a week.) Belsky theorized that the aggression may be triggered by the children's experience at the end of the day when they are reunited with their parents. But another principal investigator, Dr. Deborah Phillips of Georgetown University, speculated that the mediocre quality of child care is to blame. Belsky's opinions made it to the front page of *The New York Times*. Phillips wasn't even cited in the main news article; her analysis, no less valid than Belsky's, was relegated to an essay tucked into the science section several days later.[45]

In the same vein, the one positive finding of the study—that children who spend more time in child-care centers, as opposed to other types of child care, are more likely to display better language skills and have better short-term memory by age four and a half—was mentioned only in passing in the final paragraph of the *Times*'s news coverage.[46] In fact, other studies have confirmed that children who attend high-quality day-care centers have better language, math, and social skills than children who do not. In one study, those who received high-quality day care consistently outperformed their peers who did not on both cognitive and academic tests, and also were more likely to go on to attend college or to hold high-skill jobs.[47]

All child care should be raised to the same caliber. But that will never happen as long as it is considered a negative replacement for full-time mother care. In effect, the United States punishes families in which the mother works by forcing them to put their children in substandard care. "The underlying reason for the failure of day care programs to develop in this country is the traditional ideology that young children and their mothers belong in the home," wrote women's liberation activists Louise Gross and Phyllis Taube Greenleaf in 1970. Their words are no less true today. "That women should have to work and therefore have to put their children in day care centers are circumstances which are generally considered to be necessary evils in this society."[48] As long as mothers compete over which is "better"—to stay at home or to work for pay—and being a stay-at-home mother is idealized while being a working mother is slandered as selfish, negligent, or, God forbid, feminist, our government will continue to refuse to raise the quality of day-care centers or to subsidize the tuition for the excellent ones. We may have come a long way, baby, but our babies and children are denied the advantages to which they have every right.

STAY-AT-HOME MOTHERS

Working mothers and their families are not the only ones punished for their decision regarding work. Stay-at-home mothers also pay a dear price. In her book *The Price of Motherhood*, Ann Crittenden demonstrates that full-time mothers who either work part time or not at all are systematically disadvantaged by a society that on the one hand praises them for their unpaid labor but on the other hand punishes them economically. Her book is filled with disturbing facts about their financial losses. College-educated women who quit their jobs to tend to their children full time pay a "mommy tax" of more than $1 million in lost income when they have a child. (Crittenden arrives at this figure by looking at a couple with a total income of $81,500 and two equally capable partners. If they have a child and the wife leaves her job, they will lose $1,350,000 in lifetime income.) The wage gap between mothers and childless women is far greater than that between women and men. At-home mothers do not have the safety net of Social Security, workers' compensation, and unemployment insurance. The United States is one of only six countries of 152 surveyed by the United Nations that does not require paid maternity leave.[49] Motherhood, Crittenden warns, is now the single greatest risk factor for poverty among American women. It is a grave threat to a woman's economic well-being.

Crittenden offers her own financial facts as a cautionary tale. She had been a full-time journalist for *The New York Times* for eight years (and had worked full time for twenty years), but she resigned in 1982 after the birth of her son. When she left, she had a yearly salary of roughly $50,000. After leaving the paper, she worked part time as a freelance writer, earning roughly $15,000 a year. "Very conservatively," she writes, "I lost between $600,000 and $700,000, not counting the loss of a pension....[50] I took what I thought would be a relatively short break, assuming it would be easy to get back into journalism after a few years, or to earn a decent income from books and other projects. I was wrong. As it turned out, I sacrificed more than half of my expected lifetime earnings. And in the boom years of the stock market, that money invested in equities would have multiplied like kudzu. As a conservative estimate, it could have generated $50,000 or $60,000 a year in income for my old age."[51]

The greatest injustice of this situation is that women alone face it. Most married men with children can rise in their careers and also enjoy time with their families. They are not pressured by the society at large to curb their work hours or to quit altogether. Women, on the other hand, are expected to either scale back their career or drop it so that they can be "good" mothers—or, they *have* no choice because there is no high-quality or affordable child care available to them. As mothers, they make the ultimate sacrifice: their economic livelihood.

There is no adequate compensation for the financial sacrifice made by mothers. But at least stay-at-home mothers have the approval of America. In one recent survey conducted by *The*

Washington Post with the Henry Kaiser Family Foundation and Harvard University, two-thirds of Americans said they believed it would be best for women to stay home and care for their families.[52] In another poll, four out of five Americans agreed with the statement "It may be necessary for mothers to be working because the family needs money, but it would be better if they could stay home and take care of the house and children." Single mothers are "allowed" to work because they have no choice, most Americans believe, but if there are two parents, the mother should stay home.[53]

Because public opinion is so strongly in favor of stay-at-home motherhood, it is not a surprise that mothers who do choose to stay at home generally explain their decision as one they made because it is best for the sake of their children. But when a stay-at-home mother opens up and honestly discusses the rationale behind her choice, she nearly always divulges other reasons for quitting her job: Motherhood gave her an excuse to quit an unrewarding position (something she may have longed to do even before becoming a parent), or she was "in between" jobs because of a move or recession-provoked layoff. Or, very commonly, she felt pressured to quit or was forced out of her job because her workplace was so inflexible that she was not permitted to rearrange her work hours, even if the quality or quantity of her work would not be sacrificed. René Clawson, the former architect quoted in *Redbook* as being appalled that some parents bring their laptops and cell phones with them when they go to the park with their kids, also told the magazine that "I'm thrilled with my decision. The only time I whip out that résumé is on those bad days with my two-year-old when I feel underappreciated at home. But then I remember how underappreciated I felt at work."[54] Another woman, Julia Olkin Meza, forty, of Castro Valley, California, holds a Ph.D. in mathematics and worked at the prestigious Stanford Research Institute. She told Loretta Kaufman and Mary Quigley, authors of *And What Do You Do?: When Women Choose to Stay Home*, that when her oldest child was entering kindergarten, she took a new position at another company. She ended up quitting soon after to stay home because the job "turned out not to be what I expected. It was a small company. It sounded great, but the work was not the right match for me.... I decided I didn't want to go back to work."[55]

Being dissatisfied with work is hardly limited to mothers. In a recent survey of three thousand married and single young women by Youth Intelligence, a market research firm, more than two-thirds said they would quit their jobs if they could afford to. A poll of eight hundred women conducted by *Cosmopolitan* found the exact same statistic: Two out of three respondents "would rather kick back *a casa* than climb the corporate ladder." Women today dream of the stay-at-home life even before they have children. The president of Youth Intelligence, Jane Buckingham, attributes the fantasy to young women's high expectations of their jobs. They "are therefore more easily frustrated and prone to calling it quits," she said. "People feel less of a need to 'pay their dues.'" Buckingham found that young women want to feel passionate about their jobs and become deflated when they don't. Instead, they turn their aspirations to the home. "Home is safe and controllable, and women want that power in their lives," she explains. [56]

If a woman is dissatisfied with her job and decides she and her family would be better off if she left it for the home, she has made a decision that is best for her and her family. But staying at home is what mothers are conditioned to want to do in order to fulfill society's expectations. Kaufman and Quigley's book is an example of the kind of thinking that claims there is only one right way. Both authors quit their jobs to stay home with their children. Even though 7.7 million married mothers with children under eighteen don't work, with another 5 million working part time, and even though most Americans, as we have seen, approve of their lifestyle, the authors liken themselves to brave explorers charting new territory. "In writing this book," they state, "we often felt like Lewis and Clark, the explorers who invented terms for flora and fauna they discovered in the uncharted West." Later, they say, "It takes courage to go against the grain of what society expects of an educated woman.... The conventional expectation for a wife and mother today is that she works outside the home. To do otherwise is countercultural."[57] To the contrary, an educated mother of young children is expected to curb her work hours or take a few years' leave from her career until her children are older.

In defending stay-at-home motherhood, Kaufman and Quigley adopt a patronizing tone toward all middle-class and upper-middle-class married working mothers. They suggest these mothers have not properly calculated their household financial status. "Unquestionably, some of you work because you need the money. We're saying: Think about it. Think it through. Sharpen your pencil. You may have more options than you're aware of. Don't be so quick to assume that you can't afford to stay at home." It seems unfathomable to the authors that some mothers want to continue working for its own sake. If they can afford to live off their husbands' salaries, then "the decision to continue full-time work is based on wanting a certain lifestyle rather than an economic necessity.... [S]ome young women approach motherhood as just another item on the to-do list of accomplishments: college, check. Grad school, check. Good job with title, check. Decent apartment, great wardrobe, check. Better job, check. Nice vacation, check. Marriage, check. First condo or house, check. Baby, check—or so it seems."[58]

Kaufman and Quigley are defensive because the full-time mother is often stereotyped as a woman who packs off her kids to school and then goes shopping, plays tennis, has lunch with her friends, and watches the soaps before her kids return at the end of the day. In reality, most full-time mothers are busy at school, playgroups, or community organizations when they're not doing household chores, spending hours with children, sewing costumes, or coaching sports. If they have an infant or toddler, they are busy with the ceaseless tasks of breast-feeding, cooking, cajoling, monitoring, transporting, reading, teaching, cleaning, and wiping. It is grueling, tiring, thankless, and unpaid work.

However, women with school-age children don't spend significantly more hours with them than working-out-of-the-home mothers. A large-scale 1983 study of time use found that a typical full-time mother spends less than ten minutes per day playing with or reading to her child. She is busy with household chores, and spends more of her time watching television (an average of twenty-one minutes a day) than in any other activity. The working mother, this study found, spends as much time as the nonworking mother in direct interaction with her children. The main difference is when the interaction occurs: The working mother reads to her children and plays with them in the mornings, evenings, and weekends.[59] A more recent study from 1997, conducted by the Institute for Social Research at the University of Michigan, similarly found that today's working mothers spend about the same amount of time (26.5 hours a week) with their children as at-home mothers did a generation ago, in 1981 (26 hours). Today's fathers and at-home mothers, however, do spend an additional four to six hours a week with their children as compared with the previous generation. The only group that did not register an increase was single mothers. The study's researchers say that there is more time to spend with children today because families are doing less housework than they used to.[60]

Because there is so much misunderstanding between mothers who work for pay and those who stay at home, mothers tend to befriend only other mothers who've made the same decision they have. Thus, a thirty-five-year-old physician with four kids and a nanny sighs when I ask if she socializes with the mothers of her children's friends. Many of them are stay-at-home mothers. "It's hard for me to connect with them," she says. "There's a real division between the mommy kids and the nanny kids. Mommy kids can't play with nanny kids because nanny kids don't have a mother who's present when the kids play. So my kids only play with other nanny kids and I associate with the mothers who have nannies."

Most of us know working and stay-at-home mothers, and we know that both are too busy and have little time for themselves. Both live complicated and full lives. But what they most have in common is this: They must make significant lifestyle decisions that their partners, generally, do not. "Men get to work. They get to have a career," says a thirty-three-year-old lawyer who is planning to have a child but worries about the future of her career in which she has invested ten years. "They don't have to worry, 'Well, if I have a baby, will I take two years off? Will I not work again?' They don't have to calculate how old they will be when they start a family and how many years they have to take off and will they have to leave their kids at day care."

Whether a mother spends her weekdays working for pay or being busy with her children at home is not the real issue. The real issue is the rigid nature of the U.S. labor force that effectively discriminates against women because it forces mothers into an all-or-nothing decision and then punishes them no matter what decision they make. The paucity of child care alternatives further compels mothers to make decisions that may not be best for them or their families. Working mothers and full-time mothers, then, face enormous constraints. Both groups need to stop judging each other and band together to demand better conditions for all parents so that they can be present for their children and also continue to provide for them.

CHAPTER SIX
WHEN WOMEN WORK TOGETHER

We have examined major areas in which women tend to compete, judge, or envy other women. But what happens when women do decide to collaborate, when we work together to achieve a goal? Can we overcome our conditioning and focus on a shared agenda? There are two models of women's collaboration, one historical and one contemporary, that offer illumination: the suffrage movement (1848–1920) and women's sports.

THE SUFFRAGE MOVEMENT

American women organized to fight for their rights in 1848. Seventy-two years later, their movement culminated in the Nineteenth Amendment to the Constitution. It was a long, difficult struggle. During those years, millions of women, with a small number of charismatic leaders, united in the belief that they were entitled to full political citizenship. The right to vote would not have been signed into law had it not been for the relentlessness of women with a common agenda. Yet, had it not been for divisiveness within the movement, and the ultimate decision of a new generation of leaders to conform to "ladylike" conventions rather than fight against them, suffrage could also have marked the beginning of a new age of women's rights. Instead, the Nineteenth Amendment signaled the conclusion to the movement for women's rights.[1]

To understand why suffrage was denied women for so long, we have to understand how women were regarded at the time. In the United States in the early 1800s, it was believed that women's brains were smaller than men's and therefore inferior, and that women's most elevated tasks were parenting and taking care of the household. Thus, there was no reason for women to receive any education other than in the domestic arts, and the vast majority of girls were not educated. But as the 1800s progressed, industrial development spread, the population of our new country grew, and women were in demand as teachers and other workers. They began to undertake responsibilities in the public sphere and became essential to the smooth working of both the economy and civic life.

Still, women had very few rights. They could not control their own earnings or property, sign legal papers, bring a lawsuit, or bear witness. If a married woman worked and earned a salary, her money belonged to her husband—even if, as historian Eleanor Flexner has pointed out, her husband were a drunkard and spent every penny on alcohol, leaving no provisions for his wife and children. If she sought divorce, he would probably have been granted legal guardianship of the children, despite his inability to provide adequate care.[2]

In the 1830s, a small group of women, fed up with their situation, decided to do something about it. They learned from the growing abolitionist movement, which was holding meetings, conducting petition campaigns, and assisting runaway slaves to escape to free territory via the Underground Railroad. In fact, several prominent abolitionists were women: Lucretia Mott and the sisters Sarah and Angelina Grimké. The Grimké sisters were abolitionist celebrities who violated nineteenth-century "ladylike" convention by speaking in public and who, over time, made the practice acceptable. It was they who began to link the two issues of slavery and the status of women.

A growing number of people became aware of the injustices against women, and between 1839 and 1850 most states passed some kind of legislation recognizing the right of married women to hold property. But women's status did not become a cause of its own until the summer of 1848. That July, Lucretia Mott and Elizabeth Cady Stanton, the educated wife of abolitionist leader Henry B. Stanton, decided to convene a Women's Rights Convention in Seneca Falls, New York, in which they would present their resolutions for a better life for American women.

Over two days, an audience of some three hundred people, including men, most of them active in the abolitionist movement, came to hear discussions of women's inequalities. Stanton argued that women needed the right to vote if they were ever going to improve their conditions. Suffrage, as she saw it, was a means rather than an end in itself: It was intimately interlinked with all the other civil rights that women were entitled to possess. The proposition on suffrage, more than any other presented at the convention, was considered shocking and radical. But it was approved by the participants—by a small margin.

The Women's Rights Convention was one of the most notable events in American history because it was the first time women came together to work on changing their own status under the law. Until 1848, individual women such as Mary Wollstonecraft and the Grimké sisters had written and spoken out about women's lot, but now a group of women was determined to do something about it—together. By today's standards the goals of this movement were exceedingly tame. But at the time, they were controversial and abhorrent to most of America. If women held many of the same rights as men, then men would not be able to hold on to the privilege of their sex. No longer would they be able to control their wives and daughters as property. No longer could they reign supreme in the public world and no longer could they count on women alone to make the home a safe haven. The rights sought by members of the new women's movement meant nothing less than a vast overhaul of American life, and most Americans wanted nothing of the kind.

Two of the most important architects of the movement were Stanton and Susan B. Anthony. Theirs was an unlikely friendship, but because they saw past their differences and teamed up with a common cause, history would forever be changed. Stanton was motivated to fight for women's rights soon after she moved to Seneca Falls and was confronted with the tireless and lonely life of a housewife with many children (she would eventually have seven) in an isolated, small town. Her husband was often away on business; she had no intellectual stimulation or even an occasional opportunity to relax. Anthony, by contrast, enjoyed being single; by choice, she never married or had children. She first became aware of discrimination against women when she worked as a headmistress of a private school yet earned a fraction of the salary earned by the headmaster. Since she wasn't married and had to support herself, she was very conscious of the disparity in men's and women's earnings. The two women met in 1851 and became fast friends. Stanton persuaded Anthony to become involved in the women's movement. Anthony proved indispensable: She was to become the primary strategist and has been called the Napoleon of the movement.

Throughout the 1850s, the two women led the movement to change laws. Stanton spoke before New York State's two legislative houses to make their case. Anthony traveled throughout the state, often in harsh conditions, to gather signatures for petitions and to speak publicly to promote their cause. Because of their efforts, in 1860 the women of New York won the right to own property, collect their own wages, and sue in court.

During the Civil War, women became essential to the work force. While men were fighting, women earned wages and single-handedly managed households. They provided food and clothing to the soldiers, cared for the sick and wounded as nurses, and manufactured wartime goods. Even after the war, more and more women worked as industrialization grew at a fast pace. No longer were women necessarily confined to the home. It was becoming harder to justify their second-class treatment. Stanton and Anthony, earlier regarded as off-balance for their ideas, now appeared almost reasonable. More women saw the cause of women's rights as legitimate and followed their lead.

Members of the movement, however, were betrayed by many of the very people who should have been their natural allies—abolitionists. In the aftermath of the war, when Congress was debating granting suffrage to black men, Stanton and Anthony maintained that it would be easy to extend that right to women as well. But despite women's indispensability during wartime, the dominant belief was still that women belonged at home, not in the public sphere (particularly middle-class white women, because black and working-class women of both races always had to work outside the home as well as inside), and that therefore they should exert their influence at home and not in the men's world of public affairs. The abolitionists agreed, arguing that black men needed suffrage more than women did. Thus, the Fifteenth Amendment did not extend the right to vote to women of any race.

Just as the women's movement was gaining strength, it divided. In 1869, two separate organizations formed, each with a different ideology and strategy. This rift would have long-lasting repercussions, not only for the suffrage movement but for the direction of twentieth-century feminism. The divide began when Stanton and Anthony organized the National Woman Suffrage Association, for women only. This organization regarded the right to vote as one elemental part of the larger struggle for women's autonomy. It adopted a platform that linked women's right to vote with many other women's issues, and embraced anyone who would speak for women. Some of these issues were considered radical and shocking to middle-class Americans, such as the ability of women to seek a divorce without penalty, equal pay for equal work, and the right of women to have sex with pleasure (the latter preached most famously by the flamboyant and controversial Victoria Woodhull).

In response to the formation of the National, Lucy Stone led an alternate suffrage organization, the American Woman Suffrage Association. This organization was cautious and conservative. It worked solely for suffrage. Its leaders were not interested in working in collaboration with other women's rights groups because it feared alienating middle-class Americans. The two organizations also differed as to the most expedient strategy for achieving suffrage. While the National focused on influencing Congress, the American concentrated on trying to amend constitutions of individual states and territories. Indeed, over the next several decades, territories like Wyoming and Utah did enact women's suffrage.

Between 1880 and the early 1900s, many members of the conservative faction of the suffrage movement were also involved in the moral crusade of the social purity movement. They advanced the idea that women were morally superior to men and lacked sexual desire; they therefore needed to be protected from the lustful excesses of men. These activists sought regulations against prostitution, obscenity, even divorce and contraception—all in the name of "protecting" women. In truth, they were concerned almost exclusively with the interests of white, middle-class women, and they actually did little to advance the cause of women's equality. If anything, they hurt women more than they helped them by reinforcing the old idea that women and men belong in separate spheres with distinct roles.

By 1890, the influence of the older generation of woman suffrage leaders was on the wane, and the conservative forces overruled the radical elements of the movement. The two factions, the National and the American, merged into a new organization, the National American Woman Suffrage Association. Stanton was forced out when she published a feminist commentary on the Bible, *The Woman's Bible*, in which she analyzed the Bible through the lens of women's equality and found it sorely lacking. Enraged suffragists censured the very woman who had jump-started the entire cause of suffrage. In the early 1900s, both Stanton and Anthony died and a new generation of leaders took over the helm.

By 1913 women had suffrage in nine states. That year, new leaders Alice Paul and Lucy Burns organized a parade of five thousand women, who marched up Washington's Pennsylvania Avenue the day before Woodrow Wilson's inauguration, when the city was filled with visitors from across the country. Suffragists now worked for the sole purpose of enacting a federal suffrage amendment to the Constitution. Like their predecessors, these leaders and their constituents endured many hardships—pickets, arrests, jail sentences, even hunger strikes.

During the First World War, women took jobs in manufacturing and agriculture and in the railway, automobile, and airplane industries. As was evident during the Civil War, women's responsibilities were in severe disharmony with their lack of civil rights. After the war, women's suffrage became more tenable. In the first few months of 1917 alone, seven states granted its women the right to vote. The constitutional amendment dubbed the "Anthony Amendment" passed the House in January 1918, with exactly the two-thirds majority required to pass a constitutional amendment. It took two and a half more years, until August 1920, for the United States Senate to ratify the amendment. The vote was 49 to 47.

Because the suffrage movement in its later years concentrated solely on suffrage to the exclusion of other rights for women, its work was now done and it had no reason to exist. Voting, which Elizabeth Cady Stanton had envisioned as a means to an end, had become an end in itself. The movement fell apart; few women even sought elected office in the decades that followed. An essential right for women had been gained, but at great cost. In an effort to be cautious, practical, and "ladylike," suffragists lost the opportunity to build a long-lasting collaboration of women.

Nevertheless, women won the right to vote because women worked together town by town, state by state, and only lost momentum and passion when they became concerned about maintaining feminine conditioning and decorum. As a result, American women were pressured to retreat to their traditional role as sole protectors of family and home for the next half-century, when the "second wave" of feminism again took up the cause of women's rights—and this time, to hell with decorum.

WOMEN IN SPORTS TODAY

The second wave of feminism ushered in truly radical changes for women—the right to an abortion, the outlawing of discrimination based on sex, the surge of women in professions that had long been controlled by men, such as medicine and law. It also won the opportunity for girls and women to participate in sports. In 1972, legislation known as Title IX mandated equal financing for girls' athletics in federally funded school programs. As a result, girls in elementary and high schools and women in college have spent the past thirty years catching up with boys in developing their athletic prowess, and women's professional sports are now attracting as much, if not more, attention than their male counterparts.

Like the suffragists of yore, girls and women involved in sports today, particularly team sports, represent a massive effort of female collaboration: To win a game, they must work together with members of their team. Like the suffragists before them, females involved in sports go against the grain of what is expected, since girls and women are not "supposed" to be competitive and not "supposed" to get down and dirty, as sports often require of its participants. What's interesting about sports specifically is that it fosters both collaboration and competition at the same time, since obviously to win, one must prove herself superior to others even as she molds herself to the needs of her team. Does this tension force athletes to compete in a healthy way? Can women in sports provide a model for being collaborative while being competitive?

In our current cultural environment, there is no definitive answer. On the one hand, there are many obvious advantages to girls' and women's participation in sports. Girls and women are now given the chance to compete in the same way that boys and men have always done. They learn to compete in an aboveboard way within a rigid framework with rules and regulations. Moreover, they learn the importance of working with other females as a team, which means trusting and granting responsibilities to other females. These impulses are not automatic for many of us because we have been conditioned to divide from one another rather than unite.

On the other hand, from observations of both amateur and professional sports, women do not necessarily collaborate or compete in the most collegial way. There is often fierce hostility among competitors, and women are not naturally kind and gentle in their pursuit of winning. Most important, because of the historical exclusion of women from the world of sports, together with lingering homophobia, women in sports feel pressured to make themselves appear as "feminine" as possible, which serves only to divide women from one another in a tacit competition over who is most female.

Women's sports have surged in popularity over the last few years, especially since the 1996 Olympics. That summer in Atlanta, American women won the gold in softball, basketball, and soccer. At the winter Olympics in Nagano in 1998, the American women's ice hockey team took home the gold.

In 1999, forty million people watched the final game of the Women's World Cup in which the U.S. women's soccer team won a suspenseful victory, with Brandi Chastain making a triumphant penalty kick and then taking off her jersey, exposing her black sports bra, before being engulfed by her giddy teammates.

In a Gatorade commercial that ran in 1999, soccer star Mia Hamm and Michael Jordan challenged each other over the soundtrack of "Anything You Can Do, I Can Do Better," with Hamm matching Jordan move for move. In the summer Olympics in Sydney in 2000, the women brought home the gold in basketball and softball, and celebrity athletes Venus and Serena Williams and Marion Jones won the gold in tennis and track and field. Female athletes now enjoy lucrative commercial endorsements just as male athletes always have. The Women's National Basketball Association (WNBA) now regularly has sell-out crowds to its games, even though it's only six years old. Today, increasing numbers of women are building careers behind the scenes in the American sports industry as administrators, marketers, and executives. Seventy-five percent of tennis fans prefer the women's game, and the television ratings for the women are routinely higher than for the men.[3]

This new popularity has trickled down to school-age girls. In 1970, only one in twenty-seven girls participated in high school sports. Today the figure is one in three.[4] More than 3.5 million girls in elementary and high school play soccer in the United States. At the college level, during the 1971–72 season, fewer than 15 percent of college varsity athletes were female. Today, 41 percent are female.[5] Mariah Burton Nelson, author and former professional basketball player, applauds the new interest in sports among girls and points out that girls who are involved in sports can bond with each other instead of competing over boyfriends and diets.[6] There is also evidence that female athletes do better academically and have lower drop-out rates than their nonathletic counterparts and that exercise and sports participation can offer adolescent girls self-confidence, positive feelings about their bodies, and feelings of competency and success. In a major study conducted by the Women's Sports Foundation, researchers found that girls who are athletes are less than half as likely to get pregnant as female nonathletes, and that they are also less likely to use illicit drugs, smoke cigarettes, and be suicidal.[7] Thus, the U.S. Department of Health and Human Services counseled in 1997 that girls "should be encouraged to get involved in sport and physical activity at an early age."[8]

Women's sports enthusiasts maintain that, aside from individual benefits to the physical and mental health of girls, women in sports provide good role models because they place a greater emphasis on teamwork and less focus on aggression or thuggery than men in sports do. At the WNBA games I've been to at Madison Square Garden in New York, Liberty fans told me that they prefer women's games over men's because "the atmosphere is different." One young woman in her late twenties said, "There's not as much showing off. I think there's more teamwork and less showboating. I just feel like they're working harder because they have to prove themselves. Ever since I've been watching them, I've become more interested in sports in general. I've even started playing myself." A female season ticket holder said to me, "The women's game is different from the men's game. The women's game is more about finesse. The women have more focus and passion." Another season ticket holder told me she likes the WNBA because "The women are not downright nasty. You have to be nasty sometimes, you have to play hard sometimes, but the women don't do it without being fair." (She added that that she also prefers the New York Liberty over the New York Knicks because "the tickets are a lot less expensive.")

But is it in fact true that women in basketball are not as nasty as men? Is there really more teamwork and less showing off? At Liberty games, I've seen plenty of angry blows, sharp jabs, and out-and-out fighting. The players also seem to enjoy grabbing personal attention by arguing with referees and falling to the floor in pretend agony in bids for sympathy. It is not clear to me what makes these games "female" aside from the sex of the participants, the absence of dunking, and the extra six seconds on the shot clock. Certainly the WNBA players appear just as determined to win as NBA players do.

On the amateur level, too, women in sports are not necessarily kinder and gentler than their male counterparts. If anything, I've heard reports to the contrary. Laura Sigman, a player in an all-female amateur basketball league in Manhattan, has watched the men in her league and observes, "They go out there and play. They rarely argue a call. They rarely argue among each other, at least not publicly. But the women's games ..." Laura sighs. "The women scream at each other, they scream at women on the other team, they scream at the refs. They are really aggressive. I come home with bruises. I mean, this is not the WNBA. This is supposed to be an after-work leisure league. We do it once a week to get some exercise and have some fun. We're in the beginner level. But it's become very competitive. Very, very competitive."

Just because women may react more emotionally than their male counterparts doesn't mean they compete the "wrong" way. Men in sports, for that matter, do not necessarily compete in a "correct" way. But in general, competition is healthier and fun when it's practiced in an open environment, when everyone involved is straightforward about her goals. The women in the amateur league express themselves uninhibitedly, which is valuable: They are willing to broadcast their own competitiveness. But at the same time, they feel anxious about their competitiveness. They confuse their legitimate desire to win with an illegitimate need to insult others, emotionally and physically. As an observer I see that male athletes, by and large, are less likely to personally attack their team members or members of an opposing team. This is not because men are inherently better than women but because men have had the opportunity to engage in sports for a long time, and with tremendous social support. Unlike women, they have the privilege of confidence: They know that wanting to compete to win is a legitimate endeavor.

Marilyn Edwards, an editor who has long been involved in competitive bike racing, reports, "I've always trained with men, my training partners have been men, so I can compare the way men do sports and the way women do sports. And I find that the women are much more personal. They tend to take things more personally. Women tend to make comments about other women athletes' bodies. Cycling is a very weight-conscious sport. The muscle-to-fat ratio is very important. It's always about losing the last extra five pounds. There was this one woman who was on a national team in Canada and she was really good, but she was heavy. You wouldn't have believed the catty comments about her, that she was fat, that she needed to lose weight. But she was an exceptional athlete." Claudia Manley, a writer and editor as well as an ice hockey player, confirms Edwards's observations. When male athletes criticize other male athletes, she says, "it's about skill level, like: 'He has no sprinting speed.' But women often make comments that are based on personality or looks. I've heard women say things like, 'She's a bitch' or 'She's so ugly.'"

Female athletes, however, are not given the same opportunities as their male counterparts, which no doubt makes them particularly defensive. In the professional world of women's sports, there are huge pay discrepancies between female and male athletes. The U.S. women who won the World Cup in 1999 were paid $12,500 each. The American men would have earned $388,000 each had they won.[9] WNBA players earn salaries that are a fraction of those earned by NBA players, even though both leagues pull in sold-out crowds. Colleges and universities spend far more on men's athletics than on women's. At the college level, women receive 41 percent of the athletic scholarships, 33 percent of athletic operating budgets, and 30 percent of the dollars spent to recruit new athletes.[10] Aside from the inequality in pay and budgets, women in sports face discrimination in people's attitudes. Many people find humor in the very idea of women engaging in athletics—what could be more ludicrous? Case in point: A *New York Times* article on women preparing for the Women's Professional Football League (founded in 1999). "The ladies couldn't throw," the article began. You had to keep reading to find out that it wasn't their sex that weakened them but the forty-mile-an-hour gusts that plagued the players on the day the reporter came to visit them.[11]

Female athletes today are no longer novices or newcomers. They deserve to be treated with the same respect the men command. Their sometimes gruff attitudes stem from their second-class treatment. But it is also the result of their development as athletes. Marilyn Edwards points out that when women are novices, they go out of their way to teach one another and to encourage other women to participate in sports. "But there comes a point, and I find myself doing this too, where you see other women who are at your level and you can't be as nice and supportive as you used to be because you want to win. Sometimes I'm one of only three women in a group of seventy-five people [competing in bike racing]. There is definitely a status to being an accomplished female athlete [in bike racing] because we are so rare. And when other women enter the realm, there is competition for attention and status. I don't want too many women doing the same thing because then I won't be considered so special."

Another explanation of women's different competitive style is that, like Edwards, many women in sports feel conflicted about their desire to win—since "femininity" and competition are supposedly incompatible. Thus, when a woman has the desire to be the best— better than anyone on the opposing team and even better than everyone on her own team—she doesn't quite know how to behave. Since she has been conditioned to criticize other women who seem to pose a threat to her own success, she is likely to become aggressive toward the women with whom, according to the rules of sportsmanship, she is supposed to respect. Men in sports might not resort to personal attacks as often because, unlike women, they feel secure in their position as athletes. They have been told their whole lives that athletics is men's domain, so they feel right at home.

THE MOST FEMININE ATHLETE WINS

The female athlete today is no longer an eyebrow-raiser. She is no longer a pioneer. So how can she distinguish herself from her colleagues? One thing that professional athletes, particularly those who play in team sports, do is play up their femininity. Because of the long-held stereotype that all female athletes are lesbians, many women in sports bend over backward to show how sexy they are. WNBA and Olympic star Lisa Leslie, who plays with polished fingernails and models in her spare time, posed for the cover of the May–June 2000 issue of *Sports Illustrated Women* in a midriff-baring bathing suit. Gabrielle Reece, 1990s volleyball star, posed nude for *Playboy* in a twelve-page photo spread in the January 2001 issue. The WNBA, which consciously tries to project a "family-friendly," wholesome image, handpicks its stars for their feminine (read: heterosexual) appeal as much as for their abilities on the court.

Many professional athletes are in fact lesbians, but most remain closeted lest their fans lose interest in them and commercial endorsements and other financial opportunities dry up. The stigma surrounding lesbianism puts pressure on all female athletes, regardless of their sexuality, to look as feminine as possible, and it effectively divides female athletes from one another: No one wants to risk the chance of being seen as gay or associating with anyone who is gay. Anyone who hasn't publicly come out is under tremendous pressure to prove her heterosexuality by being as sexy as possible and by distancing herself from colleagues who are known or suspected to be lesbians.

For most of Western history, sports have been the province of men alone. Only men were allowed to compete in the ancient Greek Olympics; in fact, women were forbidden from even watching the games. When the Olympics were revived in 1896, the male-only tradition continued. The United States did not send a women's team to the Olympics until 1920.[12] In 1928, the director of physical education for New York State declared that competitive sport is an "unnatural activity for girls" likely "to distort their natures." He warned that if girls were to "ape" boys by playing competitive sports, it would be "disastrous to the welfare of...men, women, and society."[13]

If sport is men's domain, then any woman who participates is trespassing on private property, violating the norms of femininity, and "ruining" the significance of sports for men. How special can sports be if women are allowed to be involved? An easy way for men to hold on to their turf is to discredit lesbianism in general, and then to disgrace women in sports by calling them lesbians. Sports historian Pat Griffin explains:

> Stigmatizing lesbian identity serves the interests of those who want to maintain the imbalance of opportunity and power in athletics based on gender. As long as women's sports are associated with lesbians and lesbians are stigmatized as sexual and social deviants, the lesbian label serves an important social-control function in sport, ensuring that only men have access to the

benefits of sport participation and the physical and psychological empowerment available in sport.[14]

Until Title IX, when the idea of women in sports became more acceptable to the population at large, lesbians often did flock to sports, particularly team sports. It was one haven for those who did not fit feminine norms and a place for like-minded women to meet each other. Team sports continue to hold appeal for lesbians today.

Feminine women, together with men, benefit from homophobia in women's sports. Griffin cites the case study of Babe Didrikson, "arguably the greatest athlete of the 20th century," who became a national celebrity in the 1930s after winning Olympic medals in track and field. Didrikson, a closeted lesbian (her sexual identity was confirmed only after her death), was described by sportswriters as "mannish," "unfeminine," and "unattractive." Sports fans and reporters alike derided her as a "muscle moll." But in the years following World War II, when the government began cracking down on communists and anyone not part of the mainstream, Didrikson decided that she could no longer afford to be regarded as masculine. In the 1950s she began wearing skirts and makeup and she married a man. She turned from track and field to the more genteel sport of golf and downplayed her earlier Olympic accomplishments.[15]

During World War II, Philip Wrigley, owner of the Chicago Cubs, formed the All-American Girls' Baseball League (AAGBL), later sold to and administered by Arthur Meyerhoff until its demise in 1950. Meyerhoff wanted only "feminine" white women on his teams. He believed that the only way the public would buy tickets was if the players were attractive and heterosexual. The treatment of the character Marla Hooch in the movie *A League of Their Own*, a fictionalized documentation of the real-life AAGBL team the Rockford Peaches, is not far from the way unattractive players were treated in the 1940s. In the movie, Marla is a great hitter, but the manager says he can't use her because she's not pretty. She makes the team anyway, but is the butt of most of the film's jokes and sight gags. "Every girl in this league is going to be a lady," the players are told, and they are required to take regular classes in charm and beauty. The player Dottie Hinson (Geena Davis) is given preferential treatment not only because she is an ace player but because she is beautiful and married (her husband is in the Pacific fighting the war) and therefore the epitome of the "lady" the league wanted its players to be. In fact, AAGBL officials really did choose players because of their feminine appearance, and players were required to compete in a skirted uniform and makeup.

Since the 1970s, lesbianism has become less of a stigma in the culture at large, but it remains a problematic identity in the world of U.S. women's sports. In 1981, tennis star Billie Jean King revealed that she had had a lesbian lover; her commercial sponsors subsequently deserted her. The same year, fellow tennis player Martina Navratilova revealed her relationship with writer Rita Mae Brown; she, too, paid a high price in her loss of sponsors as well as fans. Officials of the Women's Tennis Association warned other players not to come out because they wouldn't tolerate any more lesbians.[16] Today on college campuses, administrators worry that their schools will develop a reputation as lesbian-friendly; they don't want a repeat of WNBA star Sheryl Swoopes's departure from the

University of Texas, which, according to her mother, was because she was "bothered by the presence of lesbians on the basketball team."[17] Colleges, therefore, are known to retract sports scholarships from students once they are discovered to be lesbians, and either refuse to hire or discriminate against coaches who are known to be lesbians. In 1991, it was exposed in the *Philadelphia Inquirer* that Penn State women's basketball coach Rene Portland did not allow lesbians on her teams.[18] Ohio State University, meanwhile, hired field hockey coach Karen Weaver in 1987. Weaver was clearly very talented and the best field hockey coach the university had ever had. Her team broke into the top five of the Division I (the most competitive grouping of the National College Athletic Association) standings. Despite the school's policy prohibiting discrimination on the basis of sexual orientation, she was attacked covertly for her alleged lesbianism and fired in 1996. Six other female coaches, all believed to be lesbians, were forced from their jobs between 1994 and 1997.[19]

Europeans are far more tolerant of lesbian athletes. French tennis star Amélie Mauresmo announced her homosexuality in 1999 at the Australian Open and publicly hugged and kissed her lover. The French have stood by her and are proud of their country's champion. She is considered a national hero. All of Mauresmo's corporate sponsors have supported her. A spokesman for Dunlop, one of her sponsors, has said, "We signed her up [because] we were attracted by her athleticism, skill, and dedication. Her sexuality is her own business and has no impact on our sponsorship." An American player who came out, on the other hand, would be deserted by at least some of her corporate sponsors, and Americans on the whole would not be very receptive. After losing to Mauresmo in one match, Lindsay Davenport has said that her "shoulders looked huge to me...I think they must have grown," and added that sometimes she feels that she is "playing against a guy." (Homophobia is hardly limited to American players, however; the Swiss star Martina Hingis has called Mauresmo "half a man" and has sneered, "She's here with her *girlfriend*.")[20]

The biggest names in women's U.S. sports are "feminine." It seems that each star has decided (or is pressured by team management) to represent a different facet of traditional femininity. There is Sheryl Swoopes, often portrayed as a homebody whose son is the most important thing in her life. A *Sports Illustrated Women* profile says that Swoopes "turned down a spot on the Olympic national team because she loves her son even more." She is one of the highest paid female team athletes in the world, the first female athlete to have a signature shoe, the Nike Air Swoopes, and one of only two women to win an NCAA title, an Olympic gold medal, and a WNBA title. But in interviews, she prefers to emphasize that she is a mother first and foremost. "When I'm done on the court, I'm going to go home and spend time with my child. I look forward to that. I could watch him play all day," she told the magazine. Not that there is anything wrong with juggling professional athletics and parenthood—far from it. It would be wonderful if male athletes boasted about their role as fathers. Think about how much influence someone like Michael Jordan could wield on teenage boys and young men if he chose to champion fatherhood and the responsibilities of child raising. However, when women in sports are represented as women first, athletes second, their athletic abilities are minimized because women are not "supposed" to be athletes in the first place. They present a picture of themselves as "soft"—and therefore nonthreatening to men. They "remind" us that women's real place is in the home, not the court or field.

Cynthia Cooper, two-time Most Valuable Player of the WNBA, member of two U.S. Olympic teams, and a huge star, has been relentlessly portrayed in the press as the doting caretaker of her sick mother and friend. Cooper's mother, Mary Cobbs, was diagnosed with breast cancer in 1997, just as the WNBA was in its first season. Cooper oversaw her mother's care and frequently traveled back and forth to accompany her mother during her chemotherapy treatments. Cobbs died in 1999, the same year that Cooper's best friend and teammate, Kim Perrot, was also diagnosed with cancer and died. Again and again, the details of Cooper's relationship with these two women have been highlighted more than her athletic achievements. Cooper herself has been complicit in the way she has been represented; the narrative of her 1999 autobiography, *She Got Game*, is anchored by her mother's illness and her influence on Cooper's life. The afterword to the paperback edition is dedicated to the memory of Kim Perrot.[21] Two weeks after Perrot's death, when their team, the Houston Comets, won their third championship, Cooper waved her friend's number-10 jersey in the air. Cooper is now an activist in raising money for cancer research. When I read about her hardships and how she channeled her emotional losses into activism, I was inspired. But why do articles about her sports achievements devote so much space to her life story and activism in the first place? Could it be that she is less threatening when she is regarded as the good daughter and devoted friend of cancer victims? By putting the emotional traumas she has experienced before her physical challenges on the court, do journalists—and Cooper herself—seek to minimize the significance of her physical prowess?

Then there are the athletes who put their sex appeal above all else. There is Anna Kournikova, the pinup tennis player who wears tight outfits. Kournikova has never won a singles title and is not one of the game's best players. Yet her sponsors include corporate heavyweights Adidas shoes and apparel, Omega watches, lycos.com, and Yonex racquets. Amy Acuff, Olympic high jumper, has been a body double for Daryl Hannah and a model for the Click agency. She has been voted one of ESPN's top twenty sexiest athletes and one of *Esquire*'s "10 Sexiest Athletes in America." Acuff has been ranked internationally among the top five in her sport, but she has chosen to grab attention by posing semiclad for *Rolling Stone* and hosting an MTV home video in which a workout demonstration is followed by a makeup session and a swimsuit fashion segment. In a profile of Olympic triathlete Gina Derks-Gardner, *Vogue* informs us that she takes her hairdresser with her everywhere, even to the Olympics. Sometimes Derks-Gardner goes straight to the salon after training.[22] Are these women supposed to be role models for their athleticism or for their perfectly groomed hair?

The two athletes who put the most effort into reminding everyone that they are women first, athletes second, are tennis stars and sisters Venus and Serena Williams. Each sister has won the U.S. Open, Venus two years in a row; Venus has won Wimbledon twice and boasts a 115-miles-per-hour serve; between the two of them, they earned over $17 million in the year 2000 alone; Venus has a $40 million endorsement contract with Reebok, the largest for a female athlete. Still, both sisters are pursuing degrees in fashion design and make it clear that fashion, not tennis, is their true love. Their professional goal is to start a clothing business together. Venus told *The New York Times* that she had to win at Wimbledon 2000 because she had already bought a dress she wanted to wear to the champions ball. "I had one dress I could wear," she said. "It was last year's, and colors have changed since then. I was scrambling. It was an extra incentive to win, because if I didn't, I wouldn't get to wear this wonderful dress."[23] According to *Vogue*, both sisters "have been known to shift out of autopilot and perk up when the subject turns from tennis to Prada and Gucci."[24] They posed seminude for *Elle*, a magazine that is less interested in their titles and more focused on the fact that they "get wonderfully agitated when they talk about handbags."[25]

There is nothing wrong with the Williams sisters pursuing fashion design; it is smart of them to plan future careers since tennis stars, like many professional athletes, have a short shelf life. However, their avid discussions of their nonprofessional pursuits, which happen to be "feminine," provide a counterpoint to their image as strong, fierce athletes. Perhaps they feel the need, as women, to downplay their physical capabilities because "real" women just don't hit a ball at 115 miles per hour. As *Ms.* magazine justifiably praises them, "Venus and Serena are big and bodacious, flailing with finesse, their nappy hair slinging pearls, later braided into crowns." These are women who "choose to destroy instead of demur."[26] But perhaps in their minds women are "supposed" to demur.

Much has been made of the fact that on occasion, the two sisters compete against each other—most notably at the 2001 U.S. Open, when Venus beat her younger sister. But despite the dramatic rivalry, they seem to sincerely love each other and get along. When Venus won the 2001 U.S. Open, she hugged Serena and said, "I love you." She patted her on the back and blamed the wind for her sister's error-filled performance on the court. In her acceptance speech, Venus said, "I always want Serena to win. It's strange. I'm the bigger sister. I'm the one who takes care of her. I make sure she has everything even if I don't. I love her. It's hard." As Venus spoke, Serena nudged her in the side and whispered, "Don't, Venus. You're making me cry."[27] Their sisterly love seems genuine and is actually quite touching. It also furthers the image both have cultivated as feminine athletes, though in this context, the image is only positive. What could be a better model to emulate than an athlete looking after her sibling, even when her sibling is her biggest rival?

Every athlete works under pressure (from sports management and from the culture at large) to prove she is an appropriate role model for girls and women, and many parents and sports professionals hold a narrow vision of what it means to be a good role model. The people who market women's sports to the public play a particularly big hand in the emphasis on femininity. In 1996, for example, Dick Ebersol, president of NBC Sports, orchestrated the media coverage of the Atlanta Olympics to focus on the personal obstacles facing female athletes. According to Mariah Burton Nelson, who was not a fan of Ebersol's coverage, "Rather than focus on [the female] athletes' strengths—as is traditionally done in sports broadcasting—he emphasized their vulnerabilities. In this way, he hoped, women in the audience would be able to empathize with the Olympians.... So in what came to be known as the Oprah Olympics, NBC told us about athletes' troubled pasts: cancer, car accidents, sports accidents, joint problems, financial problems, coaching problems, divorced parents, dead parents." Nelson observes that to allow time for all this "kinder, gentler coverage" of the athletes, NBC was forced to cut parts of the soccer and softball games, for which the Americans won the gold.[28] Can you imagine the uproar if men's games were cut to allow viewers to learn about male stars' divorced or dying parents?

Women's athletics hold much promise for all girls and women. When girls and women become involved in sports, they learn important lessons about both collaboration and healthy competition. But as long as sports are played in an environment that is overly concerned with distinguishing between "real" women and "unfeminine" women, participants will remain divided: Those who use feminine stereotypes will be rewarded while those who are gay or simply refuse to play up their femininity will be punished. Since celebrity athletes appear not only in games but in television commercials, print ads, and magazine and newspaper profiles, they effectively offer a public endorsement of the status quo for all women: To win the game, the female athlete needs to know her place. If she wants fame, she must be feminine.

When women do collaborate in movements and sports, they achieve major accomplishments. When they move together in strength, there is little they can't accomplish. But because of societal expectations about what it means to be a woman, females who collaborate are often tugged, gently or forcefully, into the traditional feminine role. It is incumbent upon us to be aware of and to fight against these societal pressures. Otherwise, we end up competing with each other for the little power we are allowed to collect.

EPILOGUE

We can see that competition between women serves only the status quo. And the status quo keeps us from gaining more power over our lives, our work, and our relationships. But if we become conscious of our behavior, we can redirect our inclinations. When men compete, they look past the trivia of personal habits. Women, too, need to get past personal attacks. What goes around comes around.

We must channel our energies to create better alliances with other women. Some actions we all can take:

☞ Compliment another woman on her appearance.

☞ Refuse to buy clothing that requires a semistarvation weight. Demand that stores carry size 14 and up.

☞ If you are single, host a party for another single friend in which friends and family join to celebrate a turning point in her life.

☞ Be friendly to your boyfriend's ex.

☞ At singles events, exchange numbers with women as well as men.

☞ In the office, tell your female supervisor how much you admire her work. Help her be a role model. Likewise, if there are women working for you, have lunch with them; offer to mentor someone.

☞ In male-dominated workplaces, form a women's caucus that meets once a month. You and your female colleagues will feel stronger as a group. Demand on-site child care, flexible scheduling, the chance to work from home when necessary, and a room at work for nursing mothers.

☞ Write to senators and representatives to demand that the government expand the Family and Medical Leave Act (which now offers only twelve unpaid weeks of parental leave) to grant universal, paid parental leave for at least ten months, as most European countries now do. Demand that the government offer more adequate subsidies or reimbursement for the cost of child care.

☞ Form a group of mothers to include stay-at-home mothers and full-time and part-time workers. Share insights and tips, and resist a culture that pressures us to make myriad sacrifices and then punishes us for the decisions we make.

☞ Share the realities of new motherhood. Tell the truth. Explain that taking care of a young child is at least as difficult as the most demanding paid job.

☞ Be a friend to someone who has given birth. Offer to watch her infant so that she can take a nap, do chores, or read a newspaper.

☞ If you are involved in amateur team sports, tell a woman on your team (or on another team) that you admire her muscles and strength. Mentor a novice so that she will be inspired to improve her skills and become a formidable competitor.

If we follow these suggestions, we will appreciate one another, rise to the top, and help other women to rise. If we stick together, we can demand that all health insurance plans cover contraceptives such as the Pill (now only 33 percent of plans do). We could shun and shame the men who abuse women, physically or emotionally, and use our institutions to do so: churches, synagogues, mosques, as well as workplaces. We could champion the Renoir bodies of Kate Winslet and Kathleen Turner instead of the emaciated ones of Calista Flockhart and Renée Zellweger. We could have a society in which single women would regard other single women as comrades, not competitors. Mothers who quit their jobs to stay home with their children would do so because it's their choice, not because there is no affordable, quality child care available. Women would applaud other women making the choices that best fit their needs.

If we end competition with each other, all women win. If we unite, we can shape the world to meet our needs.

NOTES

INTRODUCTION

1. Anne Taylor Fleming, *Motherhood Deferred: A Woman's Journey* (New York: Putnam, 1994), p. 177. This passage is an excerpt of a *New York Times Magazine* essay, "Women and the Spoils of Success," written in the 1980s when Fleming was in her thirties.

2. Phyllis Chesler, *Woman's Inhumanity to Woman* (New York: Thunder's Mouth/Nation Books, 2002).

3. bell hooks, *Feminist Theory: From Margin to Center* (Boston: South End Press, 1984), p. 43.

4. Elizabeth Wurtzel, *Bitch: In Praise of Difficult Women* (New York: Anchor, 1999), p. 49.

5. Quoted in Nancy Reagan, *My Turn: The Memoirs of Nancy Reagan* (New York: Random House, 1989). Cited in John Leland, "Gowns? What Gowns?," *New York Times*, February 11, 2001, Week in Review section, p. 2.

6. Genesis 21:9–10; Genesis 29:21–30; I Samuel 1:1–6; I Kings 3:16–28.

7. Susan J. Douglas, *Where the Girls Are: Growing Up Female with the Mass Media* (New York: Times Books, 1994), Chap. 10, "The ERA as Catfight."

8. Elaine Rapping, "You've Come Which Way, Baby?" *Women's Review of Books*, July 2000, p. 21.

9. Leslie Kaufman and Cathy Horyn, "More of Less: Scantier Clothing Catches On," *New York Times*, June 27, 2000, p. B9.

10. Letty Cottin Pogrebin, "Competing with Women," *Ms.*, July 1972, pp. 78–81. Reprinted in *Competition: A Feminist Taboo?*, edited by Valerie Miner and Helen E. Longino (New York: The Feminist Press, 1987), pp. 11–17.

11. Author's interview with Jill Nelson, February 9, 2000.

CHAPTER ONE: THE ROOTS OF THE PROBLEM

1. Alfie Kohn, *No Contest: The Case Against Competition* (New York: Houghton Mifflin, 1986, 1992), p. 100.

2. Ibid., p. 46.

3. Mariah Burton Nelson, *Embracing Victory: How Women Can Compete Joyously, Compassionately, and Successfully in the Workplace and on the Playing Field* (New York: Avon, 1998), pp. 9–10.

4. Charlotte Perkins Gilman, *Herland: A Lost Feminist Utopian Novel* (New York: Pantheon, 1979), pp. 19, 88, 69. Originally published in 1915.

5. Susan Brownmiller, *In Our Time: Memoir of a Revoluion* (New York: Dial, 1999), p. 60.

6. Ibid., p. 211.

7. Sigmund Freud, "Femininity," in *Freud on Women*, edited by Elisabeth Young-Bruehl (New York: Norton, 1990), pp. 353–54.

8. Ibid., p. 350.

9. Nancy J. Chodorow, *Feminism and Psychoanalytic Theory* (New Haven, Conn.: Yale University Press, 1989), pp. 64–65.

10. Phyllis Chesler, *Woman's Inhumanity to Woman* (New York: Thunder's Mouth/Nation Books, 2002), p. 5.

11. Frantz Fanon, *Black Skin, White Masks* (New York: Grove, 1967), pp. 146, 147, 148.

12. Jill Nelson, *Straight, No Chaser: How I Became A Grown-Up Black Woman* (New York: Putnam, 1997), p. 99.

13. Associated Press, "Income Gap Widens for U.S. Families," *New York Times*, January 18, 2000.

14. According to the Congressional Budget Office. David Cay Johnston, "Gap Between Rich and Poor Found Substantially Wider," *New York Times*, September 5, 1999, p. A16.

15. Barbara Ehrenreich, "Class Ceiling," *In These Times*, reprinted in Alternet Independent News and Information wire service, November 25, 1999.

16. Ibid.

17. May 1999 issue.

18. Susan Faludi, "Don't Get the Wrong Message," *Newsweek*, January 8, 2001, p. 56.

19. According to Edward N. Wolff, a professor of economics at New York University. Monique Yazigi, "When You Got It, Flaunt It," *New York Times*, December 26, 1999, Week in Review section, p. 1.

20. Ibid.

21. David D. Kirkpatrick, "Thy Neighbor's Budget," *New York*, August 7, 2000, pp. 33–34.

22. Friedrich Nietzsche, *The Genealogy of Morals III*, section xiv, in *The Birth of Tragedy and the Genealogy of Morals*, translated by Francis Golffing (New York: Doubleday, 1956), pp. 258–59.

23. See Alice Vachss, *Sex Crimes* (New York: Random House, 1993); and Helen Benedict, *Virgin or Vamp: How the Press Covers Sex Crimes* (New York: Oxford, 1993).

24. Nietzsche, *The Genealogy of Morals I*, section x, in *The Birth of Tragedy and the Genealogy of Morals*, translated by Francis Golffing (New York: Doubleday, 1956), pp. 170–71.

25. Sara Ruddick, *Maternal Thinking: Toward a Politics of Peace* (Boston: Beacon, 1989), pp. 150, 148.

26. Patricia Pearson, *When She Was Bad: How and Why Women Get Away with Murder* (New York: Penguin, 1998), p. 7.

27. Carol Tavris, *The Mismeasure of Woman: Why Women are Not the Better Sex, the Inferior Sex, or the Opposite Sex* (New York: Touchstone, 1992), p. 60.

28. Sara Snodgrass, "Women's Intuition: The Effect of Subordinate Role on Interpersonal Sensitivity," *Journal of Personality and Social Psychology* 49 (1985): 146–55. Cited in Tavris, *Mismeasure of Woman*, p. 65.

29. Tavris, *Mismeasure of Woman*, pp. 65–66.

30. Katha Pollitt, "Marooned on Gilligan's Island: Are Women Morally Superior to Men?," originally published in *The Nation* in 1992. Reprinted in Katha Pollitt, *Reasonable Creatures: Essays on Women and Feminism* (New York: Knopf, 1994), pp. 42–62.

31. Dana Crowley Jack, *Behind the Mask: Destruction and Creativity in Women's Aggression* (Cambridge, Mass.: Harvard University Press, 1999), p. 196.

32. Natalie Angier, *Woman: An Intimate Geography* (New York: Houghton Mifflin, 1999), p. 239.

33. Helen Ellis, *Eating the Cheshire Cat* (New York: Scribner, 2000), p. 66.

34. Terri Apter and Ruthellen Josselson, *Best Friends: The Pleasures and Perils of Girls' and Women's Friendships* (New York: Three Rivers Press, 1998), pp. 68–69.

35. Margaret Atwood, *Cat's Eye* (New York: Bantam, 1989, 1996), p. 132.

36. Ibid., p. 237.

37. Apter and Josselson, *Best Friends*, pp. 9–10.

38. Abby Goodnough, "Gym Now Stresses Cooperation, Not Competition," *New York Times*, July 5, 2000, p. B12.

39. Sylvia Plath, *The Unabridged Journals of Sylvia Plath, 1950–1962*, edited by Karen V. Kukil (New York: Anchor, 2000), p. 34.

40. Ibid., p. 38.

41. Ibid., p. 315.

CHAPTER TWO: BEAUTY

1. Pam Houston, "Out of Habit, I Start Apologizing," in *Minding the Body: Women Writers on Body and Soul*, edited by Patricia Foster (New York: Doubleday, 1994), p. 150.

2. Naomi Wolf, *The Beauty Myth: How Images of Beauty Are Used Against Women* (New York: Morrow, 1991), p. 12.

3. Barbara L. Fredrickson et al., "That Swimsuit Becomes You: Sex Differences in Self-Objectification, Restrained Eating, and Math Performance," *Journal of Personality and Social Psychology* 75:1 (1998): 269–84.

4. Sigmund Freud, Selections from "On Narcissism: An Introduction," *Freud on Women*, edited by Elisabeth Young-Bruehl (New York: Norton, 1990), p. 192.

5. Fredrickson et al., "That Swimsuit Becomes You," p. 270.

6. Barbara L. Fredrickson and Tomi-Ann Roberts, "Objectification Theory: Toward Understanding Women's Lived Experiences and Mental Health Risks," *Psychology of Women Quarterly* 21 (1997): 177.

7. Gloria Steinem, "Lovely to Look Upon—Or Else," *New York Times*, January 16, 2000, Week in Review section, p. 17.

8. Cited in Janny Scott, "Florida Face-Off," *New York Times*, December 3, 2000, Week in Review section, p. 3.

9. Steinem, "Lovely to Look Upon."

10. Elaine Sciolino, "Woman in the News: Condoleezza Rice," *New York Times*, December 18, 2000.

11. Bernard Weinraub, "Ratings Grow for a Series, Like the Hair of Its Star," *New York Times*, December 4, 2000, p. E1.

12. Sarah Bernard, "Gotham: Material Moms," *New York*, May 10, 1999, p. 13.

13. Janet Lee, "Coming Back from Pregnancy," *Us*, March 19, 2001, p. 58.

14. "Perspectives," *Newsweek*, March 5, 2001, p. 17.

15. Judith Krantz, "Just Seventy," *Vogue*, August 2001, p. 98.

16. Marilyn Wann, *Fat!So?: Because You Don't Have to Apologize for Your Size!* (Berkeley: Ten Speed Press, 1998), pp. 92–93.

17. Carlta Vitzhum, "Just-in-Time Fashion," *Wall Street Journal*, May 18, 2001, p. B1.

18. Marcelle Karp and Debbie Stoller, eds., *The Bust Guide to the New Girl Order* (New York: Penguin, 1999), p. 47.

19. Dale M. Bauer and Jean Marie Lutes, "Beauty," in *The Oxford Companion to Women's Writing in the United States*, edited by Cathy N. Davidson and Linda Wagner-Martin (New York: Oxford University Press, 1995), p. 96.

20. Kathy Peiss, *Hope in a Jar: The Making of America's Beauty Culture* (New York: Owl/Holt, 1999), pp. 22–24.

21. Fuller is cited in Bauer and Lutes, "Beauty," p. 97.

22. Peiss, *Hope in a Jar*, pp. 24–33.

23. Ibid., pp. 28-39.

24. Author's interview with Kathy Peiss, December 4, 2001.

25. Peiss, *Hope in a Jar*, pp. 142–44.

26. Ibid., p. 146.

27. Ibid., pp. 193–96.

28. Joan Jacobs Brumberg, *Fasting Girls: The History of Anorexia Nervosa* (New York: Plume/Penguin, 1989), pp. 187, 245.

29. Ibid., p. 245.

30. Joan Jacobs Brumberg, *The Body Project: An Intimate History of American Girls* (New York: Random House, 1997), pp. 99–104.

31. Brumberg, *Fasting Girls*, p. 240.

32. Sarah Banet-Weiser, *The Most Beautiful Girl in the World: Beauty Pageants and National Identity* (Berkeley: University of California Press, 1999), pp. 35–43.

33. Alan Feuer, "Miss America Official Fired After Rule Furor," *New York Times*, September 28, 1999; Robin Finn, "Here He Is, The New Chief for Miss America," *New York Times*, April 12, 2000, p. B2.

34. Banet-Weiser, *The Most Beautiful Girl in the World*, p. 57.

35. Tracy Nightingale is a pseudonym. The winner of this pageant spoke to me on the condition of anonymity.

36. Associated Press, "Miss America Winners Said Thinner," *New York Times*, March 22, 2000.

37. Carol Hanisch, excerpt from a critique of the Miss America Protest, in *Dear Sisters: Dispatches from the Women's Liberation Movement*, edited by Rosalyn Baxandall and Linda Gordon (New York: Basic, 2000), pp. 185–86.

38. Andrea Oxidant, "The Skin Trade," *Bitch*, December 2000, p. 24.

39. Amy Bloom, "The Skin Trade," *Elle*, January 2001, p. 80.

40. Karp and Stoller, eds., *The Bust Guide*, p. 47.

41. Ellen Zetzel Lambert, *The Face of Love: Feminism and the Beauty Question* (Boston: Beacon, 1995).

42. Sander L. Gilman, *Making the Body Beautiful: A Cultural History of Aesthetic Surgery* (Princeton, N.J.: Princeton University Press, 1999), p. 331.

43. Claudia Kalb, "Our Quest to be Perfect," *Newsweek*, August 9, 1999, p. 55.

44. David Noonan and Jerry Adler, "The Botox Boom," *Newsweek*, May 13, 2002, p. 52.

45. Jane Gross, "In Quest for the Perfect Look, More Girls Choose the Scalpel," *New York Times*, November 29, 1998, p. A1.

46. The one-in-5,000 fatality rate is from a January 2000 study published in *Plastic and Reconstructive Surgery*. For more information, see Ron Shelton, "Tumescent Liposuction," *eMedicine Journal*, December 5, 2000.

47. Jonathan M. Sackler and A. J. S. Rayl, "How Dangerous is Liposuction?," *USA Today*, Health section, January 24, 2000.

48. Lisa Collier Cool, "Could Breast Implants Make You Sick?" *Glamour*, November 2000, pp. 246–48.

49. Norimitsu Onishi, "On the Scale of Beauty, Weight Weighs Heavily," *New York Times*, February 12, 2001, p. A4.

50. Lori Gottlieb, *Stick Figure: A Diary of My Former Self* (New York: Simon & Schuster, 2000), pp. 90–91.

51. Kate Dillon, as told to Laurel Ives, "Why It's Better to Be a Size 12 Model Than a Size 6," *Marie Claire*, October 2000, p. 141.

52. Abby Ellin, "Dad, Do You Think I Look Too Fat?," *New York Times*, Styles section, September 17, 2000, p. 7.

53. Michelle Stacey, "The Thin Threat," *Elle*, February 1999, p. 156.

54. Ellin, "Dad, Do You Think I Look Too Fat?," p. 7.

55. "A Body to Die For," *People*, Special Report, October 30, 2000, p. 109.

56. "Merrick Ryan: With So Much to Live For, She Chose to Die," part of "A Body to Die For," p. 111.

57. Denise Grady, "Efforts to Fight Eating Disorders May Backfire," *New York Times*, May 7, 1997.

58. Linda Villarosa, "Dangerous Eating: The Results of Our Survey on Eating Disorders Show That Black Women Are at Risk," *Essence*, January 1994, pp. 19–20.

59. Ibid., p. 21.

60. Debra Waterhouse, *Like Mother, Like Daughter: How Women Are Influenced by Their Mothers' Relationship with Food—And How to Break the Pattern* (New York, Hyperion, 1997), p. xvi.

61. Anne Taylor Fleming, "Daughters of Dieters," *Glamour*, November 1994, p. 224.

62. Stephanie Gilbert, "Fear of Being Fat," *Washington Post*, April 13, 1999, p. Z12.

63. Gottlieb, *Stick Figure*, pp. 34–84.

64. Fleming, "Daughters of Dieters," p. 225.

65. Waterhouse, *Like Mother*, p. 26.

66. Fleming, "Daughters of Dieters," p. 222.

67. Ed Diener, Brian Wolsic, and Frank Fujita, "Physical Attractiveness and Subjective Well-Being," *Journal of Personality and Social Psychology* 69: 1 (1995): 120–29.

CHAPTER THREE: DATING

1. Genesis 2:18.

2. *Glamour*, September 2000, p. 160.

3. Jaclyn Geller, *Here Comes the Bride: Women, Weddings, and the Marriage Mystique* (New York: Four Walls Eight Windows, 2001), pp. 16, 8.

4. See Alan Dundes, *Cinderella: A Casebook* (New York: Wildman Press, 1983).

5. Geller, *Here Comes the Bride*, p. 26.

6. Joseph Allen Boone, *Tradition Counter Tradition: Love and the Form of Fiction* (Chicago: University of Chicago Press, 1987), p. 61.

7. Charlotte Brontë, *Jane Eyre* (New York: Penguin Classics, 1996; first published in 1847), p. 200.

8. Ibid., p. 210.

9. Ibid., p. 330.

10. Sandra Gilbert and Susan Gubar, *The Madwoman in the Attic* (New Haven: Yale University Press, 1984; first published in 1979), p. 34.

11. Barbara Ehrenreich, *The Hearts of Men: American Dreams and the Flight from Commitment* (New York: Anchor, 1984), p. 8.

12. Ibid., p. 51.

13. David Moberg, "Bridging the Gap: Why Women Still Don't Get Equal Pay," *In These Times*, January 8, 2001, p. 24.

14. Judy Mann, "Companies Could See Profit in Equal Pay," *Washington Post*, October 20, 1999, p. C15.

15. According to a study by the AFL-CIO and the Institute for Women's Policy Research, "Equal Pay for Working Families: National and State Data on the Pay Gap and Its Costs," 1999. It is available from AFL-CIO Support Services at (202) 637-5042. Cited in Moberg, "Bridging the Gap," p. 25.

16. Dorothy C. Holland and Margaret A. Eisenhart, *Educated in Romance: Women, Achievement, and College Culture* (Chicago: University of Chicago Press, 1990), p. 201.

17. Ibid., p. 109.

18. Ibid., pp. 116–18.

19. Andrew Sullivan, "The Love Bloat," *New York Times Magazine*, February 11, 2001, p. 23.

20. Katie Roiphe, "The Independent Woman (And Other Lies)," *Esquire*, February 1997, p. 86.

21. Figures cited in Tamala Edwards, "Flying Solo," *Time*, August 28, 2000, p. 48.

22. David Popenoe and Barbara Dafoe Whitehead, "The State of Our Unions 2000: The Social Health of Marriage in America," a report of the National Marriage Project. This report is available online at marriage.rutgers.edu.

23. Ibid.

24. Ibid.

25. This nationally representative survey of high school seniors is conducted annually by the Institute for Social Research at the University of Michigan. Cited in Ibid.

26. Cited in Diane White, "Being Single: A Lifestyle, Not a Sentence," *Boston Globe*, June 11, 1998, p. E1.

27. Marcelle Clements, *The Improvised Woman: Single Women Reinventing Single Life* (New York: Norton, 1998), p. 16.

28. Edwards, "Flying Solo," pp. 48–52.

29. Ellen Fein and Sherrie Schneider, *The Rules: Time-Tested Secrets for Capturing the Heart of Mr. Right* (New York: Warner, 1995), pp. 9, 19, 88.

30. Helen Fielding, *Bridget Jones: The Edge of Reason* (New York: Viking, 2000), pp. 36, 321.

31. Helen Fielding, *Bridget Jones's Diary* (New York: Penguin, 1999), p. 29.

32. Quoted in Alex Kuczynski, "Dear Diary: Get Real," *New York Times*, Styles section, June 14, 1998.

33. Suzanne Finnamore, *Otherwise Engaged* (New York: Vintage, 2000), p. 3.

34. Clements, *The Improvised Woman*, pp. 68, 309.

35. Ibid., p. 313.

36. Jonathan Tropper, *Plan B* (New York: St. Martin's Griffin, 2001), p. 47.

37. Meghan Daum, "The Ex Files," *Vogue*, July 1999, pp. 50–52.

38. Melissa Bank, *The Girls' Guide to Hunting and Fishing* (New York: Penguin, 1999), p. 50.

39. Finnamore, *Otherwise Engaged*, p. 18.

40. Ibid., p. 31.

41. Ibid., p. 176.

42. Ibid., p. 33.

43. Anna Maxted, *Getting Over It* (New York: ReganBooks/HarperCollins, 2000), pp. 6, 153, 201.

44. Denene Millner, *The Sistahs' Rules: Secrets for Meeting, Getting, and Keeping a Good Black Man* (New York: Quill/Morrow, 1997), p. xv.

45. Ibid., p. 110.

46. Monique P. Yazigi, "Bigger Diamonds Are a Girl's Best Friend," *New York Times*, February 13, 2000, Week in Review section, p. 2.

47. Penny Proddow and Marion Fasel, "Rocks of Ages," *In Style*, February 2001, pp. 274–76.

CHAPTER FOUR: WORK

1. "Facts About Working Women," AFL-CIO Fact Sheet, available online from www.aflcio.org/women/wwfacts.htm; Rashda Khan, "Women Closing in on the Gender Gap," *San Angelo Standard-Times*, October 31, 1999; Sheila Wellington and Catalyst with Betty Spence, *Be Your Own Mentor: Strategies from Top Women on the Secrets of Success* (New York: Random House, 2001), p. 3. Statistics are from the U.S. Department of Labor.

2. Associated Press, "Sexual Inequality Is Found in Medical Faculties," reprinted in the *New York Times*, February 10, 2000.

3. Susan Estrich, *Sex and Power* (New York: Riverhead, 2000), p. 16.

4. Associated Press, "Women in Board Rooms Studied," reprinted in *New York Times*, December 15, 1999.

5. Karen Jacobs, "Women Scale Corporate Ladder, But Climb Continues to Be Slow," *Wall Street Journal*, November 12, 1999; Associated Press, "Professors: Glass Ceiling in Place," reprinted in *New York Times*, January 6, 2000.

6. Reed Abelson, "Study Finds Diversity Programs Ineffective at Getting Women Minorities to the Top," *New York Times*, July 14, 1999.

7. Joan Williams, *Unbending Gender: Why Family and Work Conflict and What to Do About It* (New York: Oxford, 2000), p. 81.

8. Judy Mann, "Companies Could See Profit in Equal Pay," *Washington Post*, October 20, 1999, p. C15. Statistic is from the U.S. Department of Labor. This statistic and translation into median weekly earnings do not reflect wage differentials at different ages for women.

9. "New and Stronger Remedies Are Needed to Reduce Gender-Based Wage Discrimination," Testimony of Heidi Hartmann, Director of the Institute for Women's Policy Research before the U.S. Senate Committee on Health, Education, Labor and Pensions, June 8, 2000. A copy of this testimony is available from the Institute for Women's Policy Research in Washington, D.C.

10. "Working Women Say...," *American Writer*, Summer 2000, p. 12. This article is a summary of an AFL-CIO telephone survey of working women ages eighteen and older. The survey was based on responses of a national random sample of 765 women.

11. Amy Goldstein, "Breadwinning Wives Alter Marriage Equation," *Washington Post*, February 27, 2000, p. A1.

12. Mary Williams Walsh, "So Where Are the Corporate Husbands?," *New York Times*, June 24, 2001, Money & Business section, p. 1.

13. Kate Rounds, "Clippings," *Ms.*, October–November 1999, p. 30.

14. Tim Smart, "A New Presence in the Corporate Elite," *Washington Post*, July 20, 1999, p. A1.

15. Patrick McGeehan, "Morgan Stanley Is Cited for Discrimination Against Women," *New York Times*, June 6, 2000, p. C1; Joseph Kahn, "Morgan Stanley Is Target of Sex Bias Inquiry," *New York Times*, July 29, 1999, p. C1.

16. Reed Abelson, "If Wall Street is a Dead End, Do Women Stay to Fight or Go Quietly?" *New York Times*, August 3, 1999, p. C1.

17. Reed Abelson, "A Survey of Wall Street Finds Women Disheartened," *New York Times*, July 26, 2001, p. C1.

18. Estrich, *Sex and Power*, p. 28.

19. Associated Press, "Professors: Glass Ceiling in Place," reprinted in *New York Times*, January 6, 2000.

20. Virginia Valian, *Why So Slow?: The Advancement of Women* (Cambridge, Mass.: MIT Press, 1998), p. 5.

21. Junda Woo, "Widespread Sexual Bias Found in Courts," *Wall Street Journal*, August 20, 1992, p. B1. Cited in Kathleen Hall Jamieson, *Beyond the Double Bind: Women and Leadership* (New York: Oxford, 1995), p. 122.

22. This experiment was first conducted in 1968. In 1985, it was replicated, as were the results. Michele A. Paludi and Lisa A. Strayer, "What's in an Author's Name? Differential Evaluations of Performance as a Function of Author's Name." *Sex Roles* 12:3–4 (1985): 353–61. Cited in Jamieson, *Beyond the Double Bind*, p. 123.

23. Judy Mann, "Things Could Be Better for Women at the Top," *Washington Post*, July 16, 1999, p. C10. These concerns were revealed in a study conducted by the

Business and Professional Women Foundation and the American Management Association.

24. "Good Part-Time Jobs Scarce for Professionals," *Seattle Times*, February 19, 2000, p. A13.

25. Susan H. Greenberg, "Time to Plan Your Life," *Newsweek*, January 8, 2001, p. 54.

26. Cited in Melinda Ligos, "The Fear of Taking Paternity Leave," *New York Times*, May 31, 2000, p. G1.

27. Deborah Rhode, "Myths of Meritocracy," *Fordham Law Review* 65 (1996): 585, 588; Sue Shellenbarger, "Lessons from the Workplace," *Human Resource Management* 31 (1992): 157, 160. Both quotations cited in Joan Williams, *Unbending Gender: Why Family and Work Conflict and What to Do About It* (New York: Oxford, 2000), p. 69.

28. Paul Raeburn, "The Perils of Part-Time for Professionals," *Business Week*, March 6, 2000.

29. "Good Part-Time Jobs Scarce for Professionals," *Seattle Times*, February 19, 2000, p. A13.

30. Cited in Estrich, *Sex and Power*, p. 105.

31. Ibid., p. 75.

32. See Sylvia Ann Hewlett, *Creating a Life: Professional Women and the Quest for Children* (New York: Talk Miramax, 2002); Lisa Belkin, "For Women, the Price of Success," *New York Times*, March 17, 2002, Job Market section, p. 1.

33. Anne Roiphe, "Who's Afraid of 'Hilla the Hun'?," *New York Observer*, July 31, 2000, p. 5.

34. Elisabeth Bumiller, "The First Lady's Race for the Ages: 62 Counties and 6 Pantsuits," *New York Times*, November 8, 2000.

35. The names on this list of casualties were collected by Richard Goldstein in "Hillary's Big Problem: No Woman Has Ever Won Higher Office in New York State," *Village Voice*, July 20, 1999, p. 57.

36. The states are Arizona, Delaware, Massachusetts, Montana, and New Hampshire.

37. Gretchen Morgenson, "Barbie's Guru Stumbles: Critics Say Chief's Flaws Weigh Heavily on Mattel," *New York Times*, November 7, 1999, Money & Business section, p. 1.

38. Leslie Kaufman, "Questions of Style in Warnaco's Fall," *New York Times*, May 6, 2001, Money & Business section, p. 1.

39. Rachel Abramowitz, *Is That a Gun in Your Pocket?: Women's Experience of Power in Hollywood* (New York: Random House, 2000), pp. xi.

40. Cited in Michelle Cottle, "Sugar and Spice: Our Shy, Retiring Female Senators," *New Republic*, January 1 and 8, 2001, p. 16.

41. Kevin Gray, "The Summer of Her Discontent," *New York*, September 1, 2000, p. 34.

42. Monique Yazigi, "So Hard to Find Good Employers These Days," *New York Times*, August 15, 1999, Styles section, p. 1.

43. Associated Press, "Housekeepers Told to Speak Only English Get Settlement," reprinted in *New York Times*, April 22, 2001, p. 24.

44. Graham Staines, Carol Tavris, and Toby Epstein Jayaratne, "The Queen Bee Syndrome," *Psychology Today*, January 1974, p. 57.

45. Ibid., p. 57.

46. Abramowitz, *Is That a Gun in Your Pocket?*, pp. 55, 129.

47. Judy B. Rosener, *America's Competitive Secret: Women Managers* (New York: Oxford University Press, 1995), p. 107.

48. Solomon Cytrynbaum, Ph.D., and Max Belkin, M.A., "Gender and Authority: Implications for Group Psychotherapy and Research," presented as part of a Symposium on Gender and Group Psychotherapy to the 13th International Congress of Group Psychotherapy, London, August 24–28, 1998, pp. 4, 5. This paper was made available to me by Dr. Cytrynbaum.

49. Ibid., pp. 15, 17.

50. Sally Helgesen, *The Female Advantage: Women's Ways of Leadership* (New York: Doubleday Currency, 1995), p. x.

51. Ibid., pp. 239, 75, 31.

52. Judy B. Rosener, "Ways Women Lead," *Harvard Business Review*, November–December 1990, pp. 119–25.

53. Rosener, *America's Competitive Secret*, pp. 6, 12, 124.

54. Ibid., p. 31.

55. Jonathan D. Glater, "Women Are Close to Being Majority of Law Students," *New York Times*, March 26, 2001, p. A1.

56. Ibid.

57. Vivian Gornick, "Why Women Fear Success," in the premiere issue of *Ms.*, appearing in *New York*, December 20, 1971, pp. 50–51; Matina Horner, "Toward an Understanding of Achievement-Related Conflicts in Women," *Journal of Social Issues* 28: 2 (1972): 157–76, reprinted in *The Psychology of Women: Ongoing Debates*, edited by Mary Roth Walsh (New Haven: Yale University Press, 1987), pp. 169–84; Janet Shibley Hyde, *Half the Human Experience: The Psychology of Women*, 3rd ed. (Lexington, Mass.: DC Heath, 1985), pp. 204–207.

58. Joan Riviere, "Womanliness as a Masquerade," *International Journal of Psycho-Analysis* 9 (1929): 303–313. Reprinted in *The Inner World and Joan Riviere: Collected Papers, 1920–1958*, edited by Athol Hughes (London: Karnac Books, 1991), p. 94.

59. Mary Ann Doane, *Femmes Fatales: Feminism, Film Theory, Psychoanalysis* (New York: Routledge, 1991), p. 25.

60. Ruth Shalit, "The Taming of the Shrews," *Elle*, October 2001, p. 108.

61. Dylan Loeb McClain, "At the Top of the Executive Ladder, Many Women Experience Vertigo," *New York Times*, October 17, 2001, Workplace section, p. G1.

62. Sheila Wellington and Catalyst with Betty Spence, *Be Your Own Mentor: Strategies from Top Women on the Secrets of Success* (New York: Random House, 2001), p. 85.

63. Gail Evans, *Play Like a Man, Win Like a Woman* (New York: Broadway Books, 2000), p. 123.

64. Gloria Steinem, "Fear of Crying," *Ms.*, August–September 2000, p. 90.

65. Evans, *Play Like a Man*, p. 123.

66. Carolyn S. Duff, *When Women Work Together: Using Our Strengths to Overcome Our Challenges* (Berkeley, Calif.: Conari Press, 1993), pp. 46–47.

CHAPTER FIVE: MOTHERHOOD

1. Christina Baker Kline, "Introduction," in *Child of Mine: Writers Talk About the First Year of Motherhood*, edited by Christina Baker Kline (New York: Delta/Dell, 1998), p. 3.

2. Susan Maushart, *The Mask of Motherhood: How Becoming a Mother Changes Our Lives and Why We Never Talk About It* (New York: Penguin, 2000), pp. 115–16.

3. Shari Thurer, *The Myths of Motherhood: How Culture Reinvents the Good Mother* (New York: Penguin, 1994), p. xiv.

4. Ibid., p. 272.

5. Maushart, *The Mask of Motherhood*, p. 32.

6. Adrienne Rich, *Of Woman Born: Motherhood as Experience and Institution* (New York: Norton, 1995; first published in 1976), p. 22.

7. Denise Grady, "Something's Often Missing in Childbirth Today: The Pain," *New York Times*, October 13, 1999.

8. Margaret Talbot, "Pay on Delivery," *New York Times Magazine*, October 31, 1999, p. 19.

9. Maria Schneider, Letters to the Editor, *New York Times Magazine*, November 21, 1999, p. 22.

10. Thurer, *The Myths of Motherhood*, pp. 73–75, 173–76, 199.

11. Margot Slade, "Breastfeeding Revisited," *Child*, September 1998. Reprinted in *For Women Only! Your Guide to Health Empowerment*, edited by Gary Null and Barbara Seaman (New York: Seven Stories Press, 1999), pp. 1091–93. See also Sara Corbett, "The Breast Offense," *New York Times Magazine*, May 6, 2001, p. 84.

12. Cathi Hanauer, "Breast-Feeding: The Agony and the Ecstacy," in Kline, *Child of Mine*, p. 181.

13. Laurie Tarkan, "Research Is Urged for Healthier Breast Milk," *New York Times*, October 16, 2001, p. F6. See also Sandra Steingraber, *Having Faith: An Ecologist's Journey to Motherhood* (Cambridge, Mass.: Perseus, 2001).

14. Wendy Wasserstein, "Annals of Motherhood: Complications," *New Yorker*, February 21–28, 2000, pp. 101–102.

15. Slade, "Breastfeeding Revisited," p. 1092.

16. Pamela Gerhardt, "Momma, This Isn't Just 'The Baby Blues,'" *Washington Post*, March 14, 2000, p. Z14.

17. Susan Chira, *A Mother's Place: Choosing Work and Family Without Guilt or Blame* (New York: HarperPerennial, 1999), p. xiv.

18. Dan Balz and Edward Walsh, "Clinton's Wife Finds She's Become Issue," *Washington Post*, March 17, 1992, p. A1; Kathleen Hall Jamieson, *Beyond the Double Bind: Women and Leadership* (New York: Oxford, 1995), p. 27.

19. "Deciding to Stay Home—No Piece of Cake," Letters to the Editor written by Anne Byrnes and Anna Hewitt Wolfe, *Washington Post*, March 28, 1992, p. A19.

20. Danielle Crittenden, *What Our Mothers Didn't Tell Us: Why Happiness Eludes the Modern Woman* (New York: Simon & Schuster, 1999), p. 25.

21. Barbara Ehrenreich, *Nickel and Dimed: On (Not) Getting By in America* (New York: Holt, 2001).

22. Susan Korones Gifford, "Why Are These Moms at War?," *Redbook*, April 2000, pp. 162–67.

23. *Tanakh: The Holy Scriptures: The New JPS Translation According to the Traditional Hebrew Text* (Philadelphia: Jewish Publication Society, 1985), pp. 1337–38.

24. Tamar Lewin, "More Mothers of Babies Under 1 Are Staying Home," *New York Times*, October 19, 2001, p. A14. The figure is from a Census Bureau report, "Fertility of American Women 2000."

25. Faye Fiore, "55 Percent of New Moms Return to Labor Force Within First Year After Birth," *Los Angeles Times*, November 26, 1997.

26. Barbara Kantrowitz and Pat Wingert, "Unmarried, With Children," *Newsweek*, May 28, 2001, p. 48.

27. Rosalind C. Barnett and Caryl Rivers, *She Works/He Works: How Two-Income Families are Happy, Healthy, and Thriving* (Cambridge, Mass.: Harvard University Press, 1998), p. 45.

28. See Stephanie Coontz, *The Way We Never Were: American Families and the Nostalgia Trap* (New York: Basic, 1992).

29. 1960 U.S. Census figures cited in Barnett and Rivers, *She Works/He Works*, p. 3.

30. Julie Salamon, "Staticky Reception for Nuclear Families on Prime-Time TV," *New York Times*, July 30, 2001, Arts and Leisure section. The statistic is from the U.S. Census Bureau.

31. Barnett and Rivers, *She Works/He Works*, pp. 1–3.

32. Ibid., p. 7.

33. Kirstin Downey Grimsly, "Family A Priority For Young Workers," *Washington Post*, May 3, 2000, p. E1.

34. Barnett and Rivers, *She Works/He Works*, p. 59.

35. Ibid., pp. 24–28.

36. Ibid., p. 95. Sandra Scarr, et al., summary of a report edited by S. Kammerman and C. D. Hayes for the National Academy of Sciences, "Families That Work: Children in a Changing World," 1982. Cited in ibid., p. 99.

37. Ellen Galinsky, *Ask the Children: What America's Children Really Think About Working Parents* (New York: Morrow, 1999).

38. Ann Crittenden, *The Price of Motherhood: Why the Most Important Job in the World is Still the Least Valued* (New York: Metropolitan/Holt, 2001), p. 22.

39. Jennifer Steinhauer, "For Women in Medicine, A Road to Compromise, Not Perks," *New York Times*, March 1, 1999, p. A1.

40. Elaine Wethington and Ronald Kessler, "Employment, Parental Responsibility, and Psychological Distress," *Journal of Family Issues*, December 1989. Cited in Barnett and Rivers, *She Works/He Works*, p. 32.

41. Sue Shellenbarger, "Quality Child Care Protected Kids Caught in Terrorist Attacks," *Wall Street Journal*, September 26, 2001, p. B1.

42. Sue Shellenbarger, "Here's the Bottom Line on Child Care's Impact," *Wall Street Journal*, June 23, 1999.

43. "Working Women: Equal Pay—Working Together for Kids," AFL-CIO fact sheet, available online at www.aflcio.org/women/kids.htm.

44. The report was titled *Then and Now: Changes in Child Care Staffing 1994–2000*. Cited in Katha Pollitt, "Happy Mother's Day," *Nation*, May 28, 2001, p. 10.

45. Sheryl Gay Stolberg, "Link Found Between Behavioral Problems and Time in Child Care," *New York Times*, April 19, 2001, p. A1; Stolberg, "Science, Studies, and Motherhood," *New York Times*, April 22, 2001.

46. Stolberg, "Link Found Between Behavioral Problems and Time in Child Care."

47. A Cost, Quality, and Child Outcomes study, which tracked 800 children through second grade, was cosponsored by the University of Colorado at Boulder, the

University of California at Los Angeles, the University of North Carolina and Yale University, 1999. The study is available from the Bush Center in Child Development and Social Policy, New Haven, Conn. Cited in Shellenbarger, "Here's the Bottom Line." The second study, the Abecedarian Project, involved 111 African-American families in Chapel Hill, N.C., whose infants were medically healthy but, demographically, at risk for failure in school and beyond. Cited in Jodi Wilgoren, "Quality Day Care, Early, Is Tied to Achievements as an Adult," *New York Times*, October 22, 1999.

48. Louise Gross and Phyllis Taube Greenleaf, "Why Day Care?," 1970, Sheli Wortis personal collection, reprinted in *Dear Sisters: Dispatches from the Women's Liberation Movement*, edited by Rosalyn Baxandall and Linda Gordon (New York: Basic, 2000), p. 234.

49. Elizabeth Olson, "United Nations Surveys Paid Leave for Mothers," *New York Times*, February 16, 1998. Cited in Crittenden, *The Price of Motherhood*, p. 95.

50. At the time, the *Times* required employees to work for ten years before their pension became vested, although the law has since changed to allow vesting after five years with one employer.

51. Crittenden, *The Price of Motherhood*, p. 88.

52. Richard Morin and Megan Rosenfeld, "With More Equity, More Sweat: Poll Shows Sexes Agree on the Pros and Cons of New Roles," *Washington Post*, March 22, 1998, p. A1. Cited in Joan Williams, *Unbending Gender: Why Family and Work Conflict and What To Do About It* (New York: Oxford, 2000), p. 49.

53. Tamar Lewin, "Study Finds Little Change in Working Mothers Debate," *New York Times*, September 10, 2001, p. A26.

54. Susan Korones Gifford, "Why Are These Moms at War?" p. 163.

55. Loretta Kaufman and Mary Quigley, *And What Do You Do?: When Women Choose to Stay Home* (Berkeley, Calif.: Wildcat Canyon Press, 2000), p. 32.

56. Judy Dutton, "Meet the New Housewife Wanna-Bes," *Cosmopolitan*, June 2000, pp. 164–66.

57. Kaufman and Quigley, *And What Do You Do?*, pp. 2, 5, 22.

58. Ibid., pp. 201, 21, 116.

59. Sandra Scarr, *Mother Care/Other Care* (New York: Basic, 1994). Cited in Barnett and Rivers, *She Works/He Works*, p. 105.

60. Pat Wingert, "Study Watch: Parents Today Make More Time for Quality Time," *Newsweek*, May 21, 2001, p. 53.

CHAPTER SIX: WHEN WOMEN WORK TOGETHER

1. Sources for background on the suffrage movement: Eleanor Flexner, *Century of Struggle: The Woman's Rights Movement in the United States* (Cambridge, Mass.: Belknap/Harvard University Press, 1996; enlarged edition first published in 1959); Carol Hymowitz and Michaele Weissman, *A History of Women in America* (New York: Bantam, 1978; published in cooperation with the Anti-Defamation League of B'nai B'rith).

2. Flexner, *Century of Struggle*, p. 58.

3. Joel Stein, "The Power Game," *Time*, September 3, 2001, p. 58. The 75 percent statistic is from a *USA Today* poll.

4. Jean Zimmerman and Gil Reavill, *Raising Our Athletic Daughters: How Sports Can Build Self-Esteem and Save Girls' Lives* (New York: Doubleday, 1998), p. 10.

5. Elizabeth Crowley, "Special Report: American Opinion," *Wall Street Journal*, June 22, 2000. The figure is according to the National Collegiate Athletic Association.

6. Mariah Burton Nelson, *Embracing Victory: How Women Can Compete Joyously, Compassionately, and Successfully in the Workplace and on the Playing Field* (New York: Avon, 1998).

7. Women's Sports Foundation, "Research Report: Health Risks and the Teen Athlete," 2001. The report is available online at www.womenssportsfoundation.org.

8. "The President's Council on Physical Fitness and Sports Report: Physical Activity & Sport in the Lives of Girls," a report prepared by the U.S. Department of Health and Human Services under the direction of the Center for Research on Girls & Women in Sport, University of Minnesota, and supported by the Center for Mental Health Services/Substance Abuse and Mental Health Services Administration, Spring 1997. The report is available online at education.umn.edu/tuckercenter/pcpfs/default.html.

9. Mark Starr and Martha Brant, "Girls Rule! Inside the Amazing World Cup Victory," *Newsweek*, July 19, 1999, p. 51.

10. Verna Williams, "Decreasing Athletic Opportunities for Males?," *NCSEE News* (a publication of the National Coalition for Sex Equity in Education), Spring 2000, p. 16.

11. Tina Kelley, "To Women's Sports, Add Pro Football," *New York Times*, December 13, 1999, p. B12.

12. Pat Griffin, *Strong Women, Deep Closets: Lesbians and Homophobia in Sport* (Champaign, Ill.: Human Kinetics, 1998), p. 30.

13. Cited in Royce Webb, Introduction to special issue on women and competition, *sportsjones* magazine, January 21, 1999. Available on the Internet at www.sports-jones.com.

14. Griffin, *Strong Women*, p. 20.

15. Ibid., pp. 35, 38.

16. Ibid., p. 45.

17. Liz Galst, "The Sports Closet," *Ms.*, September–October 1998, p. 78. Swoopes's mother was quoted in the Austin *American-Statesman*.

18. Griffin, *Strong Women*, p. 46.

19. Galst, "The Sports Closet," pp. 76–77.

20. John de St. Jorre, "Out in the Open," *Women's Sports & Fitness*, September–October 1999, pp. 115–16.

21. Cynthia Cooper, *She Got Game: My Personal Odyssey* (New York: Warner, 2000).

22. Joanne Chen, "Born to Win," *Vogue*, May 2000, pp. 282, 290.

23. Selena Roberts, "Venus Williams Wins Wimbledon, Lighting Up Center Court," *New York Times*, July 9, 2000, Sports section, p. 1.

24. James Kaplan, "Dynamic Duo," *Vogue*, March 2001, p. 583.

25. Devin Friedman, "Sister Act," *Elle*, January 2001, p. 148.

26. Patricia Smith, "Venus & Serena Williams: *Ms.* Women of the Year," *Ms.*, December 2001–January 2002, p. 40.

27. Selena Roberts, "The Night Belongs to Venus," *New York Times*, September 9, 2001, Sports section p. 1.

28. Nelson, *Embracing Victory*, p. 47.

ACKNOWLEDGMENTS

I signed the contract to write this book when I was seven months pregnant with my first child. Clearly, I was naïve about the demands of raising a young child and I was presumptuous to think that no matter how hard it would be, I would somehow be able to manage. In this case, naïveté and presumptuousness served me well, for if I'd known how overwhelming raising a young child is, I would not have undertaken this project. That I did manage to write *and* be a present mother is due not to my own superhuman powers—since no woman, least of all myself, is a superwoman—but to the assistance of one invaluable person. Vaidehi (Joy) Ramlogan cared for my older son while I did most of the work for this book. I am enormously thankful to Joy; my mind was at ease because I always knew my son was in excellent hands.

A number of other people were indispensable. First and foremost, I owe a tremendous debt to my editor, Beverly Gologorsky. I am fortunate that Bev shared her abundant wisdom with me and indeed, I would have been lost without her guidance. I am particularly grateful because Bev, a noted novelist, worked on this book with me in the face of her own deadline. I also thank editor Kera Bolonik, who assisted me on an early version of the manuscript, and Jaclyn Geller, who took time from her busy academic and writing schedule to provide excellent criticism of several chapters. I am enormously thankful to Jill Aizenstein, Chai Glenn-Cook, Judy Hecker, Wendy Kesser, Marilyn Korn, Mala Mosher, Jill Nelson,

Rachel Schwartz, and Alex Sheller, who put me in touch with friends and colleagues for interviews. Jodi Golinsky in particular went out of her way to introduce me to a number of insightful women. I am, of course, indebted to all the women who shared their personal stories and reflections with me.

My agent, Jennifer Lyons, has been so supportive that I don't know how I can thank her properly. She believed in this work from the very beginning and worked tirelessly on its behalf. My friend Barbara Seaman likewise was always there for me as I struggled to shape the ideas in this book. As always, she is my role model.

Everyone at Seven Stories has been wonderful to work with: Dan Simon, publisher extraordinaire; Ruth Weiner, publicity director; M. Astella Saw, managing editor and book designer; Jon Gilbert, production editor; and Daia Gerson, copy editor. I couldn't ask for a better team.

Finally, I thank my husband, Jonathan, for his emotional support, and my sons, Sasson and Zev, for bringing me tremendous fulfillment as I worked on this project.

INDEX

A

abolitionists, 276–77, 279–80
Abrahamson, Shirley, 178
Abramowitz, Rachel, 200
Abzug, Bella, 194
Acuff, Amy, 298
admiration, 65
Adventures of Ozzie and Harriet, The, 258
Africa, 120
African-American women
    See women of color
Against Our Will (Brownmiller), 44
aggression
    in children, 265–66
    indirect, 61–64
All About Eve, 28
All-American Girls' Baseball League
    (AAGBL), 293–94
Ally McBeal, 30–31, 155
Amendments
    Fifteenth, 280
    Nineteenth, 275, 282
American Academy of Pediatrics, 242
American Bar Association, 187
American Woman Suffrage
    Association, 280–81
America's Competitive Secret (Rosener), 204,
    206–208
And What Do You Do? (Kaufman and Quigley),
    270, 271–72
Angier, Natalie, 63–64
anorexia, 127
    See also eating disorders
Anthony, Susan B., 278–79, 280, 282
"Anthony Amendment," 275, 282
Apter, Terri, 66
Aquafina ad, 29–30
Ask the Children (Galinsky), 261–62
Astra USA, 181
athletes
    See sports, women in

attorneys
    See lawyers, female
Atwood, Margaret, 67–68
Austen, Jane, 142, 162
authority, and gender, 202–203

B

Bachelor, The, 151
Baker, Charlotte, 175
Bank, Melissa, 160
Barad, Jill, 194–95, 196
Barnett, Rosalind C., 187, 257, 258–60,
    261, 263
Baumgardner, Jennifer, 86
beauty, 77–134
    beauty bind, 82–88, 93
    clothing, 94–98
    cosmetic surgery, 116–19
    dieting mothers and daughters, 130–34
    eating disorders, 126–30
    and female relationships, 85–88
    and feminism, 113–16
    ideal, 80–81, 88–94, 98–104
    Miss America pageant, 105–112
    mixed messages to women, 37
    and resentment, 56–58
    stereotypes, 84
    thinness, 91–92, 103–104, 119–26
beauty contests, 105–112
beauty education, 103
Beers, Charlotte, 207
belonging, 64–70
Belsky, Jay, 265–266
Billauer, Barbara P., 186
Birge, Miriam Bender, 254
Bitch, 114
black women
    See women of color
Bloom, Amy, 114
Blue, Yvonne, 104
blue-collar women, 152

Bluest Eye, The (Morrison), 93
Body Project, The (Brumberg), 104
Book, Esther Wachs, 204
Bordo, Susan, 33
Boston Bar Association, 185
Botox, 118
breast augmentation, 119
breast-feeding, 240–48
Brem, Marion Luna, 204
Bridget Jones's Diary (Fielding), 29, 156–57, 159, 172
Brines, Julie, 180–81
Brontë, Charlotte, 142–45, 162
Brown, Helen Gurley, 120
Brown, Jerry, 249–50
Brown, Rita Mae, 294
Brownmiller, Susan, 43–44
Brumberg, Joan Jacobs, 104
Buckingham, Jane, 270
bulimia, 126
    See also eating disorders
Bully Broads, 215–16
Burns, Lucy, 282
Burstein, Karen, 194

C

Care and Feeding of Children, The (Holt), 234–35
Catalyst, 179, 182
categorization, as part of competition, 38–39
"catfighting," as a term, 29
Cat's Eye (Atwood), 67–68
celebrity culture, 88–91, 170–71
Center for Research on Women (Wellesley College), 257, 259–60
Chastain, Brandi, 285
Chavkin, Wendy, 263
Chesler, Phyllis, 24, 46
chief executives, female, 179, 181, 194–96
    See also executives, female
childbirth, 239–40
child care, 264–67
childlessness, 188–91
Chira, Susan, 249
Chodorow, Nancy, 45–46, 58–59
Cinderella folk tale, 29, 139–40
class differences, 49–53
Clawson, René, 253–54, 269–70

Clements, Marcelle, 153, 157, 158, 159
Clinton, Bill, 249–50
Clinton, Hillary, 193–94, 250–51
clothing, 77–79, 94–98, 104
Cobbs, Mary, 297
cognitive abilities, and body image, 81–82
collaboration, 275–301
    feminine athletes, 291–301
    suffrage movement, 275–83
    suggestions for, 303–305
    women in sports today, 283–91
colleagues, female, 175–76
college sororities, 68–69
college students, 147–49
color caste system, 92–94
    See also women of color
"commercialized feminism," 52, 97
    See also feminism
Common Sense Book of Baby and Child Care, The (Spock), 235
comparing oneself to other women, 79–80
competition
    advantages, 42
    covert, 21, 26–27, 31–32
    definition, 17
    in education, 70–71
    healthy, 70–75
    as learned behavior, 39–49
    male, 21
    overt, 17–18, 26–27
    over who's worst off, 39
    positive aspects, 17–18
    and productivity, 41
    as proprietorship, 159–61
    psychoanalytic explanation, 44–46
    unresolved, 72–75
    withdrawing from, 222–24
competition roots, 37–75
    healthy competition, 70–75
    indirect aggression, 61–64
    learning to compete, 39–49
    members only, 64–70
    women and resentment, 55–58
    women divided by class and race, 49–54
    women's "essential" nature, 58–61
Conger, Darva, 150–51
consciousness-raising, 21–22
consumerism, 51–53, 97

Coontz, Stephanie, 257–58
Cooper, Cynthia, 297–98
cooperation, 17, 41
    See also collaboration
cosmetics, 99–101, 102–103, 114–15
cosmetic surgery, 116–19
Creating a Life (Hewlett), 188–89
Crittenden, Ann, 262, 267–68
Crittenden, Danielle, 188, 251
crying, 218–20
Cytrynbaum, Solomon, 26–27, 202–203

D

dating, 135–72
    economic aspects, 145–51
    Other Woman in literature, 139–45
    Other Woman is your friend, 165–69
    Other Woman today, 159–65
    singles culture, 151–59
    weddings, 169–72
Daum, Meghan, 160
Davenport, Lindsay, 296
Derks-Gardner, Gina, 298
diamond rings, 170–71
Didrikson, Babe, 293
dieting, mothers and daughters, 130–34
DiFranco, Ani, 29
Dillon, Kate, 122
Doane, Mary Ann, 215
domestic workers, female, 197–98
double standard, sexual, 23–24
Douglas, Susan, 29
Drillings, Fern, 247
Duff, Carolyn, 223–24
Dunlop, 295

E

eating disorders, 126–30
Eating the Cheshire Cat (Ellis), 65–66
Ebersol, Dick, 300–301
Edge of Reason, The (Fielding), 156–57, 159
Edwards, Marilyn, 288–89, 290
Ehrenreich, Barbara, 50, 146, 252
Eisenhart, Margaret, 147–79
Elle , 114
Ellis, Helen, 65–66
Embracing Victory (Nelson), 42
empathy, 60

Eng, Cynthia, 138–39, 168–69
engagement rings, 170–71
entrepreneurs, female, 201–202
envy, 17
Equal Employment Opportunity Commission (EEOC), 181
Erin Brockovich, 253
Essence, 129–30
Estrich, Susan, 78–79, 182–83, 187–88
Evans, Gail, 218, 219
"ex" boyfriends, 165–67
exclusion, 66–70
executives, female, 179, 181, 194–96, 200–201, 204–206
"ex" girlfriends and wives, 159–61
Eyre, Jane (fictional character), 142–45, 162

F

Face of Love, The (Lambert), 115
Faircloth, Lauch, 218
Faludi, Susan, 52
Family and Medical Leave Act, 186, 304
family wage system, 146
Fanon, Frantz, 47–48
fashion obsolescence, 95–96
    See also clothing
Fasting Girls (Brumberg), 104
fathers, 207, 208, 225–26, 241, 248, 259–260
"fear of success," 212–14
Fein, Ellen, 155
Felicity, 88–89
Female Advantage, The (Helgesen), 204–06
feminism, 21–23, 43–44, 52, 97, 113–16, 251–52
fen-phen, 127
Ferraro, Geraldine, 194
Fielding, Helen, 156–57, 159
Fifteenth Amendment, 280
film industry executives, female, 196, 200–201
    See also executives, female
films, 28, 29, 90–91, 252–53
Finnamore, Suzanne, 158, 160–61
Fiorina, Carleton ("Carly"), 179, 181
First Wives Club, The, 28
"flapper" look, 103–104
Fleming, Anne Taylor, 16

Flexner, Eleanor, 276
flirting, 214–15, 220–21
Flockhart, Calista, 305
Fortune 500 companies, 179
France, 264
Fredrickson, Barbara, 81–82
Freud, Sigmund, 45, 81
Friedman, Cindy, 245, 247
friendship, 71–72, 172
Fuller, Marce, 179
Fuller, Margaret, 99

G

Galinsky, Ellen, 261–62
Geller, Jaclyn, 136, 141
gender bias, female denial of, 201–202
gender roles, 46–47
Genealogy of Morals, The (Nietzsche), 55
Generation of Vipers (Wylie), 236
Gerhardt, Pamela, 247–48
Getting Over It (Maxted), 162
Gilbert, Sandra, 144–45
Gilligan, Carol, 59
Gilman, Charlotte Perkins, 42–43, 44
Gilman, Sander, 116–117
girls, 48–49, 118, 121–22, 152–53
Girls' Guide to Hunting and Fishing, The (Banks), 160
Glamour, 101, 131, 133, 134
glass ceiling, 176–77, 181–83, 201–202, 209
gossip, 220
Gottlieb, Lori, 121–22, 132–33
Green, Rose Davis, 216
Greenleaf, Phyllis Taube, 266
Griffin, Pat, 292–93
Grimké, Angelina, 276–77
Grimké, Sarah, 276–77
Gross, Louise, 266
Gubar, Susan, 144–45
gym class, noncompetitive, 70–71

H

H. J. Heinz Company, 103
Hamilton, Joanne, 70
Hamm, Mia, 285
Hanauer, Cathi, 244
Hand That Rocks the Cradle, The, 28
Hanisch, Carol, 113

Hanock-Jasie, Lisa, 201
Hardball For Women (Heim), 204
Harris, Katherine, 83–84
Harrison, Janet, 122–23, 160
Head, Susan, 123
Hecker, Judy, 68, 174–75
Heim, Pat, 204
Helgesen, Sally, 204–206
Here Comes the Bride (Geller), 136
Herland (Gilman), 42–43, 44
Hewlett, Sylvia Ann, 188–89
Hingis, Martina, 296
Holland, Dorothy, 147–79
Hollands, Jean, 216
Holt, Luther Emmett, 234–35
Holtzman, Elizabeth, 194
hooks, bell, 24
Hope in a Jar (Peiss), 99–101, 102
Horner, Matina, 212–13
House of Mirth, The (Wharton), 142, 162
Houston, Pam, 80
Hudson, Kate, 171

I

identity, source of, 37–38
Improvised Woman (Clements), 153
In Our Time (Brownmiller), 43–44
Inseley, Susan H., 206–207
Institute for Social Research (University of Michigan), 273
Institute for Women's Policy Research, 187
In Style, 170–71
Internet, and appearance, 101
Israel, 264

J

Jack, Dana Crowley, 63
Jamison, Ella, 93
Jane Eyre (Brontë), 142–45, 162
Jayaratne, Toby Epstein, 199–200
Jennings, Madelyn, 189, 191–92
"Jewish mother," 235
Jewish prayer of supplication, 11
Jews, and cosmetic surgery, 117
Jones, Bridget (fictional character), 29, 156–57, 159, 172
Jones, Georgina, 93
Jones, Marion, 285

Jordan, Michael, 285, 296
Josselson, Ruthellen, 66, 69
Jung, Andrea, 179

K

Kates, Carolyn, 56–58
Kaufman, Leslie, 195
Kaufman, Loretta, 270, 271–72
Kessler, Ronald, 263–64
King, Billie Jean, 294
Klein, Melanie, 214
Kline, Christina Baker, 229
Kohn, Alfie, 39–41, 70
Kournikova, Anna, 298
Krantz, Judith, 91

L

labor (childbirth), 239–40
La Leche League, 247–48
Lambert, Ellen Zetzel, 115
Lansing, Sherry, 200–201
Larsen, Nella, 92
lawyers, female
    job insecurity, 183–84
    maternity leave, 186, 190–91
    as partners, 187–88
    and power, 208–209
    reduced-hour options, 185
    sex discrimination, 178–79
Leader's Edge, The, 216
leadership styles, 194–96, 206–207, 215–16
League of Their Own, A, 294
Leave it to Beaver, 258
lesbians, 291–93, 294–96
Leslie, Lisa, 291
Levine, Suzanne Braun, 186
Like Mother, Like Daughter (Waterhouse), 130–31
"line-officer" jobs, 179
liposuction, 118
Louis Vuitton ads, 30
Lucky, 96–97

M

Madonna, 170
Madwoman in the Attic, The (Gilbert and Gubar), 144–45
Making the Body Beautiful (Gilman), 116–17

Malone, Annie Turnbo, 103
management styles, 194–96, 206–207, 215–16
manipulation, 216–18, 219–20
Manley, Claudia, 289
Mann, Traci, 128
marriage, 140–42, 145–51
Mason, Claire, 163, 164–65
materialism, 51–53, 97
Maternal Thinking (Ruddick), 58
maternity leave, 185–86, 267
Matlin, Marlee, 90
Mattel, 194–95
Mauresmo, Amélie, 295–96
Maushart, Susan, 230, 236
Maxted, Anna, 162
May, Elaine, 200
McBeal, Ally (fictional character), 30–31, 155
McCaughey, Betsy, 194
McGhan Medical, 119
Meir, Golda, 200
mentors, 176, 201
Meyerhoff, Arthur, 293–94
Meyerson, Debra, 183
Meza, Julia Olkin, 270
Mikulski, Barbara, 196–97
Mildred Pierce, 252
Million Mom March, 23, 238
Millner, Denene, 163–64
Mina Tannenbaum, 28
Miss America pageant, 105–112
Miss Teen USA contest, 106–107
Miss Universe contest, 106–107
Miss USA contest, 106–107
Mitsubishi Motors, 181
Mode, 92
"mommy tax," 267–68
"mommy track," 186–87
Morgan Stanley Dean Witter, 181–82
Morgenson, Gretchen, 195
Morrison, Toni, 93
mother-daughter relationships, 45–46, 58–59, 130–34
motherhood, 225–74
    and ambivalence, 231
    as "invisible" work, 191
    new mothers, isolation of, 228–36

sacrificial mother, 236–48
stay-at-home mothers, 267–74
as training for work, 205, 207–208
working mothers, 255–67
working outside home as issue, 249–54
mothers
"bad," 226–27, 231
and childless women, 189–91
dieting, 130–34
and empathy, 60
"good," 231, 240, 268
stereotypes, 226–27, 235, 272
Mothers Against Drunk Driving, 238
Mott, Lucretia, 276, 277
movies, 28, 29, 90–91, 252–53
Moynihan, Daniel Patrick, 194
Ms., 34–35
Mulcahy, Anne, 179
My Three Sons, 258

N

Nanny Diaries, The (McLaughlin and Kraus),
226–27
National Academy of Sciences, 260
National American Woman Suffrage
Association, 281
National Basketball Association (NBA), 287,
289
National Institute of Child Health and
Human Development, 264
National Marriage Project (Rutgers
University), 151–52
National Woman Suffrage Association, 280,
281
Navratilova, Martina, 294
Nelson, Jill, 35, 48, 94
Nelson, Mariah Burton, 42, 286, 300–301
New York, 30
New York Radical Women, 113
Nickel and Dimed (Ehrenreich), 252
Nietzsche, Friedrich, 57–58, 309
Nigeria, 120
Nightingale, Tracy, 109–112
Nineteenth Amendment, 275, 282
No Contest (Kohn), 39–41

O

objectification, 81–82, 110

O'Brien, Virginia, 204
Of Woman Born (Rich), 237
Ohio State University, 295
Olympic athletes, 285, 291, 292, 293, 296,
297, 298, 300–301
oppression, 26
Otherwise Engaged (Finnamore), 158, 160–61
Other Woman
as competition, 135–39
friend as, 165–69
in literature, 139–45
in pop culture, 29–31
and single women, 161–65
today, 159–65
Oxidant, Andrea, 114

P

Pappas, Christina, 171, 175–76
parenting guides, 234–36
See also motherhood
part-time work, 187, 262–64
See also work
"passing," 92, 117
Passing (Larsen), 92
Paul, Alice, 282
Peiss, Kathy, 99–101, 102
penis envy, 45
Penn State University, 295
Perrot, Kim, 297
Phillips, Deborah, 265–66
physicians, female, 263
physiognomy, 99–100
"pink ghetto" occupations, 147
Plan B (Tropper), 159–60
Plath, Sylvia, 73–75
Playboy, 146
Pogrebin, Letty Cottin, 33–34
Pollitt, Katha, 61
Popenoe, David, 152
Portland, Rene, 295
Portnoy's Complaint (Roth), 235
postpartum depression (PPD), 229–31,
233–34
Powell, Colin, 32, 84–85
power
and aggression, 63
and empathy, 60
lack of, 55–56

petty, 35, 189–91
real, 150–51
and women, 32, 46
and work, 177
prayer of supplication, 11
pregnancy, 89–90, 95, 236–39
Price, Aisha, 164
Price of Motherhood, The (Crittenden), 262, 267–68
Pride and Prejudice (Austen), 142
provider, fantasy of marrying, 149–51

Q

Queen Bees, 199–202
Quigley, Mary, 270, 271–72

R

race, as a division among women, 53–54
rape, 56–58
Rapping, Elaine, 31
Reagan, Nancy, 27–28
recognition, 191–92, 223
Redstockings, 21–22
Reece, Gabrielle, 291
resentment, 55–58, 88
Rice, Condoleezza, 32, 84–85
Rich, Adrienne, 237
Rich and Famous, 28
Rivers, Caryl, 257, 258–60, 261, 263
Rivers, Joan, 101
Rivers, Melissa, 90
Riviere, Joan, 214–15
Roberts, Julia, 90, 94–95, 252–53
Rockwell, Rick, 150–51
Roiphe, Anne, 193–94
Roiphe, Kate, 149
romance, 37, 149
Rosenberg, Dahlia, 154
Rosener, Judy, 201–202, 204, 206–208
Roth, Philip, 235
Ruddick, Sara, 58
Rules, The (Fein and Schneider), 155
Rumsfeld, Donald, 32
Russell, Keri, 88–89
Russo, Patricia, 179
Rutgers University, National Marriage Project, 151–52
Ryan, Merrick, 127–28

S

Sandler, Marion, 179
Schieffelin, Allison K., 181–82
Schneider, Maria, 240
Schneider, Sherrie, 155
Schneider, Wendy, 216–17
Schroeder, Pat, 218
Schultz, Charles, 189
Seaman, Barbara, 176
Seinfeld, Jerry, 170
self-abnegation, 216
self-effacement, 64–65
self-hatred, 47–48
self-improvement, 22
self-objectification, 81–82
Sense and Sensibility (Austen), 142, 162
Sephora, 114
7 Greatest Truths About Highly Successful Women, The (Brem), 204
Sex and Power (Estrich), 182–83
Sex and the City, 30, 153, 154, 155, 158–59, 172
She Got Game (Cooper), 297
She Works / He Works (Barnett and Rivers), 259
Shield, Erin, 94–95
shopping, 96–97
Sigman, Laura, 287–88
Silver, Megan, 165–66
singles culture, 137–38, 151–59
Sissy Fight (Internet-based game), 69–70
Sistahs' Rules, The (Millner), 163–64
sisterhood, universal, 23–24
Sklar, Jessica, 170
"slave morality," 55, 57–58
Smith College, 103
Snodgrass, Sara, 60
Snyderman, Erica, 167
socialization, and aggression, 63
social purity movement, 281
Sopranos, The, 29
sororities, college, 68–69
Spock, Benjamin, 235, 236
sports, women in
    and femininity, 291–301
    and healthy competition, 41–42, 70–71
    Olympic athletes, 285, 291, 292, 293, 296, 297, 298, 300–301
    today, 283–91

Staines, Graham, 199–200
Stanford University, 128
Stanton, Elizabeth Cady, 277, 278–79, 280, 281–82
Starbucks, 101
Steel, Dawn, 196
Steinberg, Lisa, 68–69
Steinem, Gloria, 83, 84, 218–19
Stepmom, 28, 252–53
stereotypes
    appearance, 84
    authority, 203
    crying, 218–19
    female athletes, 291
    feminine, 27–32
    gender, 46–47
    "kinder, gentler" myth, 60–61, 63
    mothers, 226–27, 235, 272
    nice women, 206
    single women, 154–55, 158–59
    women in power, 194–95
    working women, 184, 193
Stick Figure (Gottlieb), 121–22
Stoller, Debbie, 97, 115
Stone, Lucy, 280–81
Stone, Sharon, 170–71
students, college, 147–49
subordination, 47–48
Success on Our Terms (O'Brien), 204
suffrage movement, 275–83
Sullivan, Andrew, 149
Sunrise Drive Elementary School (Sayville, N.Y.), 70–71
supervisors
    female, 173–76
    male, 173
Survivor, 41
Swoopes, Sheryl, 294–95, 296

T

Talbot, Margaret, 240
Tavris, Carol, 59–60, 199–200, 208–209
teenage girls, 48–49, 118, 121–22, 152–53
television sitcoms, 257–58
thinness, 91–92, 103–104, 110–111, 119–26
"32 Flavors," 29
Thurer, Shari, 231, 236, 240–41
Time, 153–54

Title IX, 41–42, 283, 293
Tripp, Linda, 83
Tropper, Jonathan, 159–60
Turner, Kathleen, 305

U

undernutrition of Miss America contestants, 113
University of Illinois, 134
University of Michigan
    Institute for Social Research, 273
    Law School, 187
University of Minnesota, 132
University of the Incarnate Word, 197–98
U.S. Department of Health and Human Services, 286
utopian civilization, fictional, 42–43, 44

V

Vacco, Dennis, 194
Valian, Virginia, 183
violence, 59
Vogue, 197

W

W (magazine), 30
Wachner, Linda, 195–96
Walker, Madam C. J., 103
Wann, Marilyn, 91
Warnaco, 195
Wasserstein, Wendy, 246–47
Waterhouse, Debra, 130–31, 134
Weaver, Karen, 295
weddings, 169–72
weight, 91–92, 103–104, 110–111, 119–26
Wellesley College, Center for Research on Women, 257, 259–60
Wellington, Sheila, 218
Wethington, Elaine, 263–64
wet-nursing, 240–41
Wharton, Edith, 142, 162
What Our Mothers Didn't Tell Us (Crittenden), 188, 251
White, Kate, 204
Whitehead, Barbara Dafoe, 152
whiteness, as part of beauty ideal, 92
white women, 53–54, 147–49
Who Wants to Marry a Millionaire?, 150–51

Why Good Girls Don't Get Ahead...But Gutsy Girls Do (White), 204
Why the Best Man for the Job is a Woman (Book), 204
Williams, Jessica, 85
Williams, Serena, 285, 298–300
Williams, Venus, 285, 298–300
Winslet, Kate, 305
Wintour, Anna, 197
Wollstonecraft, Mary, 277
Woman in the Nineteenth Century (Fuller), 99
"Woman of Valor, A" (Proverbs), 255, 256
Woman's Bible, The (Stanton), 281
Woman's Inhumanity to Woman (Chesler), 24, 46
women
    divided by class and race, 49–54
    "essential nature," 58–61
    mixed messages to, 37–38
    as objects, 81–82, 110
    in politics, 193–94, 196–97, 200
    relational character, 59, 61
Women, The, 28
women of color
    and beauty ideal, 92–94, 100, 103
    college students, 147–49
    eating disorders, 128–30
    and Other Woman, 163–65
    and white bosses, 198–99
    and white women, 53–54
    in a white world, 47–48
women's liberation movement, 21–23, 43–44, 52, 97, 113–16, 251–52
Women's National Basketball Association (WNBA), 285, 286–87, 289, 291, 294–95, 296, 297
Women's Professional Football League, 290
Women's Rights Convention (Seneca Falls, N.Y.), 277–78
Women's Sports Foundation, 286
Women's Tennis Association, 294
Women's World Cup, 285, 289
Woodhull, Victoria, 280
work, 173–224
    and emotions, 218–24
    female advantage, 204–209
    job insecurity, 183–92
    mixed messages to women, 37
    and niceness, 209–18
    part-time, 187, 262–64
    powerful women, 196–203
    pressures on women, 176–77
    sex discrimination, 178–83
    toughness at, 192–96
Working Girl, 28
Wrigley, Philip, 293
Wurtzel, Elizabeth, 27
Wylie, Philip, 236

Y
Yates, Andrea, 230
youth, and beauty ideal, 91
Youth Intelligence, 270

Z
Zara, 96
Zayas, Mina, 197
Zellweger, Renée, 30, 156, 157, 305
Zeta-Jones, Catherine, 90

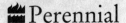 Perennial

Books by Leora Tanenbaum:

CATFIGHT
Rivalries Among Women—from Diets to Dating,
from the Boardroom to the Delivery Room
ISBN 0-06-052838-9 (paperback)

Part sociological study, part journalistic account of the American everywoman, *Catfight* explores the history and function of competition in society and the reasons why these covert, negative behaviors persist.

"**An incisive exploration of a long-taboo subject—how and why women sabotage one another.**" —Gail Sheehy

SLUT!
Growing Up Female with a Bad Reputation
ISBN 0-06-095740-9 (paperback)

Girls may be labeled "sluts" for any number of reasons, often having nothing to do with sex. In this important account of the lives of young women who stand up to the destructive power of sexual labeling, Leora Tanenbaum weaves together three narrative threads—powerful oral histories of girls and women who tell us their personal stories, Tanenbaum's own story, and a cogent analysis of the underlying problem of sexual stereotyping.

"**Tanenbaum has written an important and alarming book; it deserves serious attention and should encourage serious action.**" —*Women's Review of Books*